FILM
MARKETING
INTO THE
TWENTY-FIRST
CENTURY

nolwenn **MINGANT**
cecilia **TIRTAINE**
joël **AUGROS**

A BFI book published by Palgrave

For Francis Bordat

First published in 2015 by
PALGRAVE

on behalf of the

BRITISH FILM INSTITUTE
21 Stephen Street, London W1T 1LN
www.bfi.org.uk

There's more to discover about film and television through the BFI. Our world-renowned archive,
cinemas, festivals, films, publications and learning resources are here to inspire you.

PALGRAVE in the UK is an imprint of Macmillan Publishers Limited, registered in England,
company number 785998, of 4 Crinan Street, London N1 9XW. Palgrave Macmillan in the US is a
division of St Martin's Press LLC, 175 Fifth Avenue, New York, NY 10010. Palgrave is a global
imprint of the above companies and is represented throughout the world. Palgrave® and
Macmillan® are registered trademarks in the United States, the United Kingdom, Europe and
other countries.

Cover image: ferrantraite/Getty Images

Set by Cambrain Typesetters, Camberley, Surrey
Printed in China

This book is printed on paper suitable for recycling and made from fully managed and sustained
forest sources. Logging, pulping and manufacturing processes are expected to conform to the
environmental regulations of the country of origin.
British Library Cataloguing-in-Publication Data
A catalogue record for this book is available from the British Library
A catalog record for this book is available from the Library of Congress

ISBN 978–1–84457–838–2 (pb)
ISBN 978–1–84457–839–9 (hb)

Contents

II MARKETING FOR AND BY THE CONSUMER

Acknowledgments

The idea for this volume stemmed from a series of conferences organised by CinEcoSA (Cinema, Economy in English-Speaking Countries), a research association dedicated to studying film industries from the conjugated perspectives of economics, politics and culture. The 2010 and 2011 conferences were organised thanks to the support of the Université Sorbonne Nouvelle – Paris 3 and the Université Paris 8 Vincennes – Saint-Denis. The editors wish to thank Professor Laurent Creton (IRCAV, Research Institute on Film and Audiovisual Media), whose constant encouragement and support have been particularly determining. They are also grateful to the CiClaHo (Research Centre on Classical Hollywood Cinema), at the Université Paris Ouest Nanterre La Défense, which welcomed CinEcoSA in 2009, when it was a fledgling association. Thanks are also due to all the colleagues who participated in the film marketing conferences, as well as the other conferences organised by CinEcoSA since. The quality of their presentations, the relevance of their reflexions, their good humour and friendship have contributed to making the CinEcoSA network and events the thought-provoking and enriching locus that its founders were hoping for when they started, and herald yet more enthralling projects.

The editors would also like to express their gratitude to the BFI Publishing team as well as to the anonymous reviewers. Their comments have been very helpful in turning this book into what they hope will prove to be a useful, thought-provoking and entertaining volume.

Notes on Contributors

JOËL AUGROS is an Associate Professor at the Film Department Université Paris 8 Vincennes – Saint-Denis.. His research and teaching are mainly focused on economic aspects of Hollywood film and the French cinema. In recent years, he has been developing a more comparative approach to the different film businesses across the world.

MATTHEW BERRYMAN, PhD, works at the SMART Infrastructure Facility, University of Wollongong, and his research interests include cloud and high performance computing, and data mining.

MICHAEL CURTIN is the Duncan and Suzanne Mellichamp Professor of Film and Media Studies and director of the Media Industries Project at the University of California, Santa Barbara. His research and teaching focus on media globalisation, cultural geography, industry studies and creative labour.

MICHAEL FRANKLIN is a PhD student at the Institute for Capitalising on Creativity, School of Management, University of St Andrews. His work has been supported by the Economic and Social Research Council (ESRC). He is currently a Research Associate on a digital engagement project for Nesta's Digital R&D fund with Film London. His research focuses on digital materials, market devices and the creative industries.

BEN GOLDSMITH is a Senior Research Fellow in the ARC Centre of Excellence for Creative Industries and Innovation, Queensland University of Technology. His research interests include: media policy, creative labour and international media production.

WESLEY JACKS is a PhD candidate in the Department of Film and Media Studies at the University California, Santa Barbara. His dissertation research focuses on media distribution in contemporary China. Wes has an MA in film studies from the University of Wisconsin-Madison.

ALESSANDRO JEDLOWSKI is a Marie Curie/Cofund post-doctoral fellow in Media and Cultural Anthropology at the University of Liege (Belgium). His main research interests include African cinema, urban and popular culture in urban Africa, media and migration. He is the author of several essays on the politics and economics of Nigerian video film production published in international journals and edited collections.

KIRA KITSOPANIDOU is an Associate Professor at the Université Sorbonne Nouvelle – Paris 3 (IRCAV). She teaches undergraduate and graduate courses on the history of the film and television industries, media economics, technology and innovation. She has recently published *Les Salles de cinéma en Europe: Enjeux, défis et perspectives* (2013), with Laurent Creton.

YONGLI LI is currently a PhD candidate in the East Asian Languages and Cultural Studies Department at University of California, Santa Barbara. Her research interests include Chinese urban studies with an emphasis on modernity and the creative life of the city, as well as the contemporary Chinese film and media industry. She holds an MA from the Beijing Film Academy.

RAMON LOBATO is Senior Research Fellow in Media and Communication at Swinburne University of Technology, Melbourne. His research interests include digital distribution, copyright and piracy. He is the author of *Shadow Economies of Cinema* (2012) and *The Informal Media Economy* (2015, with Julian Thomas).

JAVIER LOZANO DELMAR holds a PhD in Communication Studies and he is an Associate Professor in the School of Communication and Education at Universidad Loyola Andalucía in Spain, where he teaches courses on Information and Communication Technologies, Television Studies and Creative Thinking. His research focuses mainly on Television Studies, analysing the use of new technologies in advertising, fandom-generated content and television promoting strategies.

NOLWENN MINGANT is an Associate Professor in American Studies at the Université de Nantes, France, and the author of *Hollywood à la conquête du monde: Marché, stratégies, influences* (2010). Co-founder of research group CinEcoSA and co-organiser of research seminar MENA Cinema, she is currently working on a book manuscript on the presence of Hollywood films in the Middle East and North Africa.

JOSÉ ANTONIO MUÑIZ-VELÁZQUEZ is an Associate Professor and the head of the Department of Communication and Education (Universidad Loyola Andalucía, Seville, Spain), PhD in Communication Studies, graduate in Advertising and Public Relations, graduate in Psychology and European Master in Direct, Interactive and Database Marketing, with work experience at several Spanish universities and advertising and communication agencies. He has spoken at several national and international seminars, workshops and conferences.

LYDIA PAPADIMITRIOU is Senior Lecturer in Film Studies at Liverpool John Moores University. She has published extensively on different aspects of Greek cinema. Her monograph *The Greek Film Musical* (2006) has been translated into Greek (2009), and she has co-edited (with Yannis Tzioumakis) *Greek Cinema: Texts, Forms and Identities* (2011). Her current research interests involve documentary, film festivals and distribution.

MIRIAM ROSS is Senior Lecturer in the Film Programme at Victoria University of Wellington. She is the author of *South American Cinematic Culture: Policy, Production, Distribution and Exhibition* (2010) and *3D Cinema: Optical Illusions and Tactile Experiences* (2015), as well as publications on film industries, new cinema technologies, stereoscopic media and film festivals. She is also co-founder of stereoscopicmedia.org

KAI SOH is currently a PhD candidate in the Faculty of Law, Humanities and the Arts at the University of Wollongong. Her thesis explores the socio-cultural and industrial implications of networking among users who comment on international co-production films on the popular Chinese social networking site Douban.

DIMITRINKA STOYANOVA RUSSELL is a lecturer in Human Resource Management at Cardiff University and an Affiliated Researcher with the Institute for Capitalising on Creativity, School of Management, University of St Andrews. Her research is in the area of creative industries: organisations and organising, work and employment. She has published on freelance work, skills, careers and social capital in the film and television industries.

CECILIA TIRTAINE is a Senior Lecturer in British Studies at the Université Sorbonne Nouvelle – Paris 3. She is a co-founding member of research group CinEcoSA and a co-founder and the associate editor of peer-reviewed international online journal *InMedia*.

BARBARA TOWNLEY is Chair of Management at University of St Andrews, Scotland, and has taught at Lancaster, Warwick and Edinburgh in the UK and the University of Alberta, Canada. She has published widely in North American and European management and organisation studies journals and has held a number of ESRC and Arts and Humanities Research Council (AHRC) grants.

HAYLEY TROWBRIDGE has recently completed a PhD at the University of Liverpool. Her research is broadly in line with the emergent media industry studies paradigm, focusing specifically on discussions of media convergence, distribution studies and American independent cinema.

YANNIS TZIOUMAKIS is Senior Lecturer in Communication and Media Studies at the University of Liverpool. His research specialises in American cinema and the business of entertainment. He is the author and editor of seven books and co-editor of two book series, most recently *The Routledge Hollywood Centenary*. He is currently co-authoring a book on acting in American independent cinema for Palgrave.

JIE YANG, PhD, has extensive experience in machine learning and cloud computing. In 2013, Jie joined the SMART Infrastructure Facility at University of Wollongong, where he is responsible for translating conceptual models into implementation programs and code prototyping. These projects involve the application of big-data processing on infrastructure planning and social media analytic.

BRIAN YECIES is a Senior Lecturer in Cultural Studies at the University of Wollongong. He is author of *Korea's Occupied Cinemas, 1893–1948* (2011, with Ae-Gyung Shim) and *The Changing Face of Korean Cinema, 1960 to 2015* (forthcoming). Currently, he is a chief investigator on the 2014–16 ARC Discovery Project 'Willing Collaborators: Negotiating Change in East Asian Media Production'.

Foreword

Janet WASKO

The study of cinema has grown dramatically since the middle of the last century, when it emerged at many universities and colleges. And while there still is a tendency by many film scholars to focus on texts, genres and authors, more attention has been increasingly directed at the institutional context in which films are produced, distributed and exhibited, as well as its social and cultural significance.

In Europe and North America (at least), important studies have dug deeper into the history of cinema exhibition and reception. A wealth of research has emerged on the media industry, especially on the film industry and especially from cinema scholars. Indeed, media industry studies has been recognised as a viable and somewhat popular approach for the study of media, despite lingering issues relating to its definition, scope and motivations. The proliferation of studies that fit under this umbrella is another encouraging sign. While not necessarily in the 'mainstream' of cinema/media research, the number of studies related to media industries has increased consistently over the last few decades. The development of new distribution outlets via digital technologies also has prompted further analysis of the ways that films are produced and how they reach and relate to audiences.

It has been argued that a full understanding of film requires an understanding of how decisions are made about what films are produced and where, how they are distributed and why. The relationships between film and other media and non-media businesses also often become important for film content and availability. And the role of the state is sometimes key in the financing and distribution of films around the world.

Despite the economic, geographical or cultural context, film marketing is an important part of this process. It seems especially important to understand commercial films, where marketing decisions often become more important than artistic, social or cultural concerns. By focusing directly on film marketing, this collection provides important information and insights that help us to understand the processes that guide the distribution of films in the current era. It is a rich and informative collection that fills a real gap in film and media studies.

The chapters that explore different elements of film marketing in various contexts are valuable contributions to our understanding of this process. A range of case studies provides details on various parts of the production and distribution process from the marketing perspective, as well as insights that help to (again) understand the marketing of different types of films in different parts of the world. There is much to be learned from case studies that take us from Nollywood to Peru, and explore issues related to everything from dubbing to advertising strategies. The interviews that are woven into the collection are especially useful and enlightening. The primary documentation of industry practices is crucial for film industry scholars and these interviews are important frames of reference for the other chapters. Finally, it is important to note the attention to changes in film marketing due to digital technologies that is explored by many of the contributors to this collection. The issues related to these changes seem endless – and include everything from the expansion of distribution outlets, to the use of digital data in marketing, to the content films, to the relationship of films and audiences.

It is possible that you may not have known much about or realised the significance of film marketing before you picked up this book. However, after reading these informative and thought-provoking chapters, I think you will appreciate the fundamental role that film marketing plays in the cinema world. Thanks to the editors, authors and interviewees for helping us to understand more about this world.

Introduction

Nolwenn MINGANT, Cecilia TIRTAINE and Joël AUGROS

While in the 1930s Bette Davis fans, enticed by posters, trailers and articles in fan magazines, had to patiently wait for her films to be released in theatres, today Julia Roberts fans can enjoy her past and current films in theatres but also on numerous types of screens, in licensed or pirated copies. They can immerse in the film's marketing campaign, by reacting on the official website, downloading applications and exchanging comments on social networks. In the early twenty-first century, films are still avidly watched, but the ways they are experienced has dramatically changed; and as the way to engage films has evolved, so have the ways to reach audiences.

Film Marketing: A Definition

Film marketer Jean-François Camilleri once described his job as 'the art of creating desire, or seducing the largest number of people'.[1] Just as the aim of marketing is to 'find the best possible match between a product and its market', film marketing strives to create 'product/market couples'.[2] Amorous metaphors thus abound, with film marketing depicted as 'large-scale flirting'[3] or 'seduction thanks to packaging'.[4] Quick seduction is required, on a 'it's now or never' principle, as people have to be enticed to go to theatres for the 'critical opening weekend'.[5] At the centre of attention is the spectator, the 'target' to reach, and film marketing can first be defined as 'consumer marketing'.[6]

Cinematic products have a number of specific characteristics. First, each film is unique: cinema is a prototype industry. For each campaign, marketers have to identify the adequate target group and create adapted material. This is called 'audience creation'.[7] Not only is each campaign unique, but it also takes place prior to the release, leaving few opportunities for ulterior changes. In the words of producer Robert Evans: 'a film is like no other product. It only goes around once. It is like a parachute jump. If it doesn't open you're dead.'[8] Second, films are cultural products. Culture can be understood as 'the works and practices of intellectual and especially artistic activity',[9] which links film to performing arts and museums, with their uniqueness, intangibility and absence of concrete utility. Film marketing, as 'cultural marketing', indeed, deals with hedonistic, emotional and symbolic experiences.[10] 'Culture' can also be understood as the common identity shared by a country's inhabitants, as a fundamental element in the very making of these nations, which Benedict Anderson defined as 'imagined political communities'.[11] In that sense, marketers have to deal with national traits and representations, and although 'marketing is universal, marketing practice … varies from country to country'.[12] Moreover, these constructed cultural elements which characterise a group[13] do not necessarily refer to a national context. The target of film marketers can, indeed, be 'affinity groups',[14] such as *Twilight* fans, or 'trekkies'.[15] With the development of social media, such affinity groups have recently gained importance. Practitioners and analysts of film marketing must thus be mindful of the link between the film, as a cultural product, and the spectator, as a culturally specific entity, whether in terms of nationality, gender, age, or affinities.

Although to the general audience film marketing is mostly visible through posters and trailers, film marketers' attempts to reach their target is a much wider-reaching activity. More than mere 'sales techniques', film marketing is about 'gathering the information and intelligence necessary to elaborate a production and commercialisation strategy'.[16] It implies the participation of many players, from the very beginning of a film's life in its author's mind, to the adoption by audiences long after they have left the theatres. For this volume, we have adopted Kerrigan's definition that film marketing 'begins at the new product development stage and continues throughout the formation of the project ideas, through production and into distribution and exhibition'.[17] Like her, we believe it is necessary to 'continue the film marketing journey unto the realm of film consumption' as consumers 'may wish to extend their consumption through visiting online review sites, discussing the films with friends or progressing with their film consumption to consumer-related films'.[18]

The Film Marketing Process
Detailed practical information on how to take a film through the different production and distribution stages is readily available in how-to guides such as Angus Finney's *International Film Business: A Market Guide beyond Hollywood* (2010), Jon Reiss's *Think Outside the Box Office: The Ultimate Guide to Film Distribution and Marketing for the Digital Era* (2011), or Robert Marich's seminal *Marketing to Moviegoers: A Handbook of Strategies and Tactics* (2013). One can also turn to the now-dated but still pertinent *Movie Marketing: Opening the Picture and Giving it Legs* (1997), in which Tiiu Lukk presents a series of case studies based on interviews with professionals. This introduction will briefly go over the different stages of film marketing.

Strategic marketing
First, the target audience is identified by analysing the 'film marketing mix' — that is, director, actors, script, genre, age classification. Marketers map out the film's SWOTs (Strengths, Weaknesses, Opportunities and Threats).[19] On the basis of these elements, film marketers operate a segmentation of the audience, identifying a core target, but also a secondary group to which the film could cross over.

Once the target audience is identified, the team determines the film's positioning, by setting its identity and defining where it stands in relation to other films on the market and in audiences' minds. Positioning relies on a film's selling points — that is, 'story elements that are easily communicated in simple terms'.[20] One film can have several types of positioning, for different target groups. *Four Weddings and a Funeral* (1994) was marketed as a comedy about single people to eighteen-to-twenty-four-year-olds, as an English-humour romantic comedy for twenty-five-to-thirty-four-year-olds and as an adult date movie for the thirty-five-plus audience.[21] A film can also have a different positioning in different countries. While *Minority Report* (2002) was sold in France on the reputation of its director, with praise from film critics printed on the poster, the highly technological elements of the films were the major selling point in the Japanese campaign.[22]

The identification of the audience segment and positioning then guides the choice of a distribution pattern or release strategy. Big-budget films for mainstream audiences usually benefit from a saturation release — that is, on a large number of screens, with a blitz television campaign. Mid-range pictures, often directed to a more adult audience, usually have

UK poster for *Four Weddings and a Funeral* (1994): an English-humour romantic comedy and an adult date movie

a more limited release. An exclusive release refers to a distribution move restricted to a few theatres, in big cities. A platform release is a limited release strategy: the film is first distributed in a few cinemas and then, as positive word of mouth expands, the number of copies gradually increases and the marketing campaign gathers pace. At that stage, a release date is selected, according to existing seasons. In the USA, summer is the peak season,[23] the time for big-budget films. A second important season for big-budget films, notably animation, is the Christmas holidays. For art-house films the peak will be autumn, on the way to the Oscar season. Although big-budget films increasingly tend to be released simultaneously around the world, or day-and-date, each region maintains its own seasons. In Europe, for example, autumn is a strong period.[24] Marketers must also take into account specific holidays such as Eid al-Fitr and Eid al-Adha in Egypt, or the summer school break in China. They must stay attuned to this seasonality, which can evolve over time. The choice of the right release date is vital, as the buzz created by the theatrical marketing push is crucial for ancillary markets such as television, DVDs and video-on-demand (VoD).

Operational marketing
Operational marketing occurs at the distribution stage. It comprises the creation of communication material (title, poster, teasers, trailers), media planning and buying (also called the media mix) and publicity. One must distinguish advertising, which marketers pay for (e.g. ads in papers or posters) and publicity, which includes all unpaid-for media coverage, TV chat shows, interviews, premiere appearances, world tours, press junkets, films reviews and awards ceremonies.[25] Trailers, which are 'probably the most important, effective, and

cost-efficient way of marketing a new film',[26] have been the object of a specific literature, with notable contributions such as Lisa Kernan's *Coming Attractions: Reading American Movie Trailers* (2004), Keith M. Johnston's *Coming Soon: Film Trailers and the Selling of Hollywood Technology* (2009) and Tiiu Lukk's chapter 'Coming Attractions: Creating the Trailer'.[27] But film promotion today relies on a wider variety of tools, as Jonathan Gray's *Show Sold Separately: Promos, Spoilers, and Other Media Paratexts* (2010) shows with his analyses of trailers, as well as spoilers, reviews or DVD bonus materials.

Operational marketing is deeply rooted in local conditions. Marketers in charge of media buying must be aware of the specificities of local media outlets. An example is how television spending is a large part of the budget in North America, while no ads for movies are allowed on French television. A central issue for the operational marketing team is, thus, how to tailor the film's campaign to a specific market, a process called adaptation or localisation. Beyond the choice of adequate media outlets for advertising and promotion, and minor adaptation of the posters and trailers, marketing teams can also use two other tools to localise their campaigns: dubbing[28] and tie-ins with local partners.

Cross-cutting practices

Some activities stand astride the division described above. For example, product placement – that is, '"placing" a product or a brand in one or more scenes of a film, in one form or another, in return for payment'[29] – is decided upon at the strategic stage and activated at the operational stage. Generally, the production company strikes a barter deal with a brand, which provides the products in exchange for their presence in the film.[30] Product placement at the production stage opens cross-promotional opportunities at the distribution stage. The James Bond franchise is probably the best-known example of product placement on a large scale, with more than twenty brands included in *Die Another Day* (2002) and the appearance of Heineken in *Skyfall* (2012).[31] As films are prepared for release, the car, food or perfume companies devise their own advertising campaigns featuring the film's characters, thus participating in the marketing push with tie-ins. Tie-in deals can also result in the creation of branded products, or merchandising.

Another activity that occurs both at the strategic and operational marketing stages is market research. As the ability to obtain information about the potential audience is vital, market research holds a central place at all stages.[32] During development, producers can resort to concept and title testing. At the strategic marketing stage, positioning studies can 'develop a detailed movie marketing plan at a very early stage based on a script and casting'.[33] Marich gives a detailed presentation of market research practices such as focus groups, test screenings, or tracking surveys.[34] Marketing material, such as posters and trailers, can also be tested. Although market research is central, film marketers equally insist on the importance of intuition and experience – personal and shared – in making decisions.

The search for predictability which guides market research has also led to a trend in academic literature whose aim is to identify the impact of the marketing mix on a film's success, such as Barry Litman and Hoekyun Ahn's 'Predicting Financial Success of Motion Pictures: The Early '90s Experience'[35] or Arthur De Vany's chapter on 'Big Budgets, Big Openings and Legs: Analysis of the Blockbuster Strategy'.[36]

Marketability and distribution choices

Given the vast array of films, not all are equally marketable. Marketability is 'a marketer's calculation of all the elements of the film than can be used in promotion and advertising':

Top Gun (1986): the prototype of the 'high-concept' film

the 'larger the number of advertising-friendly elements – including a film's imagery, storyline, music, genre and stylisation – the greater the marketability'.[37] The most 'advertising-friendly' films are 'high-concept' films, such as *Flashdance* (1983) or *Top Gun* (1986), which include striking visual and audio elements conceived to be easily used at the marketing stage.[38]

The marketing practices described above are thus used to varying degrees for each film, depending on its marketability and its distributor. Marketing strategies for big-budget films released by Hollywood studios will tend to integrate production and marketing, to devote a large budget to prints and advertising (P&A), and to rely on saturation releases. Independent distributors will tend to 'dispense with research completely',[39] have much smaller P&A budgets and fewer distribution outlets. While saturation releases rely on a massive marketing blitz, independent distribution will favour the development of positive word of mouth through limited releases and presentations in the festival circuits.

Industrial marketing

Strategic and operational marketing can be defined as 'business-to-consumer' (B-to-C) practices. They are the more visible facets of the marketing campaign. However, film marketing also encompasses 'business-to-business' (B-to-B) practices, including pitches by screenwriters to producers, screenings for sales agents or distributors, the selling of a new technology to theatre owners, as well as advocacy marketing – that is, the creation of popular and political support for Hollywood through publicised awards ceremonies and political lobbying by the Independent Film & Television Alliance and the Motion Picture Association of America (MPAA).[40]

Film Marketing Players

With such a variety of practices, film marketing involves many players. The overall strategy used is determined by the type of distributor. The largest distribution outfits are Hollywood's major studios: Disney, Paramount, Sony, 20th Century-Fox, Universal and Warner Bros. They have large marketing departments with subdivisions for creative advertising, publicity and promotion, market research and media.[41] The majors also have a large network of international distribution offices, which contributes to their continued dominance in the world markets. They own speciality divisions, such as Fine Line or Sony Picture Classics, which distribute less mainstream films. Alongside these international colossuses, there is a variety of smaller distribution companies, such as Lionsgate in the USA. To market their films abroad, US independent distribution companies rely on local distributors. While some distributors cover a regional area, such as the French company

Studio Canal which has offices in France, Germany, the UK, Australia and New Zealand, or Dubai-based Gulf Film, which covers the whole Middle East, some distributors focus specifically on their national market, such as United Motion Pictures in Egypt or Prooptiki in Greece.

Film marketing activities are often externalised to a wide range of small companies, called 'outside vendors'[42] or 'boutique agencies'.[43] Market research is largely outsourced to firms like National Research Group (NRG)[44] and Online Testing Exchange (OTX) in the USA, or Ipsos MediaCT and Dodona Research in the UK. Also often externalised is the creation of trailers, to companies such as Ant Farm in Los Angeles or Silenzio in Paris, and the film's dubbing to companies such as Dubbing Brothers, VSI Group or Arvintel Media Productions. When the distributor does not have an in-house marketing department, the marketing process can be subcontracted to advertising and communication agencies, such as Ireland's Wide Eye Media. Other types of advertising-support companies include cinema in foyer media companies (e.g. Boomerang Media in the UK), outdoor advertising companies (e.g. Primesight UK, JCDecaux or CBS Outdoor in the UK), advertising space brokers (e.g. Carat, Mediacom or Mindshare in the UK) or internet-advertising companies (France's Cinefriends).

The film's talent, the director and actors, can also be very much involved in the marketing push, through personal appearances and interviews. For small-budget films, doing the legwork can be determining, as when comedian Dany Boon toured France to promote *Bienvenue chez les Ch'tis* (2008), a medium-budget comedy which became a hit in France and subsequently experienced success in a large number of countries.

Film marketing activities do not, however, rely on film professionals only. State players also have a key role in the definition and operations of this activity. In France, the film industry is closely regulated by a public body, the Centre national de la cinématographie et de l'image animée (CNC). The ban on film trailers on television decided in order to fight inequality between small and large distributors is one aspect through which marketing is limited in France. States also intervene through censorship and quota legislations or through nationalised film distributors, such as China Film Group or Kuwait National Cinema Company. In contrast, state intervention can be enabling, especially for independent films. In 2003, the UK Specialised P&A Fund was created to support the national distribution and marketing of specialised movies, whether British or not, and of more mainstream British movies which had small P&A budgets.[45] On a pan-regional level, the Creative Europe EU initiative has a MEDIA sub-programme dedicated to distribution and marketing to encourage transnational film circulation.

A final player is the spectator. The object of constant attention from film marketers, the audience should not be viewed as a passive entity experimented upon with previews and surveys. Viewers increasingly take on an active role in film campaigns. Through positive and negative word of mouth, they can be true 'influencers',[46] a phenomenon now increased by the internet.

A Brief History of Film Marketing
Film marketing in Hollywood
Marketing developed in the USA in the 1930s. Although it did not officially reach Hollywood before the 1960s, one can consider that many current practices are as old as cinema itself, with the use of market research in production choices identified as early as the 1910s.[47] In the 1930s, stars were used as 'market strategy', while studios practised audience testing and publicity in fan magazines.[48] Before the 1970s, however, Hollywood

did not market its films, it promoted them. The publicity departments concentrated on publicity and trailers, rather than on advertising.[49] During the 'studio era', studios were, indeed, associated with particular stars – who were under contract – and genres, and each studio developed a brand identity.[50] As the studio system collapsed in the 1950s, in the wake of the 1948 Consent Decree, publicity departments could not rely on the same tools any more and had to start creating awareness for each film;[51] 'marketing services' started to be tentatively created at the very end of the 1960s.[52]

In the 1970s, two films marked the establishment of marketing practices in Hollywood: *Jaws* (1975), which launched the concept of the saturation release, with ad campaigns centred on TV spots,[53] and *Star Wars* (1977), which took the marginal practice of merchandising to previously unheard-of levels and turned it into a staple practice in Hollywood.[54] By the late 1970s, marketing had officially set foot in Hollywood, and 'publicity departments gradually evolved into "multi-disciplined" marketing departments, which include specific divisions for publicity, creating advertising, media buying and promotion (including product placement and tie-in activities)'.[55] At the same time, market research surged to become 'integral' to the film industry, in an era when conglomerate-owned studios wanted reassurance against unpredictability.[56] Today, marketing considerations guide production decisions in the Hollywood system. Janet Wasko defines this as a 'bottom-line or box-office mentality'.[57] With the development of marketing practices came the recurrent issue of constantly expanding marketing costs. Whereas studio era advertisers relied mostly on free publicity, P&A costs today represent about one third of a film's total cost by a major Hollywood studio. For big franchises, the cost can be much higher. In 1995, *GoldenEye*'s marketing costs reached 125 per cent of its production costs. In 2013, *Skyfall* kept them at 100 per cent, and relied on externalised publicity (tie-ins).

Beyond Hollywood

Given the capitalistic orientation of the US film industry, marketing found a ready ground in Hollywood. Film marketing, however, is used in film industries all over the world, as the following examples show.

Promotion of Bollywood movies has existed since the 1913 release of *Raja Harishchandra*, but film marketing actually developed in the mid-1990s, when the producer of *Hum Aapke Hain Kaun* (1994) decided to promote his film on television. Prior to the 1990s, aggressive campaigns had never seemed necessary as filmgoing was the main entertainment in the country. Since then, integrated marketing strategies have been commonly used, with previews, television appearances and dedicated websites.[58] The largest Mumbai-based distributors have adopted Hollywood-style standardised methods to promote their films in India and abroad, with P&A costs at about 10 per cent of a film's total budget.[59]

In France, another important film-making country, film marketing was first met with distrust, with cinema primarily considered as an art form and largely supported by the state. In the mid-90s, marketing was generally looked down upon by film professionals for ideological reasons: adopting marketing would mean giving in to US-style commodification, conglomeration and more generally to 'supermarket culture'.[60] The structure of the French film industry was also a factor explaining the slow adoption of marketing practices. With the exception of major companies Gaumont, Studio Canal and EuropaCorp., producers mostly work on a single project.[61] This cottage industry organisation does not allow for the allocation of large funds to marketing. The importance of state support, through French or European aid programmes, also tends to lessen the focus on the consumer in production decisions. In the 2000s, however, the development of wider releases and a cannibalisation phenomenon in peak season led to fierce competition, which pushed distributors to increasingly adopt a market logic focused on the consumer.[62]

In several countries, theatrical film marketing cannot exist as such. In Algeria, for example, the exhibition sector has collapsed over the past three decades, and only two commercial movie theatres still stand. Run by civil servants, these theatres, as well as the existing *cinémathèques* circuit, have no incentive to attract customers and simply post the day's programme outside the theatres.[63] In Nigeria, theatrical exhibition is also virtually non-existent and a flourishing local video film industry has developed since the 1990s,[64] with specific marketing practices. In recent years, Nollywood's push towards the international market has taken the form of advocacy marketing efforts, notably with the Los Angeles Nollywood Foundation.[65]

The development and range of film marketing practices can thus be correlated to each country's film production structure and culture: cottage industry vs integrated industry, art vs industry. One cannot, however, generalise, as within each country a variety of film production and marketing practices coexist. South Korea is, for example, home to both worldwide distributed, internationally co-produced sci-fi actioner *Snowpiercer* (2013) and to film-festival distributed, art-house *Moebiuseu* (2013). This volume will mostly concentrate on the marketing of English-language films, but seeks to provide reflection which can be of theoretical and practical use in various contexts around the world.

Film Marketing into the Twenty-First Century

Through academic articles and case studies, as well as interviews with professionals, this volume explores current film marketing issues, which take their roots in the 1980s wave of globalisation, characterised by 1) the opening of borders to financial, trade, population and culture flows and 2) the development of new information and communication technologies.

As borders opened, notably with the collapse of the Communist bloc, globalisation influenced the way identities were created, experienced and perceived. The easy circulation of cultural products led to the idea of the development of a 'global culture',[66] in which everyone became 'citizens of the world'. Rapidly, however, local identities claimed their place with renewed vigour.[67] Part I explores the current relevance of culture – with its diverse meanings – in film marketing decision-making and practices.

This part starts with an interview with former president of United International Pictures, Michael Williams-Jones, who shares his views on international marketing, stressing the importance of 'understanding your market and understanding your movie', and strongly defending the value of local expertise. Two articles then explore the implication of cultural differences for film marketing. Comparing the US and Greek campaigns of two Greek-oriented films, *My Big Fat Greek Wedding* (2002) and *My Life in Ruins* (2009), Tzioumakis and Papadimitriou contrast 'indie' and 'indiewood' marketing strategies in two different national contexts, and interrogate the use of stereotypes and localisation.

Stereotypes and national clichés are also at the centre of Tirtaine and Augros' article on the selling of British comedies in France. Their analysis of the main differences between the two markets and the choices made by distributors in terms of film titles and posters shows that Britishness has tended to be a major selling point when marketing British comedies in France, especially as from the 1990s.

In a case study, Mingant offers further reflexion on the localisation of campaigns through dubbing. Taking the example of the *Ice Age* franchise, she shows how the choice of famous local voices is a marketing asset for professionals in the USA and abroad.

Two essays then explore the major Hollywood studios' efforts to market their films internationally. Mingant examines Hollywood's renewed interest for non-US audiences since the mid-90s and brings to light the place of international marketing professionals and their role in the transformation of Hollywood big-budget films into highly marketable global-local films. Curtin, Jacks and Li reflect on the specific cultural and political challenges of the Chinese market, and show Hollywood operating in a highly constrained environment, by allying with local partners and relinquishing control of their products to online players.

Another market where distribution is deeply constrained by local circumstances is Nigeria. Nollywood – the Nigerian film business – is a predominantly non-theatrical industry. Jedlowski's case study shows that Nollywood, because of this, has a unique model of film marketing, which is based mostly on point-of-sale marketing strategies.

Taking a different view, the final chapter leads the reader to consider cinema as a specifically constructed culture. By detailing the marketing campaign led by Warner Bros. and Peter Jackson around *The Hobbit* 2012 and 2013 opuses, Ross shows how new technologies that revolutionise our understanding of realism can be rejected by audiences and create a marketing conundrum. This part concludes with an interview with film marketer Claudia Zavaleta, who discusses playing on audiences' expectations when distributing Bollywood films in Peru.

The second major issue since the 1980s has been the development of new communication technologies, notably the internet. In the past decades, the rapid development of social media has had a deep influence on the relationship between products and their consumers. The capacity to exchange opinion through Facebook, Twitter, YouTube or Vine has turned internet users (especially bloggers) into main players in the marketing process. Social media has made Alvin Toffler's 1980 concept of 'prosumer' – the combination of 'producer' and 'consumer' – a truism. Part II brings to light the opportunities and challenges offered by social media and user-generated content for film marketing.

Augros opens this part with a short reflexion on the interplay between official and non-official internet presence of the distributors, insisting on the blurry area of 'leaked' information. Tracing buzz-creating strategies back to the 1920s, he opens a vista on how word of mouth turned into e-WOM.

Equally insisting on the mixing of old and new strategies in the era of media convergence, Trowbridge shows how independent film-makers can tap into the internet's 'participatory culture'[68] to develop grassroots financing and distribution strategies away from the main gatekeepers.

Two shorter texts provide further case studies of marketers'/consumers' collaboration through social media. Aaron Williams relates how his SocialSamba website users can experience film and television-branded stories, as well as write their own versions of these programmes, in an example of viral marketing practice. Lozano Delmar and Muñiz-Velázquez's case study analysis of the video social network Vine shows both the opportunities offered by new technologies and the hesitations and learning processes for the distributors.

Lobato, indeed, warns that using consumers as promotional players can be 'double-edged'. He shows how distributors have to balance their desire to create e-WOM with efforts to prevent pirate access to their films through platforms such as BitTorrent.

Two final essays then take a more theoretical stand, offering new methodologies. Aiming to evaluate the value of e-WOM and user-generated content, Yecies, Yang, Berryman and Soh take the example of comments on Australian horror film *Bait* (2012) on China's Douban internet platform to propose a novel platform for social media data processing. In their chapter, based on a participant observation at the Scottish Documentary Institute, Franklin, Stoyanova Russell and Townley show how the analysis of Digital Engagement Metrics, such as Facebook Likes, influence the market, thus bringing to light the performative characteristics of social media.

Part I and II analyse the realms of culture and new technologies, focusing on the relationship between 1) the producer/film-maker/marketer and 2) their customers. An exploration of film marketing issues today, however, would have seemed incomplete without acknowledging B-to-B practices, to which a postscript is dedicated. Kitsopanidou presents the relationship between film-makers/producers and exhibitors through the case of *Avatar* (2009), focusing on Cameron's efforts in the adoption of 3D. The final article deals with an even less visible practice; Goldsmith offers insight into the work of film commissions around the world and their efforts to advertise their regions as 'film-friendly' locations for international shoots, in order to boost local economic activities. From national to virtual environments, from a culturally constructed spectator to an active prosumer, from B-to-C to B-to-B, this book proposes a journey through film marketing issues in the first decades of the twenty-first century.

Notes

1. Jean-François Camilleri, *Le Marketing du cinéma* (Paris: Dixit, 2006), p. 43.
2. Laurent Creton, *Economie du cinéma: Prespectives stratégiques* (Paris: Armand Colin Cinéma, 2005 [1994]), p. 162.
3. Camilleri, *Le Marketing du cinéma*, p. 44.
4. Nolwenn Mingant, *Hollywood à la conquête du monde: Marchés, stratégies, influences* (Paris: CNRS Editions, 2010), p. 76.
5. Robert G. Friedman, 'Motion Picture Marketing', in Jason E. Squire (ed.), *The Movie Business Book* (New York: Simon & Schuster, 1992 [1983]), p. 293.
6. Robert Marich, *Marketing to Moviegoers: A Handbook of Strategies and Tactics* (Carbondale, IL: Southern Illinois University Press, 2013, 3rd edn), p. 2.
7. Edward J. Epstein, *The Hollywood Economist* (New York: Melville House, 2010), p. 187.
8. Mark Litwak, *Reel Power: The Struggle for Influence and Success in the New Hollywood* (New York: William Morrow, 1986), p. 84.
9. Raymond Williams, quoted in John Tomlinson, *Cultural Imperialism: A Critical Introduction* (Baltimore: Johns Hopkins University Press, 1991), p. 5.
10. Hélène Laurichesse, *Quel marketing pour le cinéma?* (Paris: CNRS Editions, 2006), pp. 44–7.
11. Benedict Anderson, *Imagined Communities* (New York : Verso, 1991 [1983]), p. 6.
12. Warren J. Keegan, *Global Marketing Management* (Upper Saddle River, NJ: Prentice Hall, 2002, 7th edition), p. 2.
13. Carmel Camilleri and Margalit Cohen-Emerique (eds), *Chocs de cultures: Concepts et enjeux pratiques de l'interculturel* (Paris: L'Harmattan, 1989), p. 27.
14. Marich, *Marketing to Moviegoers*, p. 399.
15. 'Trekkies' are fans of the *Star Trek* universe.
16. Creton, *Economie du cinéma*, p. 162.
17. Finola Kerrigan, *Film Marketing* (Amsterdam: Elsevier, 2010), p. 10.
18. Ibid.
19. The SWOT analysis is a strategic management technique developed in the USA in the 1960s and 1970s.
20. Toby Miller, Nitin Govil, John McMurria and Richard Maxwell, *Global Hollywood* (London: BFI, 2001), p. 153.

21. Tiiu Lukk, *Movie Marketing: Opening the Picture and Giving it Legs* (Los Angeles: Silman-James Press, 1997), p. 5.
22. 'Rejigged Marketing Helps US Pics Soar', *Variety*, 28 October 2002.
23. Joël Augros, *L'Argent d'Hollywood* (Paris: L'Harmattan, 1996), p. 168.
24. Marich, *Marketing to Moviegoers*, p. 222.
25. Janet Wasko, *How Hollywood Works* (London: Sage, 2005), pp. 193–6. Philip Drake, 'Distribution and Marketing in Contemporary Hollywood', in Paul McDonald and Janet Wasko (eds), *The Contemporary Hollywood Industry* (Malden: Blackwell, 2008), p. 74.
26. Wasko, *How Hollywood Works*, p. 198.
27. Lukk, *Movie Marketing*, pp. 217–32.
28. See the *Ice Age* case study in this volume.
29. Jean-Marc Lehu, *Branded Entertainment: Product Placement & Brand Strategy in the Entertainment Business* (London: Kogan Page, 2007), p. 4. See also Kerry Segrave, *Product Placement in Hollywood Films: A History* (Jefferson: McFarland & Co., 2004).
30. Wasko, *How Hollywood Works*, p. 155.
31. Ibid., p. 154. 'The Skyfall's the limit on James Bond marketing', *Guardian*, 23 October 2013, www.theguardian.com/film/filmblog/2012/oct/23/skyfall-marketing-james-bond
32. Studies on audience motivation can be traced back in Hollywood to the late 1920s. For the role of George Gallup and Audience Research Inc. in the 1940s, see Susan Ohmer, *George Gallup in Hollywood* (New York: Columbia University Press, 2006).
33. Marich, *Marketing to Moviegoers*, p. 38.
34. Ibid., pp. 32–58.
35. Barry Litman and Hoekyun Ahn, 'Predicting Financial Success of Motion Pictures: The Early '90s Experience', in Barry Litman, (ed.), *The Motion Picture Mega-Industry* (Boston: Allyn and Bacon, 1998), p. 176.
36. Arthur De Vany, *Hollywood Economics: How Extreme Uncertainty Shaped the Film Industry* (New York: Routledge, 2004).
37. Miller *et al.*, *Global Hollywood*, p. 155.
38. Justin Wyatt, *High Concept: Movies and Marketing in Hollywood* (Austin: University of Texas Press, 2003 [1994]).
39. Marich, *Marketing to Moviegoers*, p. 33.
40. Miller *et al.*, *Global Hollywood*, p. 161.
41. Friedman, 'Motion Picture Marketing', p. 293.
42. Wasko, *How Hollywood Works*, p. 189.
43. Drake, 'Distribution and Marketing in Contemporary Hollywood', p. 71.
44. NRG has the same parent as trade publication *The Hollywood Reporter*, VNU. In 1997 NRG was integrated into the Nielsen Entertainment unit at VNU.
45. Cecilia Tirtaine, 'Le Nouvel essor du cinéma britannique (1994–2004): Facteurs conjoncturels et structurels', PhD Dissertation, Université Paris Ouest Nanterre, 2008, pp. 82–4.
46. Kerrigan, *Film Marketing*, pp. 115, 155.
47. David Bordwell, Janet Staiger and Kristin Thompson, *The Classical Hollywood Cinema: Film Style & Mode of Production to 1960* (New York: Columbia University Press, 1985), p. 144.
48. Cathy Klaprat, 'The Star as Market Strategy: Bette Davis in Another Light', in Tino Balio (ed.), *The American Film Industry* (Madison: University of Wisconsin Press, 1985), pp. 351–76.
49. Wasko, *How Hollywood Works*, p. 188.

50. Drake, 'Distribution and Marketing in Contemporary Hollywood', p. 67.
51. Ibid.
52. Mingant, *Hollywood à la conquête du monde*, pp. 224–5.
53. Joël Augros and Kira Kitsopanidou, *L'Economie du cinéma américain: Histoire d'une industrie culturelle et de ses stratégies* (Paris: Armand Colin Cinéma, 2009), pp. 124, 174. The national saturation technique was first experimented with by Warner Bros. with *Billy Jack* (1971).
54. Augros, *L'Argent d'Hollywood*, p. 286.
55. Wasko, *How Hollywood Works*, p. 189.
56. Wyatt, *High Concept*, pp. 155–60.
57. Wasko, *How Hollywood Works*, p. 54.
58. Camille Deprez, *Bollywood: Cinéma et mondialisation* (Villeneuve d'Ascq: Septentrion, 2010), pp. 77–9, 142.
59. Ibid., p. 72.
60. Creton, *Economie du cinéma*, p. 163.
61. Alejandro Pardo, *The Europe–Hollywood Coopetition: Cooperation and Competition in the Global Film Industry* (Pamplona: Ediciones Universidad de Navarra, 2007), p. 45.
62. Laurichesse, *Quel marketing pour le cinéma?*, p. 3.
63. Nolwenn Mingant, 'A Peripheral Market? Hollywood Majors and the Middle East/North Africa Theatrical Market', *Velvet Light Trap* vol. 75, 2015.
64. Ramon Lobato, *Shadow Economies of Cinema: Mapping Informal Film Distribution* (London: BFI, 2012), p. 57. Kerrigan, *Film Marketing*, p. 78.
65. Lobato, *Shadow Economies of Cinema*, p. 63.
66. Armand Mattelart, 'La nouvelle idéologie globalitaire', in Serge Cordellier (ed.), *La Mondialisation au-delà des mythes* (Paris: La Découverte/Poche, 2000), p. 86.
67. Benjamin Barber, 'Jihad vs McWorld', *The Atlantic Monthly*, March 1992.
68. Henry Jenkins, *Convergence Culture: When Old and New Media Collide* (New York: New York University Press, 2006), p. 331.

'My job is to find the right signals at the right moment for the right people'

An Interview with Benoît Mély

Laurent CRETON and Nolwenn MINGANT

After working for four years as Marketing Project Manager at French distributor Bac Films, Benoît Mély joined 20th Century-Fox in 2005. Since 2009, he has been Fox Searchlight Manager for France. Created in 1995, Fox Searchlight is one of the last 'independent labels' associated with a major US distributor. The company has created its own brand, notably with risky choices such as The Full Monty *(1997). It is associated with quality independent films. Although Benoît Mély's experience is linked to the French market, the practices and interrogations he describes have global relevance.[1]*

How would you define film marketing and what tools do marketers have at their disposal?
As a professional, I approach film marketing in a pragmatic way, but I also take the time to reflect on what people will think of a poster when they see it in half a second, passing in the street. Indeed, this half-second in the street is *the* crucial moment in any campaign. In a movie theatre, when the audience is eating popcorn, they are exposed to many trailers, but they remember only one out of three. We are all exposed to advertising signals linked to films, and my job is to find the right signals at the right moment for the right people. These are the fundamentals of marketing in general and of film marketing in particular.

The main tools of the trade are well known. They are the poster, the trailer, advertising in the media and on the internet. However, before using those tools, one should develop a preliminary strategic reflexion on the type of film one has to market, on how to communicate around it, on the most attractive approach to reach the public, on what should be downplayed or, on the contrary, highlighted in the final campaign.

Also, contrary to other sectors, cinema is an area where emotions, moods, conversations with other people, all determine people's choices. Each person's relationship to film is very personal. Films are products, but they are different from commodities or everyday consumer products. A central issue for marketers is thus to be able to discern what is not discernible – that is, everyone's subconscious desire, which is both personal and collective, thanks to the economic tools we have and, most of all, a reflexion on what the film conveys.

What does this strategic preliminary work consist of?
Concretely, the starting point is basic information on the film: the director, the actors, a few lines of synopsis and that's it. We haven't seen the movie or even parts of it at that point. So we start working out box-office figures thanks to that basic information only. In fact, the people on the street who see a poster while doing their shopping just take in the face or

Black Swan (2010) or 'how to sell the story of a psychotic ballet dancer'

name of the actor(s) and the visual; and they wonder whether they feel like seeing that film or not. Attendance figures are exactly that: how many people will feel like seeing the movie?

In order to estimate potential attendance figures, we use comparables. We make the lists of films by that director, or with these actors, or on similar topics. We then systematically correlate them with attendance figures. Of course, there can be no definitive conclusions, but it does give an indication.

Usually, the studio distributing the movie provides us with official comparables. For *Black Swan* (2010), Fox Searchlight had suggested *The Jacket* (2005) and *The Butterfly Effect* (2004) as comparable movies. We analysed their release dates, attendance figures, gross box office and number of prints. We then tried to define broad film categories. For example, the maximum number of tickets sold was 230,000 for Darren Aronofsky movies (*Requiem for a Dream* [2000], *The Wrestler* [2008]), 150,000 for films with strong acting performances by women (*Monster* [2003], *Antichrist* [2009], *Boys Don't Cry* [1999]), 200,000 for art-house movies starring Vincent Cassel and 300,000 for films starring Natalie Portman (except in *Star Wars* [1999, 2002, 2005] and *Closer* [2004]). This gave us benchmarks. It then appeared to us that the film should be marketed as an art-house movie, a critically acclaimed talent-loaded difficult movie, such as *The Piano* (1993) or *The Piano Teacher* (2001). We made an equation – Aronofsky + Portman + Cassel + violent movie + male and female target audience – and this became the centre of our marketing story. We felt the storyline of a swan-loving ambitious dancer didn't seem convincing enough in marketing terms. After working on the comparables, we move on to the release date, the SWOTS, the targets and the media plan.

To what extent is the release date important?

The release date is one of the most fundamental elements in the reflexion. There is a clear seasonality in movie consumption. People tend to prefer action films or monster films in the summer, but auteur films in February. Is it a real preference? Or does marketing convince people it is so? I don't know, but anyway the majors have adapted to these consumption patterns. And these patterns are always evolving. For example, up to six or seven years ago, French audiences were only offered back-catalogue films with limited appeal in August. Then, independent distributor Diaphana Films decided to try and release an auteur film, *The Page Turner* (2006), in August, betting on the absence of competition. The film sold a million tickets. Since then, each year, films shown at Cannes, such as *Melancholia* (2011), are released in French theatres in the last two weeks of August.

The release date is also important because the environment is very competitive and some weeks are unavoidable. For example, the Academy Awards have become a sort of seal of approval for film consumers. So, the French market has to follow what is going on in the USA. All important films are released between January and March. This leads to an open war situation. In fact, when I do manage to get the date I want with the exhibitors, in spite of the harsh competition, for me it is an indication that the film really has a chance to succeed at the box office.

What are the SWOTs?

SWOTs mean Strengths, Weaknesses, Opportunities and Threats. This analysis is important as positioning can transform an average film into a success or, conversely turn a good film into a box-office failure. Let me give you the example SWOTs for *Black Swan*. The strengths were the cast, the *Rosemary's Baby*-like atmosphere, the sexy and controversial quality and our positioning on the idea of a thriller in a dance environment with a strong context. The weaknesses were the lack of traction of the talents in an art-house pattern as well as the dance topic, which was too specific for film buffs but not enough for dancers. Among the opportunities, one finds the film's success at festivals, the potential tie-ins (for example, with luxury brands, although none materialised in the end) and the early availability of the film's print, which allowed us to show it to the press and various prescribers, such as bloggers. The threats were the presence of competing films in the same time-frame (*How Do you Know, The Way Back, Tron, Morning Glory, Last Night, Les Femmes du 6ème étage, True Grit* [all 2010]), the small marketing budget and the difficulty to organise personal appearances and press junkets with the cast and director.

What about the targets?

The targets are the people you are addressing. For us, at Fox Searchlight, the targets are not family audiences, but usually urban film-loving, older, frequent cinemagoers. Age is an important factor in determining a film's positioning. The age issue was central also to our campaign for *Rocky Balboa* (2006). Part of the audience was ready to go and see the film as they had grown up with the *Rocky* series. But the younger generation was likely to consider 'Rocky 6' was has-been. When we did the preliminary work, we found out, by surfing on the internet, that Rocky Balboa was a reference for rappers. They like Scarface and Rocky Balboa. He is an icon; it's the ultimate underdog story. There is a legendary aspect to that character. Plus, Stallone is widely known. Now, in *Les Guignols*,[2] Stallone is a recurrent character that makes people laugh. So, we couldn't emphasise the story of a sixty-something man making a come-back on the boxing ring. Catchphrases such as 'The Return of' or 'The New Rocky' were out of the question. We decided to erase everything related to age. Our story was 'It's Rocky, the Legend, who is back in movie theatres'. Then we thought out the media partnership. We didn't need to reach out to older generations. On the other hand, how could we appeal to the rapper, the hesitating woman attracted by the beautiful black-and-white poster? We erased all the problematic aspects of the film. We emphasised the notion of 'legend'. We didn't feature Stallone prominently, as we wanted to insist on the icon, not the man. In the end, our positioning was 'the moving story of a legend: a myth never dies'. Also this was 2006, when the French football team was on its way to the World Cup, and a prevalent story in the media was about Zinédine Zidane, one of the champions of the 1998 World Cup, about how he was too old but was participating anyway.

So the targets determine the positioning and the media strategy. Campaigns targeting women will feature posters placed near the main shopping areas, but not in business centres or along traffic lanes. Similar considerations determine the placement on the internet. To reach the female audience, ad spending will be made on websites dedicated to make-up or mothering. This is how we constitute the posting strategy.

How do you consider the use of the internet as a marketing tool?
The internet is the best medium in the world, as we can show video clips and reach specific targets. It is also … the worst medium in the world as we can never know if people have actually watched the ad. There are many banners on Hotmail and Yahoo, so people don't remember the ads they have just seen. Also people are exposed to so much information and spend such a short period of time on each page that it is far from being the ideal medium. However, it is the best way to show video clips to a potential audience, but as we release several video clips and have a different strategy for each site, this complicates the media plan operations.

Film marketing requires you to develop carefully devised, almost warlike, tactics. After years as a marketer, do you sometimes feel disconnected from the average audience?
Of course, it's very difficult to remain ingenuous. Indeed, we spend days scrutinising our competitor's campaigns, we watch hundreds of films, out of interest, passion, but also to stay informed of the competition. But, in spite of that, and maybe because my job is enthralling, I try to believe I am still the man on the street, the average person who is sensitive to a poster or not. I still go and see films on the faith of the impression their posters gave me.

Also, as marketing professionals, we sometimes need statistical tools – for example, to test a poster we have doubts about – but we can never have a mechanistic approach as there is no such thing as a unique marketing model. To come back to the issue of innocence, I also rely on my friends and relatives. When I discuss movies with people around me, I can identify the problematic elements in the films I am marketing at the moment. For example, when I told French people around me I was marketing a film called *The Descendants* (2011), they couldn't get the title; they went 'The what?' So we knew the title was going to be a problem. In the end, we decided to keep it anyway, both because we needed to stay in line with the Academy Awards campaign and because titles in English always give a cool and chic connotation. These everyday tests do feed our reflexion.

Now, it's true that the marketing vocabulary is a bellicose vocabulary, but we are closer to board games than to war. True enough, as in a war, there are objectives; there are means and logistics to reach objectives. To extend the metaphor: we use troops, orders and signals. Also, the slogans can be considered propaganda – they convince people that we are right in what we assert. The main difference is that we do not deal with politics. We do not use these warlike weapons, which affect people's intimate emotions, to defend political ideas, to urge people to buy products they don't need; we use these to support the magnificent messages conveyed by films.

Notes

1. This text is based on a 'roundtable' which took place during the CinEcoSA conference on film marketing held on 25 November 2011. Benoît Mély's presentation was chaired by Professor Laurent Creton (Université Sorbonne Nouvelle – Paris 3). It was transcribed, edited and translated by Nolwenn Mingant. The final text was approved by Benoît Mély.
2. Editors' note: a satirical puppet show, the equivalent of British *Spitting Image*. In *Les Guignols*, the Stallone puppet represents the USA.

I

MARKETING AND FILM CULTURE

'There simply isn't one-shape-fits-all for film'

An Interview with Michael Williams-Jones

Nolwenn MINGANT

Starting his career as a trainee for United Artists in Africa, Michael Williams-Jones soon became the Managing Director for Brazil, Latin America, Brazil and, later, the United Kingdom. In the late 1970s, he became president of United Artists International. He was in charge of Global Distribution and Marketing as well as Theatres and Production in certain regions. In 1981, as United Artists folded after the Heaven's Gate *debacle, he was asked by Lew Wasserman, chief executive of MCA Corporation (owner of Universal), and Charles Bluhdorn, chief executive of Gulf & Western (owner of Paramount), to head United International Pictures (UIP), their new joint venture, based in London. Williams-Jones headed UIP for fifteen years, until 1996. After years of working with major studios, he was very keen to work for a top independent company. Bob and Harvey Weinstein invited him to run Miramax International for a year before he finally retired in 2005.[1]*

How would you define film marketing?

Understanding your market and understanding your movie. Period. It goes back very early in the process of the production of a movie. The earlier the better. It's no good to start conceptual marketing at the point when the movie is made and you screen it. You have to have read the book or the screenplay and started to formulate views and ideas of how it might appeal, where its strongest and its weakest elements might be. And it *must* be examined almost forensically. And you examine it not only from one territory, but also from the points of view and interest of different markets. How would that story be best presented in Korea or Brazil or Russia or France? There is a priceless value in local knowledge. It's arrogant, but also idiotic to make critical decisions only in the so-called hallowed ground of a studio based in Hollywood. Unless you have people who genuinely know the heart and soul and character of the French or the Germans or the Italians or the British or whoever, how can you possibly make judgments affecting them? In most industries, you'll see that a great deal of respect is paid to local expertise through franchises, joint ventures or relationships to the local organisations. It is true there has been a sea change in technology which has changed marketing perceptions, but if you go around the world, you will still sense powerful differences in culture … And what you can fundamentally gain through good local knowledge is an understanding of of what these differences are and how to apply them to the marketing and selling of movies.

Can you give an example of marketing campaign adaptation?

Adaptation can be about changing the timing or the appearance of a marketing campaign, the addition of elements that are particularly appealing to local identities or the removal of elements. The first *Indiana Jones, Raiders of the Lost Ark* was a global hit in 1981, a time when we had just formed UIP. It worked in every country enormously. But I was confused by the film's failure in Japan, as it was the only country in the world where it did not perform. I ran a series of tests of the film in several cities in Japan and was astonished by the results. The original campaign showed Harrison Ford with a whip, a leather jacket and a Western cowboy hat. In fact, the Japanese reacted very negatively to the hat, very simply because hats had a very strong association with pre-war Japan. They were not fashionable and so were seen as negative in terms of seeing the film. I thought we'd have a little fun. We completely re-engineered the marketing campaign. Obviously we couldn't take the hat out of the film or the trailers. But in the presentations of the film – print ads and poster ads were very powerful in those days – we had a campaign with Harrison Ford without a hat, looking very dashing and daring. We released the film tentatively at first, then more broadly. It became a smash hit and set up the franchise. It's an illustration that you just cannot ignore local interest issues.

How do marketers get to know a specific local audience?

Back in the days of Irving Thalberg, movies were tested in front of audiences in the final stage of development, which is a very smart thing to do. It helps understand audience appeal. We would not only test the movie, but also trailers, poster concepts and various marketing concepts to selected audiences. Testing, however, should provide only additional information. Also the information obtained that way should not be read as the Bible, but put into context. You have to have the guts to put a lot of the decision-making into the hands of the people who understand the local market. Sometimes backing a local expert gives you a real added edge.

In 2001, you wrote an op-ed piece in *Variety*[2] to defend foreign marketers' expertise. What was happening at the time which made you react?

One problem was the burgeoning new philosophy that every film, or the majority of films, had to be released globally at the same time. There was this whole concept that we were in a global village and everything should be instantly made available because information was feeding around the world so quickly via the internet and if you waited the product would no longer be fresh. There was also the very real problem of piracy. So the big new idea was to release everything instantly and globally. But this doesn't take into consideration local nuances. There is, for example, the seasonality issue to examine. In certain markets, in the early 1990s, many theatres around the world were not air-conditioned, so why release in the heat of summer? Especially if this is a holiday season, like France, which empties out in August.

Now, in certain cases, global release is, of course, the right thing to do – for example, for pre-established franchises, like *James Bond* or *Spiderman*, as well as sequels or prequels and major animated events. The product is already known, so you can have a common campaign designed by a studio, which is rubber-stamped around the world. But where that studio philosophy becomes a problem is when they've got a new film, a unique product which is not known and hasn't been established with its own identity in each market. If you decide you're going to blast out with a Hollywood-designed campaign and that's it, you're actually putting the movie at risk. You need to have input from all the different markets. Not every market will create its own campaign, as there are cost issues that have to be considered. But some necessarily will. I remember, for example, Italy, France and Germany and the United Kingdom, in Europe, all had very distinctive ways of portraying a film. There is a different process. Italy and France always produced magnificent posters, stylish works of art, often abstract but connected in terms of the theme. Trailers would evolve differently, not in the more heavy-handed Hollywood style but often with European subtleties. A movie that is a new original idea, that needs to be tailored to the local market, should not be released simultaneously. There are times when it is a good idea to establish a film in a few markets and then gradually roll out the rest, basing the strategy upon the cumulative success as it builds on word of mouth, etc. One has to be sensible and nuance the release of prototype films. I think this is a very important aspect of global marketing: there simply isn't one-shape-fits-all for film.

You say marketers should be involved very early in the production process. What room are producers giving marketers in the film's production choices?
Well, that process has moved a long way. Today, with the economic growth of the global marketplace – Russia, China, Eastern Europe or Korea, the simple box-office influence of the global market is such that smart and experienced film-makers – and 'greenlighters' – have realised that input from these areas is invaluable. It need not be merely in the marketing area. It could be, for example, in the casting. For a film with a sequence shot in South-East Asia, the local marketers could suggest local actors who are at that time extremely popular in South Korea or Japan. Casting based upon international knowledge is very important. But this influence goes beyond casting, with music, with other creative areas in film production. Bringing in the input from local specialists can be profoundly important at a very early stage. More and more this is being recognised. But it's not new. Way back, United Artists, about from 1970–8, brought in marketing managers and distribution managers from all around the world to New York to grind out ideas. If there was a good thought, it would find its way to the actual film itself. So, very early on, before the product is made, marketers – in Europe and elsewhere – would understand what it is. During the production process, marketers should really be involved in designing advertising and promotional materials at the very earliest stage, from the point the project is actually being greenlit. These early initiatives can filter into the marketplace as teasers and grow the interest of newly conceived movies. By the time the film is ready to come out, you've got people who really do understand what they've got to market and sell and a public already aware of the movie …

What are the biggest difficulties for marketers?
The biggest obstacle in marketing a film is if it's a bad movie. If you've got a 'turkey', as we used to call them, it's very difficult to turn that into a rose. But film-makers will invariably blame film marketing or bad distribution for a film's failure.

The other thing that we should never forget: if you are unable to make your product stand above the clutter, you limit your chances to succeed. You've got to find something unique. Hitchcock used to call it the McGuffin, the secret alchemy that makes something special. The problem nowadays is that there is so much that looks the same. The trailers look the same. In film marketing, what you need to do is be able to have a unique identity or as unique an identity for that film in the marketplace as you can. That's got to be your first objective. How do we separate our movie from the pack? What is special or different about it? It may not even be that good, but how can we make it appear to be interesting and different?

What would you say were the most important evolutions for film marketing in the past decades?
Technologies and delivery systems and the advertising opportunities they provide. When I

came into the industry, you primarily relied on print, posters, trailers in cinemas and a few other promotional devices. Television was largely unavailable in much of the world, as it was controlled by the state or you could not advertise commercial products like films or spirits. As television became more liberated, it became a great new window of opportunity to advertise. But I think the single biggest leap has been the advent of the internet, where you can very cost-effectively reach huge audiences and almost instantly create demand. It can work both ways. It can be demand for or rejection of a film. It depends on how successful you are in its use. The internet has transformed the whole concept of marketing. I don't think we, even today, fully understand how powerful it really is. And it's not just the usual suspects on the internet. It's the social sites, the various internet magazines, which enable you to target specific films. You may have minority films dealing with minority issues, and you may be able to specifically cast your advertising strategy to minority cable programmes … to focused minority outlets on the internet that deal with certain narrower themes and issues. So it focuses in and narrows the risk to some extent if you can tap into this. It's given a whole new strategic focus to film marketing.

However, you shouldn't overwhelmingly be dominated by the internet because everybody is using it. Maybe there are occasions when you don't even want to go on the internet. In its peculiar way, this approach creates a fresh buzz, and … 'Why isn't it on the internet?' becomes a discussion point. Maybe you simply go out on billboard and print advertising and don't even touch television. Maybe you release it in a few theatres and let word of mouth build. The key is to think out of the box … always!

Another issue is that nowadays people have become very sceptical and cynical because there is so much garbage out there. The cost of going to the movies is huge and very often the result is disappointment. I think a classic example is the overabundance of 3D movies. There's nothing wrong with 3D technology. Its advancement has been exceptional. But nine out of ten movies made in 3D today are devaluing the technology. They're not adding to public interest. People have become sceptical and say 3D has become just another overpriced gimmick. And that's what killed it the last time around and the time before that. So film-makers must be very careful about how they use technologies like this to enhance film. The most important aspect of all is never to forget the art of storytelling and of character. This lies at the very core of film-making.

What are the challenges for the future?

On the positive side, the rehabilitation of movie theatres from the 1980s onwards and the wave of more imaginative film-makers from around the world. As well as Hollywood, they have expanded audiences because they understand the uniqueness of cinema. But, on the negative side, I am worried right now that some studios and film-makers are dangerously narrowing the windows – that is, the release from theatrical to home entertainment alternatives and television. They should be very wary of tampering with this. Obviously, there's a huge and essential economy in all the ancillary markets, which is an integral part of the profit cycle of film. Cinema itself will continue to evolve in terms of technology, comfort and service. It may, for example, offer multiple tiers of price-sensitive comfort and service. Some say audiovisual home entertainment, in its broadest sense is going to eventually take over and signal the decline of traditional cinema. But I don't think so at all! Cinema and its ancillaries are mutually dependent upon one another. It is an essential symbiosis. We still flock to film after more than a century in its intended venue, the cinema. And the uniqueness of that experience, seated in a darkened auditorium when the lights go out and your entire focus for two hours is on that unfolding story, is irreplaceable! If you watched that same story at home, it would be a very different experience. Theatrical viewing has got to be respected as the vehicle that establishes the fundamental life value of a film. It is what creates the excitement, the buzz and the desire to return … And theatre owners and film-makers must respect their audience and strive to give them a truly special audiovisual experience. Above all, film has to deliver entertainment in its widest context to the audience. There is nothing that is comparative to the silent but palpable tension in an audience of 500 people following a thriller or the howls of laughter when people are taken by comedy. That's an addictive quality that will keep cinema as a unique experience in the same way that opera and theatre continue to prosper. So we must believe in the future of film and cinema as a combination. It still is the launch pad that will sustain values in the rest of the industry. It requires belief with a capital B!

Notes

1. The interview was conducted by Nolwenn Mingant on 10 July 2012. The following text is an abridged version of the interview, amended by the editors and approved by Michael Williams-Jones.
2. Michael Williams-Jones, 'Global Biz Requires Global Expertise', *Variety*, 19 February 2001.

And Tom Cruise Climbed the Burj Khalifa, or How Marketing Shapes Hollywood Film Production

Nolwenn MINGANT

In the 1920s and 30s, a series of protests reached the Hollywood majors through diplomatic channels. Italians complained about being represented as clowns and gangsters, and banned offensive films such as *Top Hat* (1935) and *Star of Midnight* (1935). The French banned *Beau Geste* (1939) in all the territories under their influence. Ruth Vasey describes how, although the international market represented only 35 per cent of their worldwide revenues in the inter-war period, the majors weaved this issue into the 1930 Production Code, their code of self-censorship.[1] By instructing that 'the history, institutions, prominent people and citizenry of other nations shall be represented fairly', the majors strove to prevent any obstacle to international distribution. Vasey insists on the 'extent to which the worldwide dimensions of Hollywood's audience influenced the nature of its products',[2] through practices such as scanning scripts to erase any potentially offensive material and hiring famous non-US actors.[3] Foreign sensitivities were transmitted to Hollywood producers and creators through embassies as well as through individual experts.[4] The systematic consideration given to the international market disappeared, however, with the collapse of the studio system after World War II.[5] Over the years, the importance of non-domestic viewers has varied. Since the mid-1990s, however, the foreign market has regained importance, with the development of new distribution platforms from VHS onwards, and the opening of new markets in the former Communist bloc and in Asia. Hollywood's attention turned abroad again. As foreign spectators gradually became the focus of attention, the majors looked for foreign expertise again and found it in their international distribution offices around the world. The marketing personnel abroad gained in importance, reaching a point where their opinion is carefully listened to. Today's centrality of the role of international marketers was made possible by the importance of marketing in Hollywood over the past three decades. The aim of this chapter is to tell the story of how the international marketers have acquired a pre-eminent place in Hollywood, shaping the films that reach the screens..

Film Marketing and Film Production

The influence of advertising on film production largely pre-dates marketing. As early as the 1900s, advertising discourse, through its emphasis on novelty, realism, spectacle and stars, was shaping 'standard requirements for a film'.[6] In the 1930s, star vehicles were created around actresses such as Bette Davis.[7] Another way advertising influenced production was through the practice of previews and test screenings, which dates back to the mid-1910s, at a moment when the majors moved towards a more scientific management.[8] Previews enabled producers to test the audience's reaction and led to revisions and reshoots.[9]

Although advertising had an early influence on film production, marketing, a scientific discipline and method born in the 1930s, flourished only in the late 60s in Hollywood, at

Marketing studies led to different versions of *Fatal Attraction* (1987)

a time when the studio system had collapsed and traditional advertising and publicity patterns, based on the brand names of star and studios, had lost relevance. The establishment of marketing in Hollywood can be correlated with a movement of conglomeration in
the film industry, from the buy-out of Paramount by Gulf and Western in 1966 to the acquisition of Columbia by Coca-Cola in 1982. The acquisition of film companies by large non-
film-related conglomerates led to an evolution of the general mentality, notably to the loss
of 'showmanship' and a strong emphasis on minimising risk and fighting unpredictability.[10]
Hitherto the traditional – and somewhat mythical – model of decision-making had been
the movie-mogul, deciding with his guts. In conglomerated Hollywood, decision-making
came to rest with a 'greenlight' committee, a group of executives evaluating the break-
even potential of each project. Such committees, which are ultimately 'responsible for what
gets up on the silver screen',[11] first included the chairmen and senior vice-presidents.[12]
Marketing was welcome in this context as a scientific approach to production, a method
to fight the unpredictability of the film business, and domestic marketing executives came
to be included in the committees in the 1980s. From the 80s on, 'marketing and distribution executives have begun to dominate studio decision-making'.[13]

It is this turning point that Wyatt analyses in his seminal study *High Concept*. Tracing
this trend both to the context of conglomeration and the development of new distribution
platforms, Wyatt identifies a specific type of film 'not driven by a personal vision' but for
which 'the logic of the marketplace is clearly the author of the style'.[14] All the elements of
the film, notably striking visuals, are conceived in order to be easily extracted for marketing
purposes at the distribution stage. Citing examples such as *Top Gun* (1986), *Star Wars*
(1977), *Grease* (1978), *Flashdance* (1983) and *Ghostbusters* (1984), Wyatt calls this the
'industrial expressivity' of a 'film with marketing assets sewn into its aesthetics construction'.[15] *Fatal Attraction* (1987) is notably famous for having had four different endings proposed for test screenings.[16]

Although not all films can be defined as 'high concept', the influence of marketing on film production has been deeply entrenched for major Hollywood films since the 1980s.[17] As Kerrigan notes, film marketing 'begins at the new product development stage and continues throughout the formation of the project ideas, through production and into distribution and exhibition'.[18]

In a 2013 interview for this chapter, Randy Greenberg shared his experience as a marketing executive. Confirming that 'you cannot make a movie today without marketing and distribution agreeing to it, at least in the Hollywood world',[19] Greenberg noted that production and marketing executives are in daily dialogue. The central contribution from marketers is the creation of visually striking images, which he defines as 'iconic' or 'emblematic' and which can be used in the marketing campaigns. An example of such images is the floating candle scene in *Harry Potter*'s Hogwarts dining room. The influence of marketing can be felt from elements as diverse as casting choices, inclusion of product placement, choice of shots (for example, clearly showing actors using a product) and editing decisions. If the influence of marketing on production established itself in the 1980s, the influence of international marketers became significant only a dozen years later.

International Marketing Executives: From the Periphery to the Centre

From their very early years, the Hollywood studios have had representatives around the world.[20] After World War II, the majors quickly regained their international dominance and in the 1960s foreign markets were of great economic importance. The majors' international advertising and publicity departments, however, stood on the periphery of the Hollywood system, which enabled them to enjoy a high degree of autonomy, and routinely tailor campaigns to the local market. In the late 1970s and early 1980s, marketing executives took over the advertising offices and successfully applied techniques such as market research or advance screenings to foreign territories. A continuity from the advertising/publicity era to the marketing age was the attention given to local specificities. At a time when the domestic market was taking centre stage for the Hollywood majors,[21] international salespeople seem to have been quite autonomous. By the 1980s, their secondary and peripheral role seemed clearly established.

In the 1990s, a new wave of globalisation took place, with the opening of new markets in Eastern Europe and Asia and the development of new distribution platforms, which translated into growing international revenues for the majors. As CNN, MTV and, later, the internet actively spread images of the American culture abroad, the Hollywood majors started to consider the world as one market sharing a common cultural ground, and pushed their marketing practices towards more uniformity and standardisation. For the international marketing departments, this meant a drastic curtailing of the autonomy they had hitherto enjoyed. They increasingly started to use the original posters as well as the original English titles.[22]

The homogenisation of international campaigns was accelerated by two factors. First, major films, such as *Back to the Future, Part III* (1990), started to be released day-and-date – that is, on the same day in the USA and in the biggest international territories. The rapid and wide distribution of prints, motivated both by a desire to fight piracy and to benefit from the US buzz, led distributors to favour standardised campaigns as there was no gap any more to make local adjustments. Second, the development of worldwide merchandising plans, which turned films such as *Jurassic Park* (1993) into global brands, further pushed for the adoption of the same visuals and titles around the world. Although some campaigns were still adapted in the 1990s, localisation was not the favoured option any more.

The apparent homogenisation of the world market increasingly led the Hollywood majors to put global campaigns in the hands of the domestic marketing departments. In the early 2000s, the merging of international and domestic marketing, generally, under the supervision of a domestic market executive, enabled the majors to regain control of marketing choices for territories whose importance had become vital. It also sparked off strong protest on the part of Hollywood's foreign marketers, who warned of the diversity of the international market and the need for local expertise.[23]

At the very moment when Hollywood was dreaming of a homogenised global market, the world was actually experiencing a 'resurgence of the national',[24] which directly impacted film practices. Day-and-date releases began to be questioned by international distributors complaining about lack of time to change the campaigns in case of a flop on the domestic market, the lack of availability of stars' personal appearance tours abroad and the cannibalisation of major titles during the summer. While day-and-date remained the favoured option for big-budget event films such as *Pearl Harbor* (2001), the distribution and marketing teams were increasingly deciding on staggered releases for other types of productions, such as *Moulin Rouge* (2001). The idea of a uniform world was also belied by the fact that Hollywood started to dub films in more and more languages,[25] after the success the Hindi version of *Jurassic Park* (1993) on the difficult Indian market.[26] After the dream of a homogenised world started to bring domestic and international marketing teams closer – not necessarily to the latter's advantage – the renewed importance of localisation pushed for further collaboration.

From the 2000s onwards, the new motto became 'Think Local when Going Global'. In this new context, international campaigns came to be considered from the very beginning, at the same time as the domestic campaign.[27] Marketing teams have to prepare potential marketing material at the same time both for domestic and international purposes – for example, taking pictures of the main actors 'in various outfits to suit specific international tastes'.[28] Distributing a Hollywood film now means coordinating between a central marketing office in the USA and the multiple international marketing offices. Organisationally, each major has to strike the right balance between the 'local' pan of the weighing scales (foreign marketers and their expertise) and the 'global' pan (central decision-making offices in the USA), to reconcile centralisation and flexibility, world planning and local initiative.[29] This new organisation, with the preoccupation for the international market featured early on in campaign developments, marks a major step in the evolution of the international marketers' place in Hollywood. Leaving the periphery, they became more and more integrated in the system. As they started to collaborate more closely with the domestic marketing offices, they were increasingly consulted not only on marketing but also on production issues.

International marketers had previously had an occasional influence on production, the most famous example being *Fatal Attraction*, which was released in Japan not with the ending selected for the USA, but with the alternative ending in which Alex Forrest committed suicide.[30] It is not until the late 1990s, however, that the growing importance of the international market pushed the majors to seriously look for more information on their films' potential in specific territories. The foreign marketing departments were the ones who could answer. With their expertise in demand and their offices being merged with the domestic offices, international marketers gradually became more closely associated with production decisions, until they finally joined the greenlight committees in the early 2000s.[31]

Over the course of the twentieth century, international marketing executives have thus journeyed from the periphery of the Hollywood system to the very centre of decision-making. Today, they collaborate closely with their domestic counterparts, reading the scripts, providing estimations (ultimates) on potential international revenues and sharing their local expertise at the highest level. Although international marketers are only one of the many departments sitting in the greenlight committees,[32] their inclusion in the studios' decision-making centres has had traceable effects on production decisions.

International Influence Today

In order to grasp the extent of the influence of international market consideration on film production in Hollywood one can paradoxically start by tracing the types of films which are not made. A good example is Jon Favreau's difficulties in financing *Elf* (2003) due to the 'lack of foreign playability' of a Christmas movie with an internationally unknown actor.[33] The majors will avoid dedicating a large budget to films with genres and themes too specifically American. The victims of this 'Americana syndrome'[34] are especially movies about sports (football, baseball), trials and US history (the Civil War), as well as African-American comedies. Such genres and themes, which systematically fail internationally, are thus given limited budgets, which can be recouped on the domestic market only. The international marketers' scope of action seems, indeed, limited to big-budget movies, but, as they are Hollywood's largest films, this influence can be considered significant. In internationally oriented big-budget films, one can also start by looking at what is actually not in the film. Former UIP president Andrew Cripps thus underlines that, when reading scripts, he made sure to blot out words, phrases and sequences that could be hurtful to important markets, such as Russia or China, in order to avoid 'problems further down the line when the film is already made'.[35] In the 2012 remake of 1984's *Red Dawn*, the producers were, for example, careful to replace the Russian villains. After first choosing Chinese villains, they settled for villains from North Korea, which is not a market for Hollywood.[36] Not only do the majors try to avoid culturally hurtful references, they also fully focus their big-budget production choices on the international market.

The influence of international marketing executives on greenlighting criteria has led to the development of what I call elsewhere 'global-local films'[37] – that is, films which combine the Hollywood production values popular around the world with internationally oriented elements. The most visible of these elements is the attention given to casting. For big-budget films, studios will tend to favour American actors who are popular abroad. While for an American-oriented project, Denzel Washington would be a good choice, for an internationally oriented project, Brad Pitt would be more adequate. The global-local film also heavily relies on non-American talent, favouring actors who are popular both in the USA and abroad, such as Penelope Cruz, Javier Bardem or Marion Cotillard.[38] In a practice called 'stunt casting', foreign actors are chosen to give an international feel to a film. Their presence can subsequently be exploited in the marketing campaign. For the film *GI Joe: Rise of the Cobra* (2009), South Korean actor Byung-hun Lee features differently in US and international posters. On the US poster,[39] he appears masked and is in the background, which corresponds to the secondary importance of his character. On the other hand, prominent place is given to the heroes, whose faces are clearly visible, notably Channing Tatum's. If the US poster appears to have been used internationally, another version exists, in which Byung-hun Lee's character, although still standing in the background, is unmasked and strikes a martial pose, looking straight at the camera, thus offering the vision of a more assertive character. This version was used in Japan, Hong Kong, Singapore, Taiwan, Vietnam, China and South Korea.[40] For Japan and Korea, the local team foregrounded the local actor even more by creating posters specifically centred on his character.[41] The actor also was the main attraction during the 2009 Korean press junket.[42] Stunt casting is thus not simply conceived as directed towards a specific country, but can be exploited over larger regional areas.[43]

A second criterion influenced by foreign views is the growing tendency of Hollywood films to take place outside US territory. The increased importance of the international market is visible in franchises which start in the USA and then travel abroad, such as Soderbergh's *Ocean* series which takes its actors around Europe in its second opus (2004). Amsterdam's historical houses, Rome's palaces and the shores of Lake Como all feature in the trailer, giving an exotic touch for the international as well as the US audiences. Beyond exoticism, featuring non-US locations, such as in the *Bourne* and *Bond* franchises, can also be about staying in touch with the zeitgeist, as these films embrace 'the globe-trotting elements of their storylines to make them seem more relevant in a modern connected world'.[44] Even animation follows this mix of exoticism and internationalisation, as can be seen on the trailers of *Madagascar 3: Europe's Most Wanted* (2012), which foregrounds visually striking representations of Europe's well-known monuments (the Eiffel Tower, the leaning Tower of Pisa) and includes snippets of French, thus targeting both locals and tourists. The marketing value of foreign locations is further heightened when films are actually shot abroad, such as *Mission: Impossible – Ghost Protocol* (2011) in Dubai. The film rests on an international cast, with actors from India to Finland playing opposite American Tom Cruise, and espouses the globe-trotting rhythm of adventure blockbusters, taking the spectator from Moscow to Mumbai to Seattle. Dubai, however, takes a special importance in the film. The stage of a central episode, the highest tower of the city, the Burj Khalifa, actually becomes inscribed in the visual identity of the film. The worldwide poster[45] foregrounds the four main characters and has the tower standing tall in the background. A more breathtaking poster[46] also circulated worldwide, showing a high-angle shot of Tom Cruise climbing the tower. This scene actually became the signature of the film. In the Gulf, the presence of the American team created a buzz at the time of shooting. The buzz was kept alive with the decision to have the film's premiere take place during the Eighth International Dubai Film Festival. Tom Cruise's presence notably had large coverage in the press and on the internet. Paramount's internationalisation strategy for the film was a success, with *Mission: Impossible – Ghost Protocol* earning 84 per cent more than *Mission: Impossible III* five years earlier. Mature markets, such as Japan or Germany, showed a respectable increase of 57 per cent. Among the markets showing an impressive revenue gap between the two instalments were Middle Eastern markets: Lebanon (+160 per cent) and the United Arab Emirates (+277 per cent).[47]

The influence of the international market can also be felt in less immediately visible signs, notably in terms of genre. In 2001, Italian academic Franco Moretti made a comparative analysis of the five most successful US films per year between 1986 and 1995 in forty-six countries around the world. Focusing on the issue of genre, he notably noticed the striking success of action films all over the world, with the exception of Europe, and pronounced South and East Asia 'these films' favourite destination'.[48] While 'Americana' films tend to fail abroad, some genres are, indeed, easier to sell as they are more popular with the international audience: action/adventure, as well as visual comedies, epics, sci-fi films and franchises. With the international market representing up to 70 per cent of a film's revenues, increased attention to the genre of the films produced is in order today. In *Variety*'s International Top 100 for 2013, action/adventure films represented 51 per cent of the total. Actually, not all of theses films were American as other film industries are equally careful to cater to their local audiences' taste for action with films such as *Journey to the West: Conquering the Demons* (China) or *Dhoom 3* (India). The importance of the international market has thus accentuated Hollywood's tendency to concentrate on the action-adventure genre. Another noteworthy element is that thirteen of the top twenty films on the *Variety* list were part of franchises, which makes revenues more predictable as the domestic and international audience can be considered as pre-sold. This attention to international preference is clearly visible in *Star Trek Into Darkness* (2013). Aware that international audiences prefer fantasy to pure sci-fi, and after the failure of several opuses of the franchise, Paramount toned down the science-fiction aspect in the marketing campaign, enhancing the 'terrestrial' issues of the story.[49] It also actually wove international preferences into the very style of the movie. Journalist Brooks Barnes thus underlines how a scene in which Captain Kirk 'zooms through an asteroid field' in a space suit clearly reminds the audience of *Iron Man*, a super-hero franchise which is one of Paramount's big successes internationally.[50] The fact that *Star Trek Into Darkness* and *Mission: Impossible – Ghost Protocol* rely on a team of adventurers is also an asset in conquering the international market. The ensemble cast practice makes it easy to fit in a few foreign personalities who will appeal to different markets, such as Japanese Tadanobu Asano and Swedish Stellan Skarsgård alongside a cast of Anglo actors in *Thor: The Dark World* (2013).[51]

Action-adventure movies are also an asset as they are the ideal vehicles for cutting-edge special effects. These technological enhancements, such as 3D, are especially popular in Asia's growing markets.[52] Technology can also help in roundabout ways. While China remains quite closed to Hollywood films, with a yearly quota of about twenty films, it opened an additional quota of fourteen foreign films for IMAX and 3D formats,[53] a fact which cannot but encourage Hollywood to favour 3D-friendly genres: in 2012, China became Hollywood's top international market, ahead of Japan. The popularity of new technologies such as IMAX, Dolby Atmos sound, or 4DX in other growing markets, such as the United Arab Emirates, acts as a further incentive to favour special effects, and to publicise these new technologies on the poster and in the marketing campaign.

One should, finally, note a more occasional practice applied to markets of special interest: 'customized editing'[54] – that is, the creation of a specific version for one market. Marketing *Pearl Harbor* to the Japanese audience required culturally sensitive adaptation: repositioning the film from a war to a love story, notably by changing the poster;[55] softening offensive expressions in the translated version;[56] and inserting a new scene in which a Japanese pilot gestures to young American boys to run for cover before he starts firing on the military base.[57] With Japan as one of the top markets, a modification of the original scene was thought worthwhile. Currently, the Hollywood distributors are trying to adapt to the Chinese market, either by deleting scenes, as in *Men in Black 3* (2012),[58] or adding new ones, as in *Iron Man 3* (2013) whose local version featured two additional scenes with famous Chinese actors and tied the US hero's recovery to Chinese traditional medicine.[59] Motivated more by a desire to placate the censorship board than to reach out culturally to the Chinese audience, one cannot ascertain to what extent the local spectators embraced these particular adaptations. The large success of *Iron Man 3* in China seems, however, to validate the strategy. The strong share of the international audience in the global box-office revenues, and the official demands of certain key markets, have thus woven international consideration into the very structure of the Hollywood film production and distribution process.

Asked, in 2013, how Hollywood could reconcile different audiences today, marketing executive Randy Greenberg argued that projects designed 'specifically for one culture at the expense of others can't be exploited outside of its organic opportunity'.[60] Under the current influence of marketing executives, the international market itself is actually becoming organic to Hollywood and its production process. Big-budget films are evolving, enhancing their global colour, in order to stay attuned with the hyperconnected psyche of global citizens. Does that mean that, after having become a representation of the multicultural US society, Hollywood is now becoming a synecdoche for a global 'salad bowl'? Such a view would be ignoring the market imperatives behind the growing influence of international executives. Although the move from outsiders to insiders has meant that international marketers are now given a voice, not all territories are equally treated. Markets of lesser economic importance and in which the Hollywood majors have no direct distribution offices are left aside and unheard, as is the case with Africa. The story that these films tell us today is less that of globalisation than that of the changing geography of Hollywood's audience, as the origin of actors shows. In the 1980s, as the domestic market was foremost on the majors' minds, roles not held by US actors were filled by British actors.[61] In the 1990s, a wave of Australian and New Zealand actors took over from the British, reinforcing rather than weakening the pre-eminence of actors from the Anglo sphere. As the foreign market started to gain importance in the mid-1990s, more roles were held by non-US actors, and their national origins started to become more diverse, including Eastern Europe. The first signs of Asian influence started to be seen also at that time, with the presence of Malaysian Michelle Yeoh in *Tomorrow Never Dies* (1997) and Hong Kong Jackie Chan in the *Rush Hour* series. Ten years into the twenty-first century, the importance of the Asian market is confirmed, from the casting of South Korean Byung-hun Lee in *GI Joe: Rise of the Cobra*, to the – very brief – presence of an Indian astronaut at the beginning of *Gravity* (2013), to the Godzilla-style *Pacific Rim* (2013). A map of the world would then have Asia, Europe, Australia and North America loom large, while Latin America would stand smaller and the Middle East and Africa appear as tiny dots. The map is in constant evolution, however. As new markets are opening to Hollywood, the spectrum of potential influences is constantly widening, as the case of *Mission: Impossible – Ghost Protocol* shows regarding the increasingly profitable Persian Gulf market. Keenly aware of the box-office potential of the largest international markets, the majors have fully integrated their production and marketing procedures for big-budget films. The eagerness to open China and other emerging markets will also take them a step further, bypassing marketing executives altogether and tuning in directly to foreign producers, as the practices of co-production and local-language productions are being revived with films such as *The Karate Kid* (2010, US/China) and *My Name is Khan* (2010, US/India/UAE). From films with US protagonists capering over the world to films with multicultural casts, to co-productions and local-language productions, the international market is slowly but steadily changing the face of Hollywood films, and international marketing executives stand as one of the central instruments of this change.

Notes

1. Ruth Vasey, *The World According to Hollywood (1918–1939)* (Madison: University of Wisconsin, 1997).
2. Ibid., p. 3.
3. Ibid., p. 8.
4. Ibid., p. 81.
5. Ruth Vasey, 'Foreign Parts: Hollywood's Global Distribution and the Representation of Ethnicity', *American Quarterly* vol. 44, 1992, p. 638.
6. David Bordwell, Janet Staiger and Kristin Thompson, *The Classical Hollywood Cinema: Film Style & Mode of Production to 1960* (New York: Columbia University Press, 1985), p. 101.

7. Cathy Klaprat, 'The Star as Market Strategy: Bette Davis in Another Light', in Tino Balio (ed.), *The American Film Industry* (Madison: University of Wisconsin Press, 1985), p. 376.
8. Bordwell, Staiger and Thompson, *The Classical Hollywood Cinema*, p. 144.
9. Ibid., pp. 152–3.
10. Mark Litwak, *Reel Power: The Struggle for Influence and Success in the New Hollywood* (New York: William Morrow, 1986), pp. 96–7.
11. William Goldman, *Adventures in the Screen Trade: A Personal View of Hollywood and Screenwriting* (New York: Warner Books, 1983), p. 39.
12. Nolwenn Mingant, *Hollywood à la conquête du monde: Marchés, stratégies, influences* (CNRS Editions, 2010), p. 208.
13. Litwak, *Reel Power*, pp. 97–8.
14. Justin Wyatt, *High Concept: Movies and Marketing in Hollywood* (Austin: University of Texas Press, 2003 [1994]), p. 34.
15. Ibid., pp. 60–1.
16. Edward J. Epstein, *The Big Picture, Money and Power in Hollywood* (London: Random House Trade, 2006, 2nd edn), p. 202.
17. Janet Wasko, *How Hollywood Works* (London: Sage, 2005), p. 54.
18. Finola Kerrigan, *Film Marketing* (Amsterdam: Elsevier, 2010), pp. 9–10.
19. Phone interview with the author, 21 February 2013.
20. For a history of the studios' early efforts abroad, see Kristin Thompson, *Exporting Entertainment: America in the World Film Market, 1907–1934* (London: BFI, 1985).
21. In the 1970s, notably due to an economic crisis, the majors retrenched to Hollywood. They stopped producing foreign films, which had been an important source of foreign revenues. At the same time, foreign cinemagoing numbers started plummeting. The domestic market, however, was booming, especially with the development of ancillary markets, such as cable television and videocassettes.
22. Martine Danan, 'Marketing the Hollywood Blockbuster in France', *Journal of Popular Film and Television* vol. 23, 1995, pp. 138–9.
23. 'Global Biz Requires Global Expertise', *Variety*, 19 February 2001.
24. Michel Delapierre and Chistian Milelli, *Les Firmes multinationales* (Paris: Thémathèque, 1995), p. 185.
25. Films were traditionally originally dubbed in French, Italian, German and Spanish.
26. Toby Miller, Nitin Govil, John McMurria and Richard Maxwell, *Global Hollywood* (London: BFI, 2001), pp. 317–19.
27. 'Rejigged Marketing Helps US Pics Soar', *Variety*, 28 October 2002.
28. 'The Plots Thicken in Foreign Markets', *Los Angeles Times*, 6 October 2002.
29. 'Global Conquest: Overseas Strategy Leans on Disney Moniker, Counterprogramming', *Variety*, 27 October 2003.
30. The attempt at localisation through the reference to the practice of hara-kiri was, however, not well perceived by the audience, which clamoured for the original ending. '"Fatal Attraction" Suicide Version Finds Takers at Japan Screen', *Variety*, 16 November 1988.
31. 'The Earth Moves under their BO Feat', *Variety*, 19 November 2001.
32. Other departments represented are, for example, home entertainment, merchandising or theme parks.
33. 'Lure of Laughter Grows', *Variety*, 16 August 2004.
34. 'Travel Sickness Dogs Some Home-Grown Hits', *Variety*, 6 January 1997.
35. Interview with the author, 14 November 2013.

36. Mark Hughes, 'Red Dawn Film Replaces Chinese Villains with North Koreans', *Telegraph*, 22 November 2012.

37. Nolwenn Mingant, 'A New Hollywood Genre: The Global-Local Film', in Rohit Chopra and Radhika Gajjala (eds), *Global Media, Culture and Identity: Theory, Cases and Approaches* (New York, London: Routledge, 2011).

38. International distribution expert, email interview with the author, 20 October 2013.

39. See poster: www.movieposterdb.com/poster/bac5b7b3

40. See poster: www.movieposterdb.com/poster/4da68eab

41. See Japanese poster: www.movieposterdb.com/poster/1ff09b52. In Japan, the actor has become popular with the television series *All In* (2003). See South Korean poster: www.movieposterdb.com/poster/050bca54

42. 'GI Joe poster Featuring Lee Byung-hun', *KoreanBeacon*, 4 August 2009, www.koreanbeacon.com/2009/08/04/gi-joe-poster-featuring-lee-byung-hun/ (website no longer active).

43. The same applies to directors, especially in art-house-oriented markets, albeit to a lesser degree.

44. Email interview with the author, 20 October 2013.

45. See poster: www.movieposterdb.com/poster/60f2d489

46. See poster: www.movieposterdb.com/poster/249bfa10

47. Source: www.boxofficemojo.com

48. Franco Moretti, 'Planet Hollywood', *New Left Review* vol. 9, May–June 2001, p. 93.

49. Brooks Barnes, 'Paramount Hopes New "Start Trek" is a Global Crowd-Pleaser', *NewYorkTimes.com*, 2 May 2013, www.nytimes.com/2013/05/03/business/media/star-trek-into-darkness-aims-for-world-audience.html?_r=0

50. Ibid.

51. The presence of Hispanic actors can answer both international and domestic purposes, as Hispanics are one of the largest minority in the USA and thus a valuable audience to cater for.

52. Andrew Stewart, 'Global Box Office Hits Record in 2012 as Hispanics Attendance Grows in US', *Variety.com*, 21 May 2013, http://variety.com/2013/film/news/global-box-office-hits-record-in-2012-as-hispanic-attendance-grows-1200327049/

53. *Variety* staff, 'International Box Office Snapshots', *Variety.com*, 12 January 2013, http://variety.com/2013/film/news/international-box-office-snapshots-1118064545/

54. Joël Augros, *L'argent d'Hollywood* (Paris: L'Harmattan, 1996), p. 338.

55. 'A Kinder, Softer Movie', *Time*, 2 July 2001. 'The Plots Thicken in Foreign Markets', *Los Angeles Times*, 6 October 2002. 'Marked Territory: Japan', *Hollywood Reporter*, 15 May 2001.

56. 'Dirty Japs' became 'Japs'.

57. 'The Plots Thicken in Foreign Markets', *Los Angeles Times*, 6 October 2002.

58. 'Hollywood Takes Censorship in Stride', *Variety.com*, 7 July 2012, http://variety.com/2012/film/news/hollywood-takes-censorship-in-stride-1118056300/

59. William Wan, '"Iron Man 3" is Latest Hollywood Movie to Court Chinese Censors', *Washingtonpost.com*, 6 May 2013, http://www.washingtonpost.com/world/asia_pacific/iron-man-takes-heroic-efforts-to-satisfy-chinas-state-censors/2013/05/06/62d11e08-b62e-11e2-92f3-f291801936b8_story.html

60. Phone interview with the author, 21 February 2013.

61. Mingant, *Hollywood à la conquête du monde*, pp. 161–2.

'My Big Fat Life in Ruins'

Marketing Greekness and the Contemporary US Independent Film

Yannis TZIOUMAKIS and Lydia PAPADIMITRIOU

This chapter compares the marketing campaigns of two Greek-centred American 'indie' films, *My Big Fat Greek Wedding* (2002) and *My Life in Ruins* (2009). Its key aim is to explore the extent to which there is a difference in the approach to marketing between the USA, a large market that aims to address – initially – a niche ethnic audience, and Greece, a small, national market that identifies itself with what, in the American context, is seen as an 'ethnic' Other. Commencing from the position that when handling films with a strong ethnic minority interest US distributors tend to highlight stereotypical images in the marketing materials designed for the North American market,[1] the chapter explores how such films are marketed by local distributors in the context from which these ethnic representations originate – in this case in the Greek market. More specifically, the chapter explores how the marketing materials aimed at the North American market are adapted for campaigns in smaller, national or regional markets. In this respect, these issues are not exclusive to the Greek context, but rather reflect more broadly the nature of the relationship between the US distributor (that may also be the producer and financier, and therefore be involved with a film from the start) and the international distributors (that tend to appear in the equation after a film's US release, unless they have also had a stake in the production).

Featuring characters of Greek origin in narratives that thematise ethnic-related tensions and concerns, the respective marketing campaigns of *My Big Fat Greek Wedding* and *My Life in Ruins* in the USA and Greece can reveal a lot about the processes of appropriation and adaptation suggested above. The films are rare in their focus on characters of Greek origin, as, despite the considerable size of the ethnic Greek minority in the USA,[2] if compared to other Europe-originating ethnic minorities (such as Italian-Americans or Irish-Americans) Greek-Americans have enjoyed little visibility in US cinema, especially in central narrative roles. Therefore, prior to the release of these two films, distributors had rarely faced the challenge of having to market Greek-themed US films in Greece, which renders the two films as very useful case studies. As the analysis below will demonstrate, the campaigns for both films in the Greek context were changed minimally from the ones utilised in the North American market. The process of adaptation or appropriation of materials received from the US distributor consisted predominantly of their 'localisation' – that is, of the translation of titles and taglines. However, the analysis will also show that even such small interventions can generate connotations for the local audience that create strong paths of engagement with the film. It will also relate the differences in marketing approach between the two films to their different positioning within the context of American independent cinema.

Greeks on Film

Despite the rarity of portrayals of Greeks and Greek-Americans in US films, we can use-fully distinguish them according to whether they are set in Greece or elsewhere. Films such as *Zorba the Greek* (1963), *Captain Corelli's Mandolin* (2003) and *Mamma Mia!* (2008) were shot partly or wholly on location in Greece, and feature storylines set there, while films such as *The Postman Always Rings Twice* (1941 and 1981), *The Exorcist* (1973) and *Charlie Wilson's War* (2007) take place outside Greece (mainly in the USA) and feature characters of Greek descent, usually in supporting roles or with little empha-sis on their ethnic background. A prominent exception in this category is Greek-American Elia Kazan's *America, America* (1963), which examines Greek-American experience in a complex narrative.

In the context of such relative dearth, it was rather surprising that the 2000s saw the appearance of two US films that centred on Greeks and Greek-Americans. Despite not starting as a high-profile film, *My Big Fat Greek Wedding* became a sensational commer-cial success, posting approximately $370 million in terms of theatrical box-office gross internationally and providing Greek-Americans and Greek-American culture with global visibility. The comic story of a young Greek-American woman (Nia Vardalos) who falls in love and wants to marry a man of non-Greek origin, to the dismay of her family, the film made a particular impression in the USA, where it recorded over two-thirds of its theatrical receipts. This was followed by the higher-profile romantic comedy *My Life in Ruins*, about a stuck-up female Greek-American tour guide (Nia Vardalos, again) who works in Athens, falls in love with a local bus driver and learns to enjoy life 'Greek style'. However, *Ruins* did not manage to replicate the incredible commercial success of the earlier film, grossing slightly over $20 million at the global theatrical box office.

Besides their focus on images and narratives of Greekness, the two films displayed a number of other similarities. First, they shared a number of key contributors in their pro-duction process. Starting with Greek-American Nia Vardalos, who had written the screen-play for *Wedding* based on her own one-act play and was the female protagonist in both films, *Wedding* and *Ruins* were also co-produced by Playtone, a company co-founded by Gary Goetzman and Tom Hanks. Second, both films were distributed by 'indie' companies (IFC Films and Fox Searchlight, respectively), making them examples of contemporary American independent cinema.[3] Finally, both films presented life-affirming stories primarily within the generic framework of romantic comedy.

However, the films also display a number of differences. First, although sharing some key 'above-the-line' talent, the films were not linked narratively, with *Ruins* not being a sequel, spin-off or in any other way derivative of *Wedding*. Second, each film belongs to a different category of US films with a Greek interest: *Ruins* is set in Greece, while *Wedding* is set in the USA, with each film motivating different stereotypes in its representation of Greek and Greek-American culture. Third, the two films represent different expressions of American independent cinema: *Wedding* was a small production financed exclusively by US funds and distributed in a service deal by IFC Films, an 'indie' subsidiary of an enter-tainment conglomerate specialising in the release of low-budget US and foreign films;[4] while *Ruins* was co-financed by US and Spanish funds (with some participation in the form of facilitations by the Greek state) and distributed by Fox Searchlight. Another 'indie' sub-sidiary of an entertainment conglomerate, Searchlight was a much bigger player in spe-ciality film-making than IFC Films, having focused in the 2000s primarily on the production and distribution of 'indiewood' films, properties that held a substantial commercial poten-tial.[5] Finally, the films were also released in Greece by different distributors, with *Wedding* released by Prooptiki (1984–2006), a small to medium-sized distributor with an expertise in handling US 'indie' titles, and *Ruins* released by Hollywood Entertainment, a more main-stream-oriented newcomer (2003–) in the Greek theatrical market. As the rest of the chapter will demonstrate, this mix of similarities and differences that characterise the two films is also reflected in their marketing campaigns both in the USA and in Greece.

The US Releases: 'Indie' and 'Indiewood' Film Marketing

My Big Fat Greek Wedding represents a mature example of 'indie' cinema – here defined as a particular trend within contemporary US independent film-making that saw increasing commercialisation following the introduction of a new wave of speciality film divisions by the major players in the US film industry, such as Fine Line Features (1990) and Sony Pictures Classics (1992), and the takeover of key standalone company Miramax by Disney (1993).[6] Featuring stars and utilising genres associated with Hollywood cinema, targeting specific niche audiences and attracting funding from commercial sources, 'indie' films pop-ularised American independent cinema, making it much more accessible than in the past.[7] And even though this particular trend was superseded in the late 1990s and early 2000s by an even more commercialised 'indiewood' mode of film-making that saw the major studios and their new subsidiaries such as Fox Searchlight and Focus Features becoming producers of 'independent' films with great star power, large budgets and even more nar-ratively accessible material, 'indie' films continued to be made, albeit mostly outside the limelight.

    Wedding carries well the 'indie' label in an 'indiewood'-dominated American indepen-dent cinema in the 2000s. Its $5 million budget was low compared to 'indiewood' hits of the period such as *Eternal Sunshine of the Spotless Mind* (2004) and *Sideways* (2004), which cost between three and four times as much. It does not feature any major stars, though protagonists Nia Vardalos and John Corbett had enjoyed some visibility, especially in the film's primary demographic groups – Greek-Americans and mature women (with the latter recognising Corbett from his role in the HBO hit series, *Sex and the City* [1999–2005]). While its narrative and style are straightforward and accessible, the strong focus on an ethnic minority locates it within US independent cinema, especially as Hollywood has rarely provided central roles for ethnic minority women. This is reinforced by the fact that the film was a small-budget production, of the kind that is often released straight to video or on cable television. As a result, the film's links with Hollywood (part-financed by Time Warner subsidiary HBO, co-produced by major Hollywood star Tom Hanks and his Greek-American wife Rita Wilson, and distributed by Rainbow Entertainment subsidiary IFC Films) were not deemed strong enough to change the per-ception of the film as an indie.[8] Opening in just 108 theatres and adopting (initially) a set of 'grassroots' techniques in its marketing campaign aimed at targeting the substantial Greek-American community, the film had few points of contact with the more heavily cap-italised, and, by the early/mid-2000s often highly successful commercially, 'indiewood' expression of US independent cinema. Still, despite its much lower budget and absence of major stars, *Wedding* was consciously marketed as an 'indiewood' picture, positioned, in Alisa Perren's words, as 'simultaneously commercial and independent'.[9]

    This, more specifically, means that the film's marketing campaign drew on techniques and practices associated both with the independent sector and the major studios – the former consisting of a more targeted and gradual build-up of audiences, and a platform release; and the latter with more aggressive and cost-intensive marketing practices, and a wide or saturation release. Adopting a method from the independent sector, the first aim of the distributor was to target directly the projected core audience, the Greek-American community, most of which is located in the metropolitan areas of New York and Chicago (the latter also being the location of the film's narrative). The promotion consisted of advertising in Greek churches, dances and festivals and offering Greek community leaders advance screenings of the film so they could spread word of mouth through the Greek-American community networks.

However, adopting techniques used by the studios, the distributor utilised localised saturation advertising (for example, local cable television advertising spots) in the key markets where the film opened, a method of advertising normally inaccessible to relatively low-budget 'indie' productions. With the film posting extremely encouraging results in the first few weeks of its US theatrical release, its producers decided to invest further marketing funds that reached $20 million in the first five months of release, aiming to maximise the crossover into a more general audience. This included mobilising the film's other core demographic – adult women – primarily through advertising on extremely successful syndicated television morning shows such as *The Oprah Winfrey Show* and *Live with Regis and Kelly*.[10] As the film's unprecedented durability for such a low-budget production became evident, the marketing funds were exponentially increased, through network television advertising (a standard, but very costly, technique of studio-driven marketing for saturation releases), while its distribution gradually reached saturation levels, as the film played in over 2,000 theatres in mid-October.

It is at this point that the actual content of the marketing materials and the key concept in the marketing design of the film become particularly important, as the focal points of the campaign do, indeed, emphasise a stereotypical representation of ethnicity in the generic context of a romantic comedy. In the film poster the two protagonists, Toula and Ian, are placed at the centre, dressed as bride and groom. To the left of Toula, seven members of her family are crammed on top of each other, trying to burst their way to the foreground (and by extension to the couple's life), while Toula extends her hands backwards trying to keep them away. Although Toula's family are formally dressed as befits a wedding, the figure of the grandmother, traditionally clad in black and a headscarf, offers a clear marker of ethnicity. To the right of the image, the background behind Ian (whose long hair stereotypically suggests modern or progressive WASP masculinity) shows the Chicago cityscape, locating the film in the USA. The title of the film, partly inscribed in a font reminiscent of ancient Greek scriptures, is placed above the characters, and against the background of a blue sky reminiscent of Greek weather. Also, the emphasis on blue (the sky and the fonts) and white (the clouds and the dress) alludes to the colours of the Greek flag. The film's tagline, which reads 'Love is here to stay … so is her family', foregrounds the interfering function of the family and connects it with stereotypical markers of ethnicity.

The main trailer also follows the same approach. It starts in typical romantic comedy fashion with Toula and Ian's first meeting, before introducing us to the main obstacle for the couple's formation – her family. Here, the non-diegetic narrator's utterance of the name 'Toula' provides the film with an ethnic, initially unidentified, focus. Brief shots of ethnic customs and behaviour are then showcased for their comedy value, such as, the performance of crucifix sign and Toula's father's expectation to give permission for his adult daughter to date. It is only when Toula utters that she is the first in her family to date a non-Greek, that the specific ethnicity is indicated. From then on, stereotypical markers of Greekness abound, with the brief shot of Ian baptised in the Greek Orthodox Church being arguably the most iconic. However, the visual and narrative focus on the wedding ensures that these comic markers of ethnicity are contained within the more broadly recognised, and inoffensive, framework of a romantic comedy.

My Life in Ruins, in contrast, had a very different marketing trajectory in the USA, one that reflected its 'indiewood' status. This is evident in its $20 million transnational production financing; the profile of its director, Donald Petrie, whose experience ranged from independent film-making (Mystic Pizza [1988]) to Hollywood genre pictures (Miss Congeniality [1999]); and its casting of veteran Hollywood star, Richard Dreyfuss, in an important supporting role. With leading studio speciality film division Fox Searchlight orchestrating its distribution and marketing, it was clear that Ruins was conceived and promoted as an 'indiewood' production, aiming to emulate the remarkable success of Wedding. Another romantic comedy, focusing on the experiences of a displaced, sexually frustrated, female Greek-American tour guide in Athens, the film provided ample opportunities for stereotypical representations of contemporary Greece and native Greeks (and a host of other nationalities portrayed as tourists), as well as foregrounding the differences between Greek-Americans and Greeks. Despite the absence of any narrative links with Wedding, the star's presence and its comic perspective on an 'other' culture, seemed to be borrowing heavily from the earlier film's winning formula. Furthermore, the location of the film's narrative in Greece opened up new commercial opportunities, especially as Ruins became the first film in almost fifty years to be granted permission to shoot on a number of world-known archaeological sites, such as the Acropolis, Delphi and Olympia.

Reflecting its status as an 'indiewood' production, Ruins was marketed more upfront and aggressively, in ways that aimed to ensure rapid international visibility, and that were in clear contrast to the cautious, gradual, grassroots-based, platform release of Wedding. First, the film became the latest addition in an increasing number of 'indiewood' films (The Spanish Prisoner [1998], O Brother, Where Art Thou? [2000], Memento [2001], etc.) that were released first outside the USA, before their distribution in the North American market. This strategy is based on the expectation that a successful European release can generate additional interest in a film in the USA and increase its box-office potential. With Ruins achieving 'event film' status in Greece, following the well-publicised news of the location shooting on heritage sites, it made marketing sense to hold the film's world premiere in Greece, with great fanfare and a significant marketing push.[11]

Second, and as befits an 'indiewood' production, the film's US release (which followed the Greek premiere by two months, and the official release in Greece by a week) was wide: Ruins opened in 1,164 venues, clearly suggesting that Fox Searchlight went for a strong opening weekend designed to bring in the largest possible audience upfront. Equipped with the significant funds it secured following the ultra-successful releases of Juno (2007) and Slumdog Millionaire (2008), Fox Searchlight placed Ruins in an ambitious programme of wide and saturation releases of films with significant commercial potential in its 2009 slate (also including Whip It, (500) Days of Summer, Amelia and a few others, all of which opened in between 800 and 1,200 theatres), in the process investing large amounts of money in P&A costs.[12]

Fox Searchlight's optimism that the film could also become a box-office champion was reflected in its choice not to target the Greek-American community specifically, but to aim at a wider audience, right from the start. Aside from mature women, the traditional audience group of romantic comedies, the distributor anticipated that the film would attract a much younger demographic, through its representation of Greece as a place of sensual pleasures and sexual liberation, as well as its instances of scatological humour, with Toula's romantic interest named Poopy. It is, therefore, not surprising that the marketing materials used to advertise the film relied almost exclusively on tourist-inspired imagery of Greece, portraying it as an exotic place of summer fun and archaeological ruins – a stereotypical set of representations of Greece familiar to US audiences.

This is seen clearly in the main poster of the film that circulated in the USA, which features Georgia (Vardalos) sitting on the window sill of a traditionally white Greek island house, behind which a panoramic view of the island, the sea and a striking blue sky can be seen. Unlike *Wedding*, there is no male character occupying the central position in the poster next to Georgia, with Poopy relegated on the far right side of the poster alongside three other characters whose costumes suggest they are tourists. Apart from underlining the increased star-status of Vardalos after the success of *Wedding*, the poster also foregrounds generic contexts other than romantic comedy, such as the travelogue and the holiday film, both of which rely on stereotypical images of Greece derived from its promotion as a summer holiday destination. The film's tagline, 'The star of "My Big Fat Greek Wedding" is finally going to Greece', brings together the discourses of star and genre, though it privileges the travelogue rather than the romantic comedy as the film's main generic identity.

But if the poster seems to target a broad demographic in its emphasis on holiday escapism, the trailer redresses the balance by also foregrounding the romantic dimension of the film, therefore targeting more specifically the mature women audience group. Starting with brief shots of internationally recognisable ancient Greek monuments, and musically accompanied by bouzouki music, Georgia's voiceover explains that she came to Greece to find her long-lost 'mojo'. The following shots, however, show her doing a thankless job as a tour guide and being still far removed from finding meaning in her life. At this point the trailer introduces the romantic storyline, using many hallmarks of the romantic comedy genre, such as the first meeting between the two characters and their apparent incompatibility. While maintaining references to romance, the trailer mixes them with allusions to the travelogue and the holiday film and firmly situates the film as taking place in Greece by including shots of ancient monuments, white sandy beaches, a musician playing bouzouki, irresponsible driving, characters eating souvlaki and a brief instance of Greek dancing by Georgia, who, by the end of the trailer, seems to have rediscovered her 'mojo' and struck a romantic relationship.

However, despite the similarities with *Wedding* and the generous use of stereotypes, *Ruins* did not prove to be a commercial success. Far removed from the box-office results of *Wedding*, it opened with $3.2 million at the North American box office and lasted only four weeks at the Top 20, before finishing its theatrical run in the USA with a gross of $8.66 million, eight weeks after its release.

Release and Marketing of *My Big Fat Greek Wedding* and *My Life in Ruins* in Greece: Discreet vs In-built Localisation

Wedding was distributed in Greece by Prooptiki, a stand-alone, medium-sized theatrical distributor with a mixed portfolio of US indie and studio films, and world cinema titles. The company acquired the film during the early stages of its US release (21 April 2002), before the film had shown its commercial potential, which made it affordable for a distributor of Prooptiki's size. The film was released in Greece in the summer season (opening on 19 July 2002), predominantly in open-air cinemas, initially in city locations in Athens and Thessaloniki, and then in regional cinemas. The distributor optimised the generic appeal of the film as a comedy and 'light entertainment' by releasing it at a time of the year associated with holidays and relaxation. Parallelling the pattern of its box-office success in the USA, *Wedding* was also a 'slow burner' in Greece. Released initially on fifteen screens, it gradually expanded onto thirty-five. It remained on release for thirty-nine consecutive weeks – having reached the peak of its box office on its seventeenth week (that is, in mid-November 2002),[13] and finally grossing $4,640,000, making it one of the most commercially successful films of all time.

The contexts of the film's acquisition and the strategy of its release by the Greek distributor Prooptiki suggest that while the film was deemed a valuable asset, the company invested moderately in its promotion, reflecting both the modest expectations for its success and the limited financial muscle of the company. Specifically, beyond the cost of its acquisition, the P&A budget of the film was €133,000 ($180,000) of which €77,000 ($105,000) were spent on publicity, with the rest covering the cost of prints, trailers, subtitling, transport, etc. According to Dimitris Kominis, who was responsible for the promotion of the film in Prooptiki, this budget was relatively high for an independent film, but almost half that of blockbusters at the time (as those used high exposure on Greek television channels).

Following the established pattern of the marketing of foreign acquisitions (especially from the USA) by Greek distributors, the marketing of *Wedding* relied almost exclusively on materials provided by the original production and distribution companies. These were predominantly the poster (which was used for print media promotion and in the cinemas) and the theatrical trailers. As there were no television spots, the only other media presence was radio advertising and minimal online exposure. A lot of emphasis was placed on the theatrical premiere; both invitations to the premiere and the press release were presented as a wedding invitation. The wedding theme was also used for the distribution of promotional leaflets in central parts of Athens and Thessaloniki, which were given away by live models dressed as brides and grooms.

According to Kominis, the film's trailers reached the screens in May 2002. These were based on the original American trailer, with occasional re-edits to vary their duration. The main aspects of localisation in the promotional campaign consisted of the translation of the film's title, the promotional texts and the subtitling of the dialogue in the trailers. It is within this limited framework of localisation that the distributor managed to give certain inflections in the promotional material that had particular resonances for the Greek audience, thus, arguably, contributing to the film's successful box office.

Starting with the title, the translation as *Gamos ala ... Ellinika* (*Wedding ... Greek Style*) was effective in implicitly alluding to the use of stereotypical representations of Greekness in the film, but also in associating the film with the popular tradition of Greek romantic comedies of the 1950s and 60s.[14] Furthermore, the tagline 'papoutsi apo ton topo sou' replaced the American one on the posters. Literally translated as 'shoe from your homeland', the expression refers to the idea that anything that comes from 'home' – your ethnic and national community – is desirable, irrespective of its possible lack of certain qualities. The expression implicitly positions the enunciator as someone displaced, away from home – an immigrant, or a diasporic, Greek – thus signalling the ethnic identity of the main characters in the film's storyline as people displaced from their original home. Furthermore, it alludes (once again) to the family comedies of the 50s and 60s, not only because of their storylines referring to Greek emigration to the USA (for instance, *I Theia apo to Chicago/The Aunt from Chicago* [1957]), but also because they often thematised tensions between young people's embrace of a modern lifestyle originating from the West and their parents and extended families' disapproval of foreign customs. Thus the tagline efficiently connects the film with a cinematic tradition with which Greek audiences are very familiar, while also positioning them as bearers of a particular set of values – and also as Greeks. And yet, as the playful gaze of Nia Vardalos in the film's poster indicates, matched by her posture that holds off all her extended family behind her, the expression is there only to imply its ultimate subversion: that, after all, marrying 'your own' is not actually as desirable as it may seem!

This example of localisation suggests that even though the Greek distributor's intervention was minimal, it was efficient because the ethnic Greek identity of the film's characters allowed a set of allusions and generic expectations to be created by very simple means. However, the extent to which the film's success at the box office was the result of its marketing campaign or not is difficult to gauge. According to the distributors, the film's phenomenal success was the result of very positive word of mouth, an argument that is reinforced by the fact that, just as in the USA, the film's box office grew slowly and steadily. And it is evident that audiences did not find the ethnic stereotyping and the comedy at the expense of the supposedly typical Greek characteristics that appear in the film problematic; instead, they happily embraced the overall feel-good comedic tone that predominates, and the chance to see their Greek-American 'cousins' represented on the screen – albeit in an often rather unflattering way.

The campaign for *My Life in Ruins*, however, was localised from its inception, through a number of promotional strategies driven by its US distributor Fox Searchlight. This localisation started with extensive coverage in the media – especially in Greece – of the special permission granted to the film for shooting on archaeological sites. This permission was largely granted as the result of a change in state policy with regard to the commercial exploitation of its heritage, and aimed to enhance the visibility of Greece for tourist purposes.[15] While the media represented the granting of such a permission as a result of Vardalos's personal involvement and perseverance with the authorities (a claim that may have some truth in it), it is also clear that the arrangement was mutually beneficial for the producers and for the Greek state – ensuring location authenticity for the former, and guaranteeing extensive publicity for the publicly owned monuments for the latter.

The film's poster, analysed above, was the main one used for the US market and promoted an image of Greece associated with summer holidays. In Greece, a different poster was adopted, which was less widely used in the USA. Instead of being set on an island and positioning its audience (and the scantily clad Georgia) as consumers of a tourist experience, the Greek poster focuses on Georgia in her work attire, performing her job as a tourist guide (as the large map of Greece that she holds suggests), thus showing the labouring side of the tourist industry.[16] Furthermore, it offers the opportunity to showcase the Parthenon, one of the key sites where the film was shot, but also a symbol of Greece's national pride. This poster, in other words, invites a different kind of identification with the main character, which stresses the Greek rather than the American side of the hyphen. A tourist bus placed between the Parthenon and Georgia alludes to the travelogue dimension of the film, while the smaller size of the image of the two male characters at the bottom right of the poster indicates their lesser narrative significance.

The poster offers no visual clues as to the romantic dimension of the film, so it is the tagline's role to do this. In the US version of the Parthenon poster the tagline enigmatically states 'Falling in love … in all the wrong places', possibly seeking to remind the US audience that Georgia is away from home – America. The Parthenon-set Greek poster localises this tagline as 'Love finds you where you do not expect it', playing upon a hallmark of the romantic comedy genre that wants love taking place unexpectedly. Besides the tagline, the other two elements of localisation here are, first, its Greek title *Erotas … ala*

Ellinika (*Love ... Greek Style*), which clearly alludes to the Greek title of *Wedding* and reinforces the implied links between the two films; and, second, a title positioned at the top of
the poster that reads: 'From Tom Hanks and Rita Wilson, producers of *My Big Fat Greek
Wedding* and *Mamma Mia!*. Apart from explicitly connecting *Ruins* with two other Greek-
themed films, this title foregrounds the name of a well-known star – Hanks – and his
Greek-American wife, adding further to the assumed star power involved with this
indiewood film.

As noted above, the international premiere of *My Life in Ruins* took place in Athens on
3 April 2009 in the prestigious Megaron Mousikis, the Concert Hall, in the presence of
Nia Vardalos, Donald Petrie and Rita Wilson – an event that attracted significant media
attention.[17] The press release that preceded the premiere took place in one of Athens'
main museums (Mouseio Goulandri), in an attempt to associate the film with the cultural
capital of antiquity, as well as promote the museum itself and the image of Greece as a
land of treasures.[18]

In what is a clear example of a saturation release in the Greek market, *Ruins* opened in
120 cinemas on 27 May 2009, a week before its US release. Averaging just under $6,000
per screen, the film's gross of almost $700,000 in its first week was respectable. As
opposed to *Wedding*, though, *Ruins* had no 'legs'. Attendance dropped by 46 per cent in
the following week, and the film disappeared from the charts after five weeks. It grossed
a total of $1.8 million in its theatrical release in Greece, which places it in twentieth posi-
tion in the annual charts. While this is a better average than its performance in the USA,
its total worldwide theatrical gross barely exceeded its total production costs of $20 mil-
lion. Taking into account its future sales on cable and home video, the film probably
recouped its costs, but in no way can it be deemed a financial success.

The two case studies of US 'independent' films with a Greek related-theme and their
respective marketing campaigns in the USA and in Greece demonstrated a number of
points. First, they showed that the different profile of the two films in terms of their industrial positioning in US independent cinema impacted significantly on their marketing
approach, especially in the USA. Second, they showed that, while the Greek distributors
were provided with the materials and the techniques used by their US counterparts, they
were also responsible, to varying degrees, for the campaigns' localisation process. It also
demonstrated that the localisation of *Wedding* managed to tap into subtle cultural references specific to the Greek audience, while that of *Ruins*, despite being much more
dynamic and visible, was designed in advance with different national – including Greek
– audiences in mind and was then utilised practically unchanged in Greece. Third, the
discussion also showed that, ultimately, whether 'indie' or 'indiewood', the scope for
adapting a US marketing campaign in different national contexts is very limited (even if
within those limitations some effective choices can be made), which reinforces the role
of the US distributor as the dominant force in a film's marketing on a global level. Finally,
the chapter demonstrated that marketing to a national audience an ethnic image of itself,
as created by US media – however unflattering or stereotyped – can be successful if
some cultural references familiar to the national audience can be cultivated. If nothing
else, this clearly suggests that stereotypical representations of ethnicity or ethnic identity
are not necessarily offensive to the people represented; indeed, they can often be posi-
tively embraced, as the marketing and the box-office success of *Wedding* in Greece
implied.

Irrespective of the marketing approach, however, the ultimate factor in the success of a
film (or lack of it) is the product itself and what it offers to its audience. A clever marketing

campaign that draws on stereotypical representations of a subject in order to attract particular demographics may lead a film to a strong opening weekend, but it will not contribute to an overall successful run if the film fails to deliver on the audiences' expectations in terms of genre, narrative, style and subject matter, making audiences feel misled and cheated. But there is something uniquely satisfying when a phenomenon such as the success of *My Big Fat Greek Wedding* exceeds expectations to such a degree that it makes even marketing people wonder what they have done to deserve such rewards.

Acknowledgment

We would like to thank Mr Dimitris Kominis (Audiovisual) and Mrs Eirini Souganidou (Feelgood Entertainment), both of whom were involved with the promotion of *My Big Fat Greek Wedding* in Prooptiki, for their invaluable assistance in providing us with information and data about the marketing and release of that film in Greece.

Unless otherwise stated, all references to box-office data are from www.boxoffice mojo.com

Notes

1. See Alex Sutherland, '"Country" Continues Orion Classics' Art-house Success', *Screen International*, 6 October 1984.
2. Approximately 1 per cent of the US population, or close to 3 million. See US Department of State, 'US Relations with Greece', 2 October 2012, www.state.gov/r/pa/ei/bgn/3395.htm
3. 'Indie', here, connotes companies that are divisions of larger conglomerates, but operate and trade in the independent film sector. See Alisa Perren, 'Last Indie Standing: The Special Case of Lions Gate in the New Millennium', in King, Molloy and Tzioumakis, *American Independent Cinema*, p. 108.
4. At the time of *Wedding*'s release, IFC Films was part of Rainbow Media Holdings, a joint venture of Cablevision Systems Corporation, General Electric/NBC and MGM. See Alisa Perren, '"A Big Fat Indie Success Story?" Press Discourses Surrounding the Making and Marketing of a "Hollywood" Movie', *Journal of Film and Video* vol. 56 no. 2, 2004, p. 22.
5. Yannis Tzioumakis, *Hollywood's Indies: Classics Divisions, Specialty Labels and the American Film Market* (Edinburgh: Edinburgh University Press, 2012), pp. 141–2.
6. Yannis Tzioumakis, '"Independent", "Indie" and "Indiewood": Towards a Periodisation of Contemporary (post-1980) American Independent Cinema', in King, Molloy and Tzioumakis, *American Independent Cinema*, p. 34.
7. Tzioumakis, *Hollywood's Indies*, p. 8.
8. Perren, 'A Big Fat Indie Success Story?', p. 24.
9. Ibid., p 28.
10. All information about the marketing techniques used in *Wedding*, from ibid., pp. 27–8.
11. Alexis Grivas, '*My Life in Ruins* Holds World Premiere in Athens', *Screendaily*, 3 April 2009, www.screendaily.com/my-life-in-ruins-holds-world-premiere-in-athens/4043906.article
12. All figures obtained from the Internet Movie Database (www.imdb.com).
13. Data according to Dimitris Kominis. Information from Box Office Mojo is slightly contradictory, positioning *Wedding* at the top of the box office on the eleventh weekend of its run.

14. *Gamos ala … Ellinika* (Vasilis Georgiadis) is the title of a 1964 Greek romantic comedy. Despite being unintentional, the coincidence reflects the spirit in which the choice of title was made.

15. See the Hellenic Film Commission Office, available at www.hfco.gr

16. On this distinction in the representation of tourism in Greek musicals, see Lydia Papadimitriou, 'Travelling on Screen: Tourism and the Greek Film Musical', *Journal of Modern Greek Studies* vol. 18 no. 1, 2000, pp. 95–104.

17. Grivas, '*My Life in Ruins* Holds World Premiere in Athens'.

18. For a discussion of the ideological investment to this project by the Greek state, see Erato Basea, '*My Life in Ruins*: Hollywood and Holidays in Greece in Times of Crisis', *Interactions: Studies in Communication and Culture* vol. 3 no. 2, 2012, pp. 199–208.

Carry On Laughing

Selling English Humour in France

Cecilia TIRTAINE and Joël AUGROS

As French humourist Pierre Desproges once stated, humour is one of the two essential char-acteristics of the Englishman. The other is lawns.[1] Although humour seems to be inherent to the English and the English seem to possess a superior sense of humour – according to them, but also many non-English people[2] – *defining* English humour is a difficult task. Those who attempt to do so often end up with tautological definitions, such as English humour is the humour you find in England or the English have an English sense of humour. Analysing French people's perception of English humour is difficult also because it has evolved over time. The huge popularity of the *Benny Hill Show* on French television in the 1980s[3] and the success of Mr Bean in the 1990s, for example, have contributed to changing the image of the English comedian and of English comedy in France and to changing French audiences' expectations and the clichés about the English. This chapter aims to examine how marketing tries to sell a humour which is difficult to define in a specific national market, France. In order to do so, we have tried to quantify the marketing of British films in France by compiling sta-tistics that have allowed us to distinguish different groups of films and determine trends. Have all the British comedies which attracted large audiences in the UK also been popular at the French box office? Have they actually all been distributed in France? Have distributors and marketers used specific strategies to sell those movies on the French market? We will see that, from the mid-1990s especially, Englishness (or Britishness – both nouns tend to be, mistakenly, interchangeable for most French people and for most marketers) seems to have become a selling point in the marketing campaigns of British comedies in France.[4]

Comedy, a Staple British Genre

The definitions of genres in British cinema, and notably of comedy, vary depending on their authors. According to French authors Raymond Lefèvre and Roland Lacourbe, British comedies are characterised by:

> a rational comic, where laughing is very self-conscious and well thought-out. That genre calls for a perfect setup, which is organized around an absurd starting point leading to logical extensions and consequences. The funnier the joke, the more seriousness must be used to crack it.[5]

Twenty-five years later, Marcia Landy gives a much wider definition of 'film comedies':

> [A]s a major genre in the British cinema, comedy is represented in a variety of forms: romantic comedies, comedians' films, musicals, genre parodies, comedies of manners, family comedies and satires.[6]

The production of British comedies has always been very prolific. Before World War I, comedies already dominated the production sector. In 1914, they accounted for about half the films produced in Britain. This genre was the first in terms of number of films produced (crime films came far behind, followed by drama).[7] Today comedy remains a staple genre in Britain. Between 2009 and 2011, comedies represented 16.9 per cent of all films shot in Britain. Although they came second behind the rather motley category of 'drama' (22.1 per cent of the total number of productions), they led all the other genres ('documentary' came third with 15.7 per cent of films produced). [8] Several reasons can account for the large presence of comedies in British production history.

A first reason might be linked to the British film industry. British cinema has had a rocky history, punctuated with several almost fatal crises often followed by revivals. It is a creative and prolific cinema, but it is also dependent on foreign capital, mostly on US funds. Moreover, it is in direct competition with US cinema, a competition which is more acute than for other national cinemas because both share the same language. As a result, British cinema has often tried to juggle two opposed strategies to better attract audiences: some films are Hollywood or Hollywood-*style* movies, others are 'typically British' in the sense that they wish to distinguish themselves from Hollywood movies. 'British' comedies can thus be understood as a specifically national type of film, one fit to compete with Hollywood (but sometimes actually produced by Hollywood studios) or, simply, to attract audiences who are fond of comedies.

Second, UK audiences have always been very keen on comedies. In 2010, comedy was the genre which attracted the most cinemagoers, with a total of 19.1 per cent of box-office receipts.[9] It came ahead of animation, a genre which is more often than not treated as comedy (18.6 per cent of box-office receipts). Between 2002 and 2010, comedy reaped an overall average of 24.6 per cent of box-office receipts.[10]

Comparing the French Market and the UK Market: A Statistical Approach

With British comedies being so successful on their home market, their popularity in foreign countries – more specifically France – attracted our attention. In order to identify the marketing efforts necessary to sell these comedies on a different market, we created a database listing all the British comedies produced between 1909 and 2012. For each film, it details the release date in France and in the UK, the titles chosen by distributors for the two different territories, the director, the names of the production companies and of the companies which distributed it in the UK and in France, its box-office performance on the two markets, the number of tickets sold in the two countries and the ratio between those two figures.[11] Determining a film's nationality was tricky from a methodological point of view. According to CBO, a company which collects attendance figures for films released in France, the most successful British comedy of all time in France is *La Grande vadrouille* (1966), a film co-produced by Rank and Films Corona, but whose stars (Louis de Funès and Bourvil) are French and whose story focuses on the trials and tribulations of two French characters in occupied France during World War II.[12] The same type of questioning arose with films such as *Mamma Mia!* (2008), which we decided not to feature in the database because we deemed them not British enough. Conversely, films such as *The Full Monty* (1997), entirely financed by Fox Searchlight, and *Four Weddings and a Funeral* (1994), financed by European capital but produced by British company Working Title Films, were included in our research. We did not always stick to the official/legal definition of the British movie given by the British Film Institute or the UK Film Council, as we thought it slightly too wide – for example, *Star Wars* (1977) or *Fargo* (1996) are considered British

Table 1: The most popular British comedies in the UK and France (1980–2011)

UK market		French market	
Films	Tickets sold (estimated)	Films	Tickets sold
1 The Full Monty	14,166,965	1 Four Weddings and a Funeral/ 4 mariages et un enterrement	5,791,534
2 Bridget Jones's Diary	10,070,675	2 Notting Hill/Coup de foudre à Notting Hill	4,532,898
3 Love Actually	8,161,886	3 Bridget Jones's Diary/Le Journal de Bridget Jones	4,489,484
4 Four Weddings and a Funeral	8,105,472	4 The Full Monty	3,489,384
5 Inbetweeners	8,038,461	5 Chicken Run	3,192,445
6 Notting Hill	8,001,006	6 Bean	3,169,258
7 Bridget Jones: The Edge of Reason	7,931,431	7 Billy Elliot	2,514,645
8 Wallace & Gromit: The Curse of the Were-Rabbit	6,784,863	8 Wallace & Gromit: The Curse of the Were-Rabbit/Wallace et Gromit et le mystère du lapin garou	2,280,291
9 Bean	6,756,602	9 A Fish Called Wanda/Un poisson nommé Wanda	2,212,414
10 Chicken Run	6,591,932	10 Bridget Jones: The Edge of Reason/Bridget Jones: l'âge de raison	2,133,018
11 Calendar Girls	4,543,723	11 Secrets and Lies/Secrets et mensonges	1,471,933
12 Mr Bean's Holiday	4,377,857	12 Flushed Away/Souris City	1,302,832
13 Johnny English	4,326,485	13 Valiant/Vaillant, pigeon de combat	1,163,655
14 Hot Fuzz	4,117,343	14 Shallow Grave/Petits meurtres entre amis	1,113,351
15 Billy Elliot	3,857,393	15 Monty Python's The Meaning of Life/Monty Python, le sens de la vie	1,091,468
16 About a Boy	3,819,999	16 Mr Bean's Holiday/Les Vacances de Mr Bean	1,066,963
17 Nanny McPhee	3,488,049	17 Trainspotting	1,051,859
18 Sliding Doors	3,162,504	18 Love Actually	966,488
19 The Best Exotic Marigold Hotel	3,134,393	19 Johnny English	960,912
20 Snatch	2,758,567	20 Much Ado About Nothing/Beaucoup de bruit pour rien	930,526

Table 2: Discrepancies between the performance in the French market and the UK market
(ε: ratio under 0.01)

Some films which were much more successful in France than in the UK	Ratio	Some films which were much more successful in the UK than in France	Ratio
Secret and Lies/Secrets et mensonges	2.68	Lucky Break	0.01
Looking for Eric	2.09	Don't Go Breaking My Heart/Amour sous influence	0.01
Another Year	1.65	Kevin & Perry Go Large/Kevin & Perry	0.01
Tamara Drewe	1.35	The Damned United	ε
Death at a Funeral/Joyeuses funérailles	1.33	Confetti	ε
Happy-Go-Lucky/Be Happy	1.14	Fever Pitch/Terrain d'entente	ε
Beautiful Thing	1.05		

by the BFI. We took into account a combination of factors, but mostly the content, story material and setting of the movies, and their degree of Britishness. In doing so, we assumed that, for French audiences, a film's Britishness does not depend on the 'nationality' of the funds invested in the movie, but on its content, characters and setting – that is to say Britain, be it real or fantasised. The database has allowed us to distinguish several trends concerning British comedies and their popularity in the UK and in France, which, in turn, has helped us comprehend marketers' practices when selling British comedies in France.[13]

First, Table 1 shows that the majority of the highest-grossing British comedies released after 1996 which were successful in the UK were also successful on the French market (fourteen films out of the twenty listed).

Our database also showed some discrepancies between the two markets for specific films, as Table 2 illustrates. For example, Secrets and Lies (1996) attracted much larger audiences in France than it did in the UK (the ratio is 2.68 to 1).[14] On the other hand, a film such as Lucky Break (2001) was much more successful in the UK than it was in France: it sold a hundred times more tickets in the UK than in France.

These findings led to our focusing on the difference of reception between the two markets, a difference that marketers must be aware of to be able to devise suitable and potentially successful campaigns.

Hits in the UK, flops in France – and vice-versa

Some comedies were huge hits in the UK and were then distributed in France but attracted only small audiences in that market. This was the case, for example, for some popular television show spin-offs of the 1990s and 2000s, with characters such as Ali G and Kevin & Perry, the features starring Simon Pegg and Nick Frost and directed by Edgar Wright (Shaun of the Dead [2004] and Hot Fuzz [2007]) – all three famous for TV series Spaced (Channel 4, 1999 and 2001) – and more recently the spin-off of TV sitcom The Inbetweeners (2011). Two comedies directed by Guy Ritchie also strikingly – and rather surprisingly – feature in this category (Lock Stock and Two Smoking Barrels [1998] and Snatch [2000]). Several factors might explain those differences of reception between the two markets. Language is a significant one. Translating the comic, especially comedy based on language – puns, wit, understatement, etc. – is no easy task, whether the film is subtitled or dubbed. It is sometimes impossible to do, due to cultural differences and a lack of common references. Translation necessarily means adaptation to the culture, tastes and humour of the target audience. English humour, when 'translated' for foreign audiences, is, in most cases weakened, diluted and sometimes cannot reach the foreign audiences at all, as it simply cannot be adapted. When the film is dubbed it is also difficult for the dubbing actors to find the right 'tone', especially with understatement. Besides, accents may be a problem. It can be tough for distributors to know which accent dubbing actors should opt for, especially when this accent is noticeable in English and often reinforces the comic (see, for example, Ali G, whose 'Jafaican' accent was very difficult to put across in French,[15] or just plain Cockney, Geordie or Brummie accents). The cultural referents are different and it is tricky to find equivalents that would convey exactly the same comic feel. This is why, generally, slapstick, physical and mime-oriented comedy can be exported much more easily – hence the international success of Mr Bean.

Also, many of the movies in the category of comedies which were huge hits in the UK but made poor showings at the French box office are film spin-offs of TV shows. Often these shows had high audience ratings in the UK and a real fan base. Producers adapted them for the big screen, knowing they had a ready audience. Even when the adaptations for the big screen were not particularly imaginative and the films had negative reviews, they attracted the crowds of regular fans of the TV show. When those shows were not broadcast in France – which was the case for the majority of them – or could only be seen by cable or satellite subscribers and so had a limited number of viewers, the potential attractiveness of their film spin-offs was drastically reduced. In recent years, the changes in access to and consumption of films have also had an impact on audience figures. The way people access films (TV, video/DVD, VoD and streaming) and information on films and the way they discuss films (forums on the internet, fan groups on social networks, etc.) has fundamentally changed. 'Rom-com' *Martha Meets Frank, Daniel and Lawrence* (1998) and rom-zom-com *Shaun of the Dead* (2004) had poor performances at the French box office, with 125,622 tickets sold for the former and only 41,000 for the latter, but they do strongly on VoD websites (ranked eleventh and fourth, respectively, in the list of best-selling movies of Virgin's VoD French site in 2011).[16] We assume also that Pegg–Frost movies, widely appreciated by young male viewers (fifteen to thirty-five age group) – with a large proportion of geeks, like the characters embodied by Pegg and Frost in *Paul* (2011), for example – are frequently downloaded and shared on illegal platforms.

As for the comedies which had a better box-office performance in France than in the UK (Table 2, films with a ratio over 1),[17] the vast majority are 'social comedies', directed by Ken Loach, Stephen Frears or Mike Leigh. The most extreme case is that of *The Navigators* (2001), which attracted 312,052 cinemagoers in France but was not even distributed in the UK. One reasonable explanation for this striking difference is that those films are directed by auteurs, who are recognised and appreciated in France and have had a faithful audience for decades. Those films are generally less well distributed in the UK. With UK cinemagoers tending to be less interested in social movies depicting a less that rosy picture of the UK than French audiences are, there is less demand for them and, consequently, little incentive for cinema circuits to screen them. Despite international recognition, Loach, Leigh and, to a lesser extent, Frears do not attract wide audiences in their home country – even if their films have reaped dozens of awards. Their movies are more appreciated outside the UK. Had *Secrets and Lies* not been awarded the Palme d'Or in Cannes in 1996 it most likely would not have been distributed outside London. This award earned it a distribution in one cinema in Sussex. But the film was screened only one night, and the poster promoting it stated: 'Tonight Only: Ken Loach's *Secrets and Lies*'![18]

Changes in perception

When studying the marketing campaigns for British films, one has to take into account the evolution of the way the French see Britain, the British and British culture – most notably fashion and music. They were, at times, very popular. Three main periods can be distinguished: the 1960s (the 'Swinging' 60s), the 1990s (with Cool Britannia) and, to a lesser extent, around 2012 (Prince William and Catherine Middleton's wedding, Queen Elizabeth II's Diamond Jubilee and the London Olympics).[19]

Success might come from changed perceptions, but also from a change in the producers' and distributors' strategies. As was the case in the 1970s, the need to reach international audiences became more critical for the British film industry. One of the most successful British production companies of the past thirty years has been Working Title Films, which has managed to produce British movies aimed at international audiences.[20] Their biggest hits are romantic comedies or mid-Atlantic comedies, which generally feature Hugh Grant and a Hollywood star. Those films give an idealised image of England, the English and English humour, and are mostly stereotypical. They convey images which audiences abroad wish to see. The 'magic formula' they are based on caters to international audiences, who are keen on those postcard pictures. In these rom-coms, the gap between what audiences expect and what they are actually offered no longer exists. This, in part, explains why the latter are and have been, in the past, very popular in France.

Marketing British Comedies in France

What's in a title?

The choice of film titles is part of marketing strategies to better sell movies and is crucial as it often plays an important role in the potential cinemagoers' decisions to go and see a movie. It catches the passer-by's attention and has to talk instantly to their imagination, reach out to their unconscious. When a film travels outside its original country, the marketing team has three options: keep the original title, give a literal translation or adapt the title. We compiled a list of British films distributed in France until 2013 containing the words '*anglais*', '*anglaise*', '*britannique*', 'British', 'English', '*Angleterre*' or 'England'. Table 3 below lists the results of this compilation classified by genre. It shows that the reference to the cultural origin of the films is a major selling point.

Some distributors decided to keep the original title. In most cases it is intelligible for French audiences. Of those we listed, two original titles in English were kept (both contain the words 'English' and 'England'): *Johnny English* and *Mike Bassett: England Manager*. Titles are rarely translated literally. Only one of them was: *L'Anglais qui gravit une colline **et** descendit une montagne/The Englishman Who Went Up a Hill **But** Came Down a Mountain*. However, the translation is imperfect as the conjunction 'but' is replaced by another ('*et*'/'and') in the French title – thereby changing the meaning of the sentence slightly.

The most common practice is a change of titles, with adaptations – which sometimes distort the original meaning. A handful of titles contain the phrase '*à l'anglaise*' in the adapted French title when the actual original title did not allude to England at all:

- *Wild Target* ➜ *Petits meurtres à l'anglaise*
- *Greenfingers* ➜ *Jardinage à l'anglaise*
- *This Year's Love* ➜ *Mariage à l'anglaise*

Table 3: French titles *'à l'anglaise'*

COMEDIES

Title in France	Title in the UK	Year of release*
Mariage à l'anglaise	*I Give It a Year*	2013
Gambit: Arnaque à l'anglaise	*Gambit*	2012 (2013)
Johnny English, le retour	*Johnny English Reborn*	2011
Petits meurtres à l'anglaise	*Wild Target*	2010
Good Morning England	*The Boat That Rocked*	2009
Un Anglais à New York	*How to Lose Friends & Alienate People*	2008 (TV/DVD)
Tournage dans un jardin anglais	*A Cock and Bull Story*	2006 (2005)
Jardinage à l'anglaise	*Greenfingers*	2004 (2001)
Johnny English	*Johnny English*	2003
Mike Bassett: England Manager	*Mike Bassett: England Manager*	2001 (video/DVD)
Maybe Baby ou Comment les Anglais se reproduisent	*Maybe Baby*	2000
Mariage à l'anglaise	*This Year's Love*	2000 (1999)
Trois Anglaises en campagne	*The Land Girls*	1998
L'Anglais qui gravit une colline et descendit une montagne	*The Englishman Who Went Up a Hill But Came Down a Mountain*	1996 (1995)
Deux Anglaises en délire	*Smashing Time*	no theatrical release (1967)
La Merveilleuse Anglaise	*The Fast Lady*	no theatrical release (1963)
Deux Anglais à Paris	*To Paris with Love*	1956 (1955)

OTHER GENRES

Title in France	Title in the UK	Year of release*
The Sins of the Father – A Very British Gangster II	*The Sins of the Father – A Very British Gangster II*	#
England, My England	*England, My England*	DVD (1995)
Braquage à l'anglaise	*The Bank Job*	2008
A Very British Gangster	*A Very British Gangster*	2007
This is England	*This is England*	2007
Le Patient anglais	*The English Patient*	1997
The Last of England	*The Last of England*	1987
Meurtre dans un jardin anglais	*The Draughtsman's Contract*	1984 (1982)
La Bataille d'Angleterre	*Battle of Britain*	1969
Le Jour où l'on dévalisa la banque d'Angleterre	*The Day They Robbed the Bank of England*	1961 (1960)

* Between brackets: year of theatrical release in the UK, when different

Half a dozen titles feature the adjective '*anglais*' (sometimes nominalised):

- *How to Lose Friends & Alienate People* ➜ *Un Anglais à New York*
- *A Cock and Bull Story* ➜ *Tournage dans un jardin anglais* (this title is an obvious reference to *Meurtre dans un jardin anglais*, the French title chosen by distributors for *The Draughtsman's Contract* [1980])
- *Maybe Baby* ➜ *Maybe Baby ou Comment les Anglais se reproduisent* (here the distributor decided to add a subtitle, in order to explain the title which also allowed to introduce the selling point, '*les Anglais*')
- *The Land Girls* ➜ *Trois Anglaises en campagne*
- *Smashing Time* ➜ *Deux Anglaises en délire*

Those phrases and adjectives were deliberate choices. They did not feature in the original title.

One very noticeable title is the one chosen for *The Boat That Rocked*. In France the film was distributed with a completely different title, in English: *Good Morning England*. This choice was made, quite blatantly, in reference to a very successful US comedy on the same theme (the radio), *Good Morning Vietnam* (1987). The aim was for potential audiences to be attracted to the movie because of this parallel drawn between the two comedies thanks to the choice of title. Also, the word 'England' in the title is used as a signal that oriented the audiences towards a 'type' of movie, English comedy, and a type of humour, English humour. One other reason, maybe, for opting for an adaptation in French and not keeping the original title in English is that it is much easier for a French person not only to understand but also to pronounce and remember *Good Morning England* than *The Boat That Rocked* and a literal translation could definitely not render the pun contained in the original title. The point for marketers is to grab potential audiences' attention and make sure they remember the title, even if it means opting for a slightly twisted choice, as was the case for *East Is East* (1999), which became *Fish and Chips*[21] in France. Ocean Film, which distributed the movie in France, had decided the marketing campaign would focus on the film's humour – and not some of the more serious and thought-provoking issues, such as religion, difficulty to adapt to different cultures, generation gaps, racism, etc.[22] The distributors had also decided not to keep the original title which, according to them, might be problematic in terms of meaning, cultural references and pronunciation.[23] They had tried to find titles with the word '*Pakistanais*', but thought they might also be problematic. Finally, they opted for *Fish and Chips*, because the fish and chip shop is the main setting of the film and plays an important role in the plot, and because the expression, for French people, immediately conjures up Britain.

Translation and adaptation usually aim to help the French gather what the film's genre and main theme are clearly and immediately. The titles in Table 3 show that the words 'English', 'England', '*anglais*', '*Angleterre*', 'British', 'Britain' and '*britannique*', beyond the mere nationality of the movies, connote their 'type' of humour – hence these choices, made by distributors deliberately. Those words were also probably considered selling points in the marketing campaign and were used in order to attract wider audiences. Those titles started to proliferate as from the mid-1990s, that is to say just after the release of *Four Weddings and a Funeral* and, later, *Shallow Grave* and *The Full Monty* – British comedies which were all huge box-office hits. New comedies were produced to ride this wave of success and were also successful on the UK market. In general, also, Britain, the British culture and British cinema became fashionable again as from around that period (cf. Cool Britannia). The French distributors of some British comedies, even if they were not always good films, used this technique in order to attract audiences. This strategy is even more blatant in the poster campaigns used to promote British comedies in France.

What's in a poster?

In France, where advertising for films is prohibited on television, posters are critical in a marketing campaign. There again, the distributor may choose to keep the original poster campaign or to adapt it or to change it radically. Many of the British comedies distributed in France had poster campaigns which used Englishness and symbols of England as selling points. As was the case for titles, this strategy became more recurrent especially from the mid-1990s, when British cinema started being successful again at home and internationally – most notably comedies. One can distinguish several patterns in the poster campaigns, broadly from the most patent to more subtle approaches.

The most notable poster campaigns, which are totally different in the two territories and which make conspicuous and rather unsubtle use of UK/British/English symbols are those of *Bhaji on the Beach* (1993/1998), *Still Crazy* (1998/1999), *Maybe Baby* (2000) and *Lesbian Vampire Killers* (2008/DVD release only in France).[24] The 'nationality' of the movies is immediately apparent. The Union Jack features ostentatiously on those posters, in the background. The flag did not feature in the UK campaigns, but some determining elements, which point to comedy and Englishness and English comedy, and which are selling points on the UK market, prominently stood out: Ben Elton, Rowan Atkinson and Hugh Laurie, James Corden and Matthew Horne, the actors of TV series *Gavin & Stacey*, comparisons with *The Full Monty* or *Four Weddings and a Funeral*, which are *the* reference in terms of an international box-office hit for British comedies, an allusion to striptease, etc.

Other French poster campaigns were more subtle. They featured the words '*comédie*' and '*britannique*' or '*anglais(e)*' or '*British*', more or less discretely, sometimes in clever taglines with puns. '*Une comédie anglaise bien roulée*', '*La comédie anglaise la plus mortelle de l'année*', '*Une comédie so british*', respectively, for *Saving Grace*, *Death at a Funeral* and *Easy Virtue* or '*la nouvelle comédie hilarante du réalisateur de* The Full Monty' for *Lucky Break*. All these comedies were released in France after *The Full Monty* and mostly tried to cash in on its success and, before this movie, that of *Four Weddings and a Funeral*.

A third type of campaign might appear more surprising. It was used for some of the films which were big box-office hits in the UK, especially with audiences in the fifteen to thirty-five age group, and which were dark comedies, such as *Shallow Grave* and *Lock, Stock and Two Smoking Barrels*. They were marketed specifically as British comedies in France, whereas they were not in the original poster campaign. This was a blatant strategy to attract more potential spectators, the 'British comedy' being a genre in itself, much appreciated in France, especially from the mid-1990s (in those cases here, a subgenre: the British dark comedy) – it almost became a brand used by distributors. The tagline on the French poster of *Shallow Grave* made the adjectives 'British', 'ironic' and 'diabolical' rhyme ('*Une comédie britannique, ironique, diabolique …*'). The French poster of *Lock, Stock …* did not feature a tagline but a quote taken from *The Sun* and translated into French: '*La meilleure comédie noire de l'année! Sans doute le film britannique le plus divertissant de tous les temps!*'[25] The original UK poster was very different from the one used in France. Also, the quote was different: it did state the fact that it was 'the year's best British movie', but then compared it to cult gangster/crime movies, British (*The Long*

The posters used in the marketing campaigns of *Bhaji on the Beach* (1993/1998) and *Maybe Baby* (2000) were very different from those used in France, which made ostentatious use of the Union Jack[26]

Good Friday [1980]) and American (*Reservoir Dogs* [1992]). It was marketed as a gangster movie that would appeal to a young generation sensitive to the humour and darkness of Tarantino movies. In France, it was marketed as a British (dark) comedy.[27] Similar strategies were used for more 'social' comedies, with a reflection on social issues but aimed at a broad audience, in the same vein as *The Full Monty*: extensive use of the adjectives 'anglais' or 'British' (or both, in the case of *Shooting Fish*: '*une very British comédie*' and '*mais où les Anglais vont-ils encore pêcher tout ça?*') in quotes and/or catchphrases (the poster of *Four Lions* [2010] featured another interesting pun: '*Ils sont dangereux, ils sont organisés, ils ont fait exploser de rire l'Angleterre!*[28]), the mention of awards (mostly because they are comedies, but dealing with social issues) and the patent use of yellow as an obvious reference to the poster of *The Full Monty*, which everyone remembers – passers-by could then easily associate the comedy with *The Full Monty*.

British comedies that were considered 'art-house' by the French distributors, aimed at a niche market, were marketed the same way (minus the use of the flashy yellow background), with even more extensive use of references to festivals and awards – to which the niche audience targeted is more sensitive – and congratulatory quotes, but taken from 'quality', mostly specialised papers and magazines. For example, the poster of *Submarine* (2010) is topped with four references to festival selections. These are immediately identifiable by the targeted audience.[29] As for the art-house movies, which, as mentioned previously, have generally been more successful in France than in the UK, their poster campaigns merely highlight the name of the director, and sometimes of the screenwriter (Paul Laverty, for many films directed by Ken Loach). They do not feature the usual markers used for selling British comedies.[30] Because the films address an informed niche audience, there is no need for them. The selling point is the name of the director. The targeted audience knows what to expect when it goes to see a Loach, Leigh or Frears movie, and that it is – most of the time – a British/European movie.

The signals in the French poster campaigns of the British rom-coms are different. Their main selling point is the reference to the previous success(es) of this subgenre, the reasoning behind this strategy being that if you liked that movie, you will also like this one, which uses the same formula and more or less the same 'ingredients'. The same kind of marketing was used for all the Working Title Films rom-coms, whose reference point is *Four Weddings and a Funeral*.[31] The reference point is also Hugh Grant, the archetype of the Englishman – according to international audiences – with a specific kind of humour. After *Four Weddings*, all the Working Title rom-coms, even the films without scriptwriter Richard Curtis or Hugh Grant, were marketed the same way and mention the former successes and related information (producers or screenwriter). The French distributors of the latest Working Title rom-com *I Give It A Year* (2013) accumulated all the usual selling points used for British comedies: not only did they adapt the title of the movie in order to introduce the adjective 'English' (*Mariage à l'anglaise*), but also the poster is overloaded with markers.[32] It features the Union Jack – on an umbrella – and matching colours, a quote referring to comedy and Englishness ('*Le film anglais le plus drôle depuis des années!*[33]), clichés (umbrellas and rain), London in the background (but the more modern, hip, updated version, with the 'London Eye' and the 'Gherkin' – which no camera could actually possibly frame together[34]), the reference to an award ('*Grand prix du Festival de la Comédie de l'Alpe d'Huez*') and the usual allusion to former successful Working Title rom-coms (no longer *Four Weddings*, deemed too dated now, despite its cult status, but *Bridget Jones* and *Love Actually*). This excessive use of codes was probably meant to compensate for the lack of big bankable stars such as Julia Roberts or Hugh Grant.

This chapter aimed to show how a specific genre is sold on a foreign market. Even if, as we have seen, the biggest hits in the UK have also often been successes in France, there remain discrepancies between the two markets. They can easily be related to cultural differences between the two countries and, most likely, to differences in spectatorship on either side of the Channel. We then aimed to show how marketers tried to work with those, thanks to two main tools: titles and posters. Most marketers in France have tended to emphasise Englishness in their campaigns, using it as a selling point. The question of selling English or British comedies on the French market involves not only taking into account purely commercial considerations, but also, and maybe especially, specific cultural relationships between the two geographical areas and the way consumers from one area may appreciate or ignore entire parts of the other culture.

An analysis of the other tools used by film marketers – most notably teasers and trailers, but also press kits, interviews given by the film crew in various media, the choice of release dates and of the number of prints for each film – would certainly support our main argument. Film festivals also play a major role in promoting the films. There are now several major film festivals in France devoted to British cinema – Dinard, Nantes and Nîmes, most notably. Their increasing popularity and reputation, combined with the wealth of British film cycles on offer in cinemas across France, illustrate that the French are keen on British cinema as a distinct 'national' cinema, a characteristic which marketers emphasise, especially when it comes to selling British comedy.

Notes

1. 'The two essential characteristics of the Englishman are humour and lawns. Without humour and lawns the Englishman wilts and withers away and becomes as hollow as a Schönberg concerto. … English humour underlines the world's absurdity with bitterness and despair.' Pierre Desproges, *Les Etrangers sont nuls* (Paris: Editions du Seuil, 1992), p. 13. Pierre Desproges (1939–88) was famous for his aphorisms, his sarcasm and his mostly nonsensical humour. All translations in this article were made by Cecilia Tirtaine.
2. See, for example, Kate Fox's study on the English, *Watching the English* (London: Hodder & Stoughton, 2004), pp. 64–5: 'The popular belief is that we have a better, more subtle, more highly developed sense of humour than any other nation, and specifically that other nations are all tediously literal in their thinking and incapable of understanding or appreciating irony. Almost all of the English people I interviewed subscribed to this belief, and many foreigners, rather surprisingly, humbly concurred.'
3. In France, *The Benny Hill Show* was broadcast every Sunday evening on FR3 from 1980 for over a decade. Its ratings reached an average 3.9 million viewers per show, which was and still is considered a very strong performance for a public television broadcaster. The show was popular among most families. Parents and children alike would gather round the television set to watch it – it was a way of rounding off the weekend. As from the 1990s and until December 2004 the show was broadcast daily, usually after the 1 p.m. news programme. See http://inatheque.ina.fr/
4. In this chapter, the adjective 'British' is used generally for films as productions, and 'English' for the 'type' of humour, as referred to by Fox and Desproges above. The box-office statistics we use concern the UK – unless otherwise stated.

5. Raymond Lefèvre and Roland Lacourbe, *30 ans de cinéma britannique* (Paris: Editions cinéma 76, 1976), p. 51.
6. Marcia Landy, *British Genres: Cinema and Society, 1930–1960* (Princeton, NJ: Princeton University Press, 1991), p. 329. Marcia Landy's book and Lefèvre and Lacourbe's work both focus on approximately the same period. However, the contours of the genre may be slightly different because Landy has hindsight; comedies have acquired academic recognition and some have even since become 'cult' movies.
7. Sarah Street, *British National Cinema* (London: Routledge, 2009 [1997]), p. 41.
8. *BFI Statistical Yearbook 2012* (London: BFI, 2012), p. 159.
9. Comedy represented 21.4 per cent of all movies distributed in 2010 (figure for the UK and Ireland).
10. Over the same period, comedy represented an average 23.7 per cent of the total film output. See *BFI Statistical Yearbooks*, 2002 to 2010.
11. The list was compiled thanks to data taken from www.cbo-boxoffice.com and www.allocine.fr, the *Statistical Handbooks* published annually by the British Film Institute and the UK Film Council, Phil Wickham, *Producing the Goods? UK Film Production Since 1991, An Information Briefing* (London: BFI National Library, 2003), Phil Wickham, Erinna Mettler and Elena Marcarini, *Back to the Future: The Fall and Rise of the British Film Industry in the 1980s, An Information Briefing* (London: BFI National Library, 2005), the Internet Movie Database (www.imdb.com), *Screen International* (www.screendaily.com) and *Variety* (www.variety.com).
12. The film remained the highest-grossing French comedy for decades. 17.27 million cinemagoers saw *La Grande vadrouille. Bienvenue chez les Ch'tis* (2008) outperformed the 1966 comedy, with 20.41 million tickets sold in 2008.
13. Our chapter focuses on films released after 1996 only because statistics before then – especially for the UK – are too sparse to allow relevant comparisons. We analyse the fate of the *Carry On* series and the Monty Python movies in France, as well as the reasons for their failure or success, in another article (to be published in 2015).
14. Ratio = number of tickets sold in France/number of tickets sold in the UK. Films with a ratio over 1 were more successful in France than on their home market. Films with a ratio under 1 were more successful in the UK than in France.
15. The French actor who dubs the voice of Sacha Baron Cohen (in *Ali G Indahouse* [2002], *Brüno* [2009], *The Dictator* [2012] and *Les Misérables* [2013]) is Emmanuel Curtil, who is also the 'French voice' of Jim Carrey, Ben Stiller, Mike Myers, Johnny Knoxville and Matthew Perry, among other famous actors – mostly comedy stars. The accent he uses in *Ali G Indahouse* sounds artificial. It is the sort of accent that young people in the street have or rather that of young people in the street as represented or caricatured in films or television programmes, with a specific accent and vocabulary. Just like Sacha Baron Cohen's accent in the original version, it sounds fake – but in the French case there is no real or realistic referent, whereas in the original there is. This artificiality and lack of reference may explain why the film was a relative failure in the French market.
16. Figures for November 2011.
17. Note, however, that these films were only *relatively* successful in France. The good performances of those films at the French box office does not mean that they are among the top twenty English comedies at the French box office during that period (except *Secrets and Lies*); see Table 1.
18. *Today In English*, February 1998.

19. The impact of these events around 2012 is difficult to assess, especially in terms of popularity of British movies in France, but it is reasonable to say that Britain and its culture were very popular in France then – and film marketers made the most of this to sell the British movies they handled to the French public.

20. The strategy used by Working Title Films and the reasons why many of the films it has produced in the past three decades have been so successful internationally were analysed by Cecilia Tirtaine in a paper entitled 'Working Title Films: des productions "britanniques" au succès international', International Conference, Université de Caen, 12–13 March 2009.

21. It does not feature in Table 3 as it does not contain the words '*anglais*', '*anglaise*', '*britannique*', 'British', 'English', '*Angleterre*' or 'England', but it is definitely worth mentioning.

22. Adam Minns, 'Four goes East', *Screen International*, 5 November 1999, p. 7.

23. The film is the adaptation for the big screen of an autobiographical play by Ayub Khan-Din, *East Is East* (1997). The phrase 'East is East' refers to a recurring line from 'The Ballad of East and West' (Rudyard Kipling, 1890), which alludes to the difficulty of adapting to other people's customs.

24. For the posters of *Still Crazy*, see www.movieposterdb.com/poster/fdf70e9e (France) and http://phubb.blogspot.fr/2014/09/still-crazy-1998.html (UK). For *Lesbian Vampire Killers*, see www.movieposterdb.com/poster/fb0f9b4f (France) and www.impawards.com/intl/uk/2009/lesbian_vampire_killers_ver2.html (UK).

25. 'The best dark comedy of the year! Probably the most entertaining British movie of all time!'

26. For the posters used in the French marketing campaigns, with the Union Jack, see: www.cinefil.com/film/bhaji-une-balade-a-blackpool for *Bhaji on the Beach* and www.cinemotions.com/Maybe-Baby-ou-Comment-les-Anglais-se-reproduisent-tt13657 for *Maybe Baby*.

27. On the French poster, the source of the quotation is *The Sun*; on the UK poster it is the *Evening Standard*. For the French campaign, the source did not matter that much as the majority of the French public does not necessarily know the tabloid. What mattered was the use of emphasis, laudatory superlatives and the words 'comedy' and 'British movie'.

28. 'They are dangerous, they are organised, they made England explode with laughter!'

29. See the poster used for the French campaign here: www.cinemotions.com/affiche-Submarine-tt111934

30. The exception is the Frears movies, whose posters feature the word 'comedy'.

31. The two *Bridget Jones* movies are the exception, although they were produced by Working Title Films and were based on the same type of 'magic formula', as stated previously. Their marketing campaigns focused mostly on Helen Fielding's bestsellers and on the US star, Renee Zellweger. They did also mention Hugh Grant and Colin Firth, signals of Britishness and of a specific kind of humour, and obvious selling points, but less conspicuously than in the other campaigns.

32. The poster used for the French market is very different from the original UK one, which simply used the usual Working Title marketing strategy described above. See the two different posters here: www.movieposterdb.com/poster/68517e07 (for the UK) and http://www.movieposterdb.com/poster/aa7ec467 (for France).

33. 'The funniest English film in years.'

34. Danny Boyle had them side by side with Big Ben, in one of the last tableaux of the opening ceremony of the 2012 Olympics in London, which was watched by millions of TV viewers across the world.

Hearing Voices

Dubbing and Marketing in the *Ice Age* Series

A case study by Nolwenn MINGANT

Animation films represent a specific challenge for marketers with no live actors to build the promotional efforts on. Traditionally, campaigns have been based on the film's story (well-known children's tales) or on the film's production company (most notably Disney and Pixar). Since the early 1990s, when Robin Williams voiced the genie in *Aladdin*,[1] a new strategy has been to hire famous talent to lend their voices to the animated characters. The very successful *Ice Age*[2] animated franchise offers a rich example of the links between dubbing and marketing.

Ice Age centres on three characters: Manny the Mammoth, Sid the Sloth and Diego the sabre-toothed tiger. In the original version, they are all voiced by comedians. Ray Romano, John Leguizamo and Denis Leary were selected not only for their abilities at imitating voices, but also for their popularity and persona. The voice of Ray Romano, for example, brings to mind his performance in the TV series *Everybody Loves Raymond*. Other characters have the voice of known actors. Young and unruly possum Crash is voiced by Sean William Scott, one of the wild teenagers of *American Pie* (1999). Spooky one-eyed Buck is voiced by British actor Simon Pegg, whose name is associated with offbeat quirky films (*Shaun of the Dead* [2004], *Hot Fuzz* [2007]). Silas, a bird from the South of France, is voiced by French actor Alain Chabat, known in the USA for his performance as Napoleon in *Night at the Museum: Battle of the Smithsonian* (2009). By associating the animated characters to these actors, the aim is thus to attract the fans of their live-action films.

As each film in the *Ice Age* series adds new characters, the production team, in an effort to go beyond the initial child audience, has been selecting talent appealing to different age groups. Whereas parents will be entertained by Fast Tony, a cameo character voiced by comedian and TV host Jay Leno, the younger generation will more readily identify to the groups of teenage mammoths voiced for *Continental Drift* by actors and rappers Nicki Minaj and Drake. The large casting also enables the film's characters to be culturally diverse. African-Americans are largely represented, not only by hip-hop star Queen Latifah (Ellie), but also by singer Keke Palmer (Peaches) and comedian Wanda Sykes (Granny). Hispanic voices are also to be heard through the characters of Shira (Jennifer Lopez) as well as Sid's uncle, voiced by Eddie Piolin Sotelo, a Mexican radio host whose Spanish-language show *Piolín pol la Mañana* is very popular in California. *Continental Drift* also features two talents of Indian origin, *Big Bang Theory*'s Kunal Nayyar (Gupta) and stand-up comedian Aziz Ansari (Squint).

With the voice casting for such animation films conceived strategically to attract audiences from different generations and ethnicities, the marketing campaigns have come to increasingly resemble those of live-action films. The names of the actors feature prominently on the top of the posters. Actors are also expected to participate to the promotional push. They appear in numerous interviews and behind-the-scenes featurettes, in which they develop the psychology of their characters and the challenges in interpreting them, just as they would for a live-action role. Ray Romano, for example, explains: 'Manny comes out of me. ... I hear a different guy [than me] when I do Manny. He is stronger, he is confident, but he still has a neurotic side, which is easy for me to tap into. He has a good heart.'[3] For John Leguizamo, promoting the film included stunts as diverse as appearing on *Today* to explain how he put food in his mouth to find the perfect voice for his character[4] or flying to Alaska to unveil a 14-foot ice sculpture of Scrat, the squirrel character.[5] Marketers thus fully relied on the 'all-star cast' assembled by the production team.

This recent strategy has strong cultural implications as the films prepare to travel abroad.[6] A closer examination of the type of personalities cast shows the films to be embedded in US popular culture. *Ice Age* refers to the world of television (Ray Romano, Jay Leno, Kunal Nayyar) and radio (Eddie Piolin Sotelo) – two media which are much more parochial than films – as well as music (Queen Latifah, Drake). It is thus a very local aspect of US culture that *Ice Age* is wired to. These strongly local roots are also very visible in the choice of comedians, such as African-American Cedric the Entertainer (Carl the dinosaur) and Indian-American Aziz Ansari. Besides, the choice of representing the American cultural diversity furthers the local anchorage of the film, as this notion is not constructed in the same way in other countries. Thus, although the carefully crafted voice strategy of *Ice Age* fully resonates in an American context, it appears inadequate in other national contexts.

A second implication comes from the particularity of animation films, in that a character's image can be dissociated from its voice. When they are distributed internationally, US films are often dubbed. Although they were traditionally dubbed only in five languages, they are now dubbed in numerous versions in order to reach the largest possible international audience. Dubbing is of particular necessity for animated films as their primary audience cannot read – or at least not fast enough for subtitles. For marketers of live-action films, dubbing is not problematic as their campaigns can rely on the visual performance of the actors and their pictures appear prominently on the promotional material. Although it is not the actor's voice the audience will hear, it is still him or her they will see. In the case of animation, however, the actor is nowhere to be seen. Thus the talent associations created for the US version fully disappear and the whole strategy needs to be rethought.

Following the US trend, international distributors and marketers are now increasingly turning their back on the tradition of redubbing by professional voice actors and favour the choice of famous local talent. Here are a few examples of how the *Ice Age* voices were selected in different national contexts. In the Mexican version, the three main characters are interpreted by famous local telenovela actors. Manny is voiced by Jesús Ochoa (*Por ella soy Eva*), Diego by Sergio Sendel (*Una familia con suerte*) and Sid by Carlos Espejel (*El Privilegio de mandar*). Ellie is interpreted by singer and telenovela actress Angélica Vale (*La fea más bella*). In the same way, the Portuguese-language version is dubbed by famous Brazilian telenovela actors. In Norway, Manny is Otto Jespersen, a comedian and TV presenter (*OJ*). Sid is Dagfinn Lyngbø, a many-times-rewarded stand-up comedian. Diego is Sven Nordin, an actor famous for his role in the TV sitcom *Mot i brøstet*. Ellie is Linn Skåber, a singer and comedian who starred in the TV series *Sejer, se degikke tibake*. In Turkey, Manny is voiced by Ali Poyrazoğlu, an actor, writer and stage director who starred in numerous TV series; Sid is voiced by Haluk Bilginer, considered as one of Turkey's sexiest actors; and Diego is Yekta Kopan, a writer and television host, who is also

Voice dubber and comedian Otto Waalkes with 'Sid' at the opening of the show *Ice Age* Live: Ein Mamutiges Abendteur in Hamburg, 9 September 2012 (© Radio Hamburg)

the official Turkish voice of Jim Carrey and Michael J. Fox. In the Cantonese version, the three main characters are dubbed by pop talent in their late twenties: Hong Kong singer and TV host Edmond Leung (Manny), Taiwanese DJ and singer Sam Lee (Sid) and Hong Kong DJ, radio actor and TV host Shao Yezhan (Diego). As can be seen, local distributors and marketers embed the films in their own national context, by using the same techniques as US marketers, notably by hiring talent from the very local worlds of television and national music. And local talent can appropriate the roles to the point that they reinvent it in their own language. Just as Leguizamo created a specific lispy elocution for Sid, German comedian Otto Waalkes has the sloth yoddling through the four episodes.

As each film is extracted from its US context to be reinserted into a different national context, the local voices become the new stars of the marketing campaign.[7] On the film's posters the phrases 'avec la voix française de', 'Türkçe Seslendirme', 'Norske Stemmer' and 'Magar hangok' feature prominently. The trailer for the first *Ice Age* film similarly mentions 'with the voices of' as a selling point. In Turkey, Serbia and Norway, the posters go one step further by putting the names of the local dubbers at the top, where the names of the US talent had first been situated. The process of localisation of the film is thus complete. The local talent is then expected to perform the same promotional effort as US stars have in the USA. In France, the actors participate to shooting sessions with puppets of their characters. They fool around the dubbing studio in 'Making of' videos. They attend the film's previews with their children, as reported by the celebrity and gossip magazines. They discuss with their interviewers the psychological development of their characters and how they actually echo their own personalities. French comedian Elie Semoun, for example, explains how Sid corresponds to his own image, as a short and agitated guy, but also a character who needs affection. 'In fact, he is like me,' he ingenuously confides.[8] In Germany, the campaigns have similarly relied on the fame of Otto Waalkes. Not only do the posters mention 'Otto Spricht Sid', but the German comedian also fully involves himself in the promotional efforts: 'Besides online chats, Waalkes went on radio and TV to stump for the film. He produced funny jingles. He showed the movie trailer on his comedy tours. At the premiere, he autographed posters.'[9] In the end, each version of *Ice Age* rests on an 'all-star cast', a cast which is to be reinvented for every individual market.

Although dubbing is not technically considered part of marketing, it is increasingly becoming integral to the promotional effort. The case of animation is specific in that it rests on the sound atmosphere and the connotation of voices. As this case study shows, the soundscape one lives in is rooted in a popular culture which is eminently local. Films such as *Ice Age* thus need to be recreated to adapt to the specific cultural context of each country, an adaptation facilitated by animation's disconnection between image and voice. Although *Ice Age* comprises four episodes, it actually exists in a myriad of other versions, all as authentic as the original.

Notes

1. Joël Augros, 'Le toon c'est de l'argent', in Pierre Floquet (ed.), *CinémAnimationS* (Paris: CinémAction no.123, 2007), pp. 61–8.
2. This 20th Century-Fox franchise is constituted of four films: *Ice Age* (2002), *The Meltdown* (2009), *Dawn of the Dinosaurs* (2009), *Continental Drift* (2012). A twenty-six-minute TV special was also created in 2009, *Ice Age: A Mammoth Christmas*. With budgets between $59 million and $95 million, the four episodes have been very successful, especially outside the USA. The domestic grosses for the first opus amounted to about $176 million, the non-US grosses to $206 million. For the following films, the domestic and foreign grosses are as follows: $195 million/$460 million for *Meltdown*, $196 million/$690 million for *Dawn of the Dinosaurs*, $161 million/$715 million for *Continental Drift*. Source: www.boxofficemojo.com
3. 'Ray Romany "Manny" Ice Age Interview', posted 13 July 2012. www.youtube.com/watch?v=6RuubT21R3Q
4. 'How John Leguizamo found his voice in "Ice Age"', *Today.com*, 12 July 2012. www.today.com/video/today/48162533#48162533
5. 'Close-up: "Ice Age"'s John Leguizamo', BoxofficeMojo, 29 March 2006, www.boxofficemojo.com/features/?id=2033
6. Many thanks to Xiao Qing Huang, Xiaoya Sun, Philipp Kling, Elodie Martins, Carole Granier and Samuel Bréan for their linguistic insights.
7. The logic favouring famous voices sometimes leads to an interesting cultural twist. Among the dubbers, one can find actors who are not famous, but whose *voice* is because it is associated with an American actor. In Mexico, Silas the bird is dubbed by Humberto Vélez, the official voice of Homer Simpson in that country. In France, Buck is dubbed by Emmanuel Curtil, the French voice of Jim Carrey, Mike Myers, Ben Stiller and Matthew Perry, among others. Although the presence of these voice actors will not be advertised, it will lead the audience to unconsciously associate the *Ice Age* character with previous movie experiences.
8. 'L'Age de glace 3', *Commeaucinema.com*. www.commeaucinema.com/bandes-annonces/l-ge-de-glace-3-le-temps-des-dinosaures,94068-video-15733
9. 'The Plot Thickens in Foreign Markets', *Los Angeles Times*, 6 October 2002.

Hollywood in China

Continuities and Disjunctures in Film Marketing[1]

Michael CURTIN, Wesley JACKS and Yongli LI

At the turn of the twenty-first century, China was seen as a highly speculative prospect for Hollywood studios. Film revenues were relatively inconsequential, partly because of government import quotas and partly because the country had few cinema screens. Although a wave of new theatre construction had begun, most existing cinemas were outdated or in poor repair. What's more, the People's Republic of China (PRC) was already renowned for its lively and growing pirate video market, which had been a recurring source of tension between US and Chinese trade representatives since the early 1990s.[2] Although most US movie industry leaders acknowledged China's vast potential, they saw little reason to deploy marketing resources in a country that was under-screened, highly regulated and remarkably unruly.

Over the past few years, however, China has quickly grown to become the world's second largest theatrical market while the online video market has become the largest and arguably most sophisticated in the world. Yet problems remain. The state not only regulates the number of imported films, it also controls release dates and marketing practices, making it extremely difficult for foreign distributors to mount worldwide theatrical and ancillary campaigns. Thus the challenges for marketers are both cultural and political.

Much of the scholarly literature on film marketing focuses on marketing challenges in the USA, providing history, analysis and practical guides for professionals. As such, it describes the marketing within a context that has largely been governed by market forces. In some cases the literature offers perspectives on the challenges of transnational marketing, pointing to the cultural and sometimes political obstacles that distributors confront.[3] The PRC stands out, however, as a fairly distinctive case. As this chapter demonstrates, it is an extraordinarily attractive and lucrative opportunity for US distributors, yet it poses numerous cultural and political challenges that are far more exacting than those in other territories, making it perhaps the most demanding marketing environment that Hollywood has ever faced. Moreover, it has been until recently one of the most unruly cinema industries due to the rampant circulation of unlicensed content.[4] It is also a market that is growing and changing quite rapidly, making it a global trendsetter worthy of close examination.

This chapter begins with a discussion of the obstacles that marketers confront when they release a film theatrically. Then we will describe the journey from theatres to online environment, which is where Chinese viewers are most likely to encounter Hollywood titles, before examining the central role of online and mobile (O&M) providers in marketing US films online.[5] In China, viewers may be exposed to information about a film at three moments: the global premiere, the PRC theatrical release date and the premium SVoD release. First, international trailers, posters and online discussions may engage viewer interest but the film may not arrive in Chinese theatres for months. Second, the title becomes available in local cinemas, but average ticket prices are high and therefore consumers are cautious about when (and on what) to spend. Moreover, information about the film is sometimes sketchy as international distributors have little control over the release date and marketing campaigns are often patched together in a hasty and haphazard fashion. Third, the film is available at a more affordable price point, but marketed by an SVoD service whose interests may not coincide with those of the US distributors. At each of these three moments, online or physical pirate providers make it difficult for marketers to ensure that their best efforts result in licensed transactions. Instead, marketing may foster awareness that increases searches for unlicensed content. Hollywood films, although increasingly available and popular, are therefore marketed in China under conditions that engender institutional, cultural and political disjunctures.

Theatrical Marketing in China
In 2013, *Iron Man 3* grossed $1.2 billion in worldwide box office, reaping more than twice as much in theatres abroad ($806 million) as it did in the USA. The second biggest market for the film after the USA was the PRC, where it enjoyed record-breaking ticket sales during its opening weekend in May 2013 and ended its run with over $120 million in gross receipts. Many calculations about the Chinese market had shaped the early stages of the film's development and financing. The producers were aware of potential profits in the mainland market but also of its unique distribution challenges.

The first hurdle is the import quota system and local distribution monopoly. Each year, the major Hollywood studios produce close to 200 features, but only thirty-four foreign films (up from twenty in 2012) are granted access to the PRC on a revenue-sharing basis. The central enforcer of this import policy is the China Film Group Corporation (CFGC), a government-backed media enterprise that selects from hundreds of films worldwide based both on economic and political criteria. CFGC uses the money it earns from foreign films to support the growth of the domestic film business and provides popular titles to managers of the burgeoning exhibition chains who are anxious to fill their theatre seats.[6] Yet these economic motivations are also tempered by cultural concerns. Films must be acceptable to audiences of all ages, since China has no rating system, and acceptable to Communist Party officials as well. Even films that earn initial approval may be edited to eliminate content that is considered excessively violent, sexually explicit, or politically sensitive.

CFGC is the sole licensed importer of foreign films, which it then distributes, along with its junior partner Huaxia Film Distribution. As part of its distribution purview, China Film oversees the release dates for all films, an opaque form of leverage that makes it possible for the government to time theatrical runs so as to maintain a balance in box-office tallies between foreign and domestic product. With this tool at its disposal, CFGC often clears the schedule of foreign competitors so that domestic films can enhance their revenue at the box office, a practice which, when spread across several weeks or months, is referred to as a blackout period. Although some domestic films (such as *So Young* [2013]) perform well in the face of import competition, others (especially government-favoured pictures) sometimes see their fortunes boosted by blackout periods, favourable release dates, elaborate promotional campaigns and fabricated box-office data.[7] Meanwhile, Hollywood studios complain behind closed doors about CFGC's import selections and manipulation of release schedules. Adding to their frustrations, most US titles are assigned a release date four to six weeks in advance, which makes it difficult to develop a coordinated marketing campaign that builds momentum for the opening weekend.

The autumn of 2012 offered an example of CFGC's protective powers and Hollywood's frustrations. Thanks to an especially strong performance by imports in the first half of the year, January to June box-office numbers showed domestic films had earned only 35 per cent of gross revenue.[8] This was far below the unwritten governmental goal of 50 per cent, so a long late summer import blackout period quickly followed the announcement. In the middle of this period, Wu Ershan's big-budget fantasy film, *Hua pi 2* (*Painted Skin: The Resurrection*, 2012), had an extensive marketing campaign and a wide, uncontested theatrical release to record returns. The film's success pulled domestic box-office totals closer to parity with imports but challenges for maintaining the strength of local receipts remained. By the time the blackout period ended, only nineteen of the thirty-four import quota films had been released. This left fifteen imports to be released in about four months' time, a rapid pace for a territory used to releasing twenty imports over a full year.

In the midst of the blackout period, Warner Bros. and Sony were engaged in desperate negotiations with Chinese authorities over the release of *The Dark Knight Rises* (2012) and *The Amazing Spider-Man* (2012). Although the films had already enjoyed large international premieres early in the summer, their distributors were still without confirmed quota slots and release dates by mid-July. Lacking both, the studios put their Chinese marketing campaigns on hold. Early rumours implied a 30 August release for both films, an outcome Warner Bros. in particular, seemed desperate to avoid.[9] Intense lobbying behind closed doors reportedly ensued, but these efforts ultimately failed. On 21 July, CFGC announced the films would both open on 27 August, leaving only five weeks for local advertising campaigns.[10] In addition to the head-to-head face-off and short marketing window, *Prometheus* (2012) and *The Expendables 2* (2012) (featuring Jet Li) were slotted into release dates a week later. The clustered premieres allowed Chinese industry leaders to zoom through their remaining quota responsibilities and use intense competition to kept potential revenues of each blockbuster to a minimum. For the studios, the schedule was a nightmare, generating direct competition over billboard space, trailers, television advertising and theatre screens.

In addition to competition for publicity and exhibition space, the lag time between the international premieres and the PRC release left the films open to widespread consumption through unlicensed distribution in DVD and online formats. Film buffs regularly track upcoming Hollywood films, viewing trailers and following pre-release publicity, and then discussing the titles via social media.[11] After the premieres, fans follow box-office figures and criticism online, and search for and share unlicensed copies well before the titles have received a PRC release date. If the film receives an import slot, local marketing again increases awareness, driving enthusiasts and upmarket consumers to theatres but at the same time encouraging a second audience segment (casual film fans) towards unlicensed consumption.

In the face of these challenges, studios have turned to innovative positioning in concept, production and distribution phases to improve an import's chances of success at the box office. One of the best ways to do this is by bringing aboard a PRC partner such as Beijing-based DMG Entertainment, a company founded as an advertising firm in 1993. Its mixed American and Chinese leadership embodies the intermediary role the company often fulfils.[12] DMG produced hundreds of local commercials before undertaking its first co-produced feature with the China Film Group Corporation (CFGC), *Jian guo da ye* (*The Founding of a Republic*, 2009). Released as a central piece of the government-led celebration of the sixtieth anniversary of 'New China', this 'main melody film' (a film that upholds central tenets of the Communist Party) was produced and directed by Han Sanping, former chairman of the CFGC and the most influential PRC film official of the past two decades. DMG's participation in such a prestigious and politically revered project indicated the company's close connections to the dominant powers in Chinese media.

Since 2010, DMG has become a Chinese partner for several international producers looking for smoother entry into the local market. After successfully guiding mid-budget sci-fi *Looper* (2012) to a coveted holiday release, DMG partnered with Disney-Marvel for the promotion and release of its next tentpole, *Iron Man 3*. The announcement of DMG's participation was paired with the news that Chinese stars Wang Xueqi and Fan Bingbing were slated for supporting roles and that second-unit film-making would take place in Beijing for several weeks. DMG and Disney were also granted privileged access to the national television audience during the China Movie Channel's (CCTV-6) 2013 New Year's Gala. Robert Downey Jr appeared in a scripted segment promoting the film.[13] A few weeks later, a ninety-minute documentary on the production of the film began airing on CCTV.[14] This level of TV exposure for a Hollywood import had been virtually unheard of prior to *Iron Man 3*. The final release date remained unclear, however, and marketing material could only promise 'Summer 2013'. Rumours and anonymous quotes in industry trade journals suggested a Friday premiere before a long-weekend holiday release in late April was hoped for.[15] Ultimately, however, DMG's connections proved fallible as China Film announced the long weekend would belong exclusively to *Zhi wo men zhong jiang shi qu de qing chun* (*So Young*, 2013), the much anticipated directorial debut of the enormously popular star Vicki Zhao Wei. The Marvel tentpole was pushed back to Wednesday, 1 May. Despite the brief delay and mid-week opening, *Iron Man 3* enjoyed positive buzz and garnered $60 million in its first five days.

Inspired by the *Iron Man 3* strategy, Paramount pictures allied with non-theatrical distributors for the *Transformers: Age of Extinction* (2014) China release. The studio struck a high-profile deal with CCTV-6, a government-owned network with longstanding ties to Hollywood studios but without a track record of big-budget production. As with the DMG pictures mentioned above, Paramount announced the inclusion of Chinese production sites and local stars (Li Bingbing). To help the studio steadily build local awareness and allow CCTV to take advantage of Hollywood glamour, the producers launched a reality show featuring aspiring Chinese actors vying for roles as extras in the blockbuster movie. The show began airing over a year before the film's release, providing regular promotional exposure.[16] The film's release date was again an issue of great importance. Thus, CCTV provided Paramount with an influential partner at the epicentre of the country's media infrastructure. Announcing their collaboration in April 2013, they pegged the film's release for 'on or about 27 June 2014',[17] which was unusual compared most studios, which struggled to predict release dates even six weeks prior to their PRC premieres. Yet *Transformers* rolled out on schedule, earning a record-setting $95 million in three days.

Such successes continue to be the exception rather than the rule, and Hollywood studio executives remain anxious about their future earnings in the world's fastest-growing theatrical market. The importance of making direct overtures to the Chinese audience, regardless of how little marketing time is available before the local premiere, has become clear. When Robert Downey Jr appeared at the Beijing premiere of *Iron Man 3*, a star appearance was still rare. A year later it had become almost routine, with leading actors from *The Amazing Spider-Man 2*, *Captain America: The Winter Soldier*, *Transcendence* and *X-Men: Days of Future Past* (all 2014) all appearing at local events within a span of three months.

As the significance of Chinese movie audiences continues to grow, Hollywood marketers are finding some successful avenues through the complex web of restrictions and relationships that affect theatrical releases. In some cases this has paid off handsomely at the multiplex and, because home video licensing deals are often tied to box-office metrics, in the downstream value of ancillary markets. Box-office strength used to be of little concern to video distributors when television was the primary release window, since government-controlled stations set restrictions on licence fees.[18] Over the past few years, however, commercially owned O&M platforms have become the viewing option of choice for audiences under the age of thirty-five.[19] With licence fees rapidly rising, this could be a potential boon for foreign distributors. Yet the marketing obstacles they face remain daunting.

From Theatres to O&M

Disney's international hit *Frozen* (2013) offers an illustration of a film's journey to China and its marketing challenges on different platforms. Disney is one of the most prominent Hollywood brands in China, visible through theme parks, merchandise and dedicated television programming. As the studio's fairy tale musical built momentum in North America through the winter of 2013, Disney executives seemed confident they could secure a PRC quota slot, but faced continued uncertainty in obtaining a favourable release date. The film premiered in the USA on 27 November 2013, receiving positive reviews and enjoying a twelve-week run in the top five at the domestic box office. As the film's popularity soared, Chinese fans expressed eager anticipation to see the film and frustration that the PRC release date remained unclear. It was not until 3 January 2014 that Disney was able to confirm a mainland theatrical run, but the premiere date remained in doubt until the middle of January when it was announced that it would open on 5 February in the latter part of the Spring Festival 'Golden Week'.[20]

The mainland premiere was set for the peak of the Chinese New Year celebrations, but it was also more than two months after its global release. During that time, the film was widely and easily available to audiences in unlicensed streaming, download and DVD formats. Disney officials publicly expressed satisfaction with the premiere date, since it was scheduled during a holiday week, which generally favours family-friendly fare. Behind closed doors, however, concerns were expressed about the fact that *Frozen* would open in direct competition with some of the strongest domestic film offerings of the year, such as *Xi you ji: Da nao tian gong* (*Journey to the West: Conquering the Demons*), a big-budget remake of a literary classic, and *Baba qu nar?* (*Where Are We Going, Dad?*) (both 2014), the film adaptation of a local TV hit.[21] Moreover, the marketing window for *Frozen* was exceptionally narrow, leaving less than three weeks from announcement to opening for Disney to put together a full-scale campaign during one of the busiest and most competitive advertising periods of the year.[22]

During its first two weeks *Frozen* grossed $30 million,[23] a respectable performance, but far short of what studio executives expected from a title that garnered almost $1.3 billion in ticket sales, most of it ($873 million) in international markets.[24] Overall, Disney's most successful animated feature film in years tallied only $48 million at the PRC box office,[25] putting it behind much less bankable imports released in close proximity like *Despicable Me 2* and *Need for Speed* (both 2014).[26] Some of this underperformance must be chalked up to the tough holiday competition, but just as likely the film suffered from the ten-week delay between its global release and its PRC premiere, during which time *Frozen* was widely available online and on the street.

On 29 April, *Frozen* finally was rolled out as a premium SVoD offering, more than four months after it first appeared online in unlicensed formats. Revenue figures have not been made public, but they were most likely underwhelming, much like other Hollywood titles that have been released under similar circumstances. *Frozen* will eventually become available for free on ad-based O&M services, bundled together with other Buena Vista productions to bolster the library of titles offered by the six major platforms. By then *Frozen*'s distinctive value will have been diminished substantially, leaving little hope that its O&M revenues will make up for its weak box-office performance.

Like the theatrical market, the O&M market has exploded across China over the past decade, notably due to the growth of broadband, WiFi and 3G networks in the late 2000s and early 2010s. It reached 428 million viewers by the end of 2013,[27] with legal and illegal consumption habits coexisting, with thirteen- to thirty-year-old viewers exhibiting scant loyalty to particular web providers and consuming mostly unlicensed content. As viewers age, as their incomes rise, and as demands on their time increase, they tend to migrate towards licensed providers who offer an increasingly vast library of titles. The O&M environment, therefore, offers tremendous opportunities to movie distributors, but presents them with specific challenges. While Hollywood films currently enjoy scarcity advantages in modern multiplex theatres, where the number of available options is limited, in the O&M space, US films and TV shows vie with thousands of titles from Korea, Japan, Hong Kong and other foreign locales. Moreover, O&M viewers exhibit strong affinity for local and national products, especially content that is actively promoted by Chinese stars, critics and bloggers via complementary media.[28] However, as only a relatively small number of US films have been released theatrically in PRC, most arrive online with limited pre-awareness among O&M audiences. Foreign distributors would, therefore, need to aggressively promote their products to succeed in this environment.

Furthermore, revenues from the O&M market are relatively low. Most Hollywood films do not receive a quota slot and, therefore, their best hope for distinctive revenue in the PRC is when they are offered as pay-per-view (PPV) titles on O&M platforms, often as soon as two weeks after the global premiere. Consumers pay very little for PPV access, only 80 cents per film, which is equivalent to the price of a pirated DVD, a clear concession to the continued importance of unlicensed consumption. Titles are also available to those that subscribe to premium SVoD services, which, at $3 per month, is about half the average movie ticket price in China. Despite the fact that PPV and premium subscription fees are priced attractively for the market, the uptake has still been slow. By the end of 2013 only 11.7 per cent of O&M viewers reported paying regularly for PPV content and 23.7 per cent had either monthly or yearly subscriptions.[29] Although many have sampled these services, O&M pay models are still in their infancy. Sai Yin, senior manager of the movie centre at Youku, says the biggest challenge in the next five to ten years is for video sites to expand their paid services. For now, however, Hollywood films earn little distinctive revenue through premium O&M windows and those that fail to gain theatrical release earn virtually nothing on their own. Most of these films attract only a trickle of revenue when they are bundled with a collection of studio titles for sale to the major platforms. Under these conditions it makes little sense for the US studios to invest in the marketing of their films to O&M audiences. Once the bundle is sold, the responsibility for marketing falls to the licensee, which is more interested in promoting its service rather than particular films. Given these conditions, *Frozen* appeared briefly in premium services during April of 2014 and since has been withdrawn from the O&M market. Films that fail to achieve a theatrical release tend to fare even more modestly in the SVoD window.

Marketing to O&M Viewers

The early years of video streaming were characterised by a rapid proliferation of competing services. Since 2009, six industry leaders have emerged, offering similar services and

interfaces. As O&M viewing increases, competition among the leading services is also rising, with each platform angling to secure titles that are performing well on competing sites
and to score some exclusive titles that will help them stand out. Exclusivity, however, is
expensive, since an international distributor offering such a deal would need to secure a
fee that would be comparable, if not greater than if it made the content available to all of
the big six platforms. O&M services are cautious about paying such high prices.
Consequently, the major video sites tend to provide similar content, subscription services
and interfaces. Moreover, the range of titles is expansive, covering most popular domestic
film and television titles, as well as popular products from East Asian neighbours.
Hollywood TV shows (all of them free to stream on an ad-supported basis) are well represented and US films are slowly becoming more accessible. In 2014, Youku-Tudou, the
market leader, proclaimed the 'year of international acquisition', earmarking nearly $50 mil-
lion to secure rights to new international content.[30]

The growth of licensed content consumption has also been supported by the advertisers, who prefer to market their products on sites that abide by international copyright
conventions and are actually the main source of revenue for online video websites.
Video delivery platforms favour licensed content both to boost their reputations for providing exclusive content to viewers and to develop their reputations with international
advertisers. Mobile apps are another driver of licensed content consumption. Among
new internet users, 70 per cent come online via smartphone, where they are served by
streaming video apps maintained by the major platforms.[31] These portals only feature
licensed content, which they similarly provide on an advertising-supported basis. Given
their strong commitment to licensed content, the main video website providers are careful to protect their investments by being active advocates of IP regulation.[32] In 2013, five
of the six main providers took legal action against search engine Baidu for steering
users towards pirated content.[33] The case resulted in regulatory sanctions and a substantial fine for Baidu, marking a significant milestone in the evolution of streaming
video in the PRC.

As the amount of readily available licensed content expands, viewers are developing
loyalties to particular providers and spending less time grazing the internet. Over 30 per
cent of O&M viewers are now selecting content through websites or mobile apps
offered by licensed providers, which means they are moving away from internet search
engines and piratical content, and instead spending most of their time on licensed
sites.[34] In order to encourage this trend, it is important for video sites, which design all
marketing for the entire slate of international titles in their libraries, to come up with
innovative and proactive marketing strategies to promote their ad-based programming
and premium paid services. Video sites, therefore, promote the trendiest, most recently
available licensed content, placing special emphasis on their exclusive titles.[35] They
also favour box-office hits, award winners and, especially, films that feature popular
stars or familiar franchises. The platforms are pragmatic in their promotional strategies,
showing no observable preference for domestic, regional, or international fare. Much of
the marketing takes place on the gateway screens to their services and the various
sections of content. They promote eight to twenty films on the front page of these
movie sections and update them with new content once or twice a week, emphasising
content that is an 'online premiere', 'online exclusive' or 'free streaming premiere'.[36]
They also actively promote their premium services. Platform providers make short video
commercials about their newly available content and run them as pre-roll ads before
showing a title that a viewer selects. Services also engage social media, such as

WeChat and Weibo, to send out information and updates about content of interest to particular groups of viewers.

As mentioned above, although each site works hard to make its services stand out, exclusive content tends to be exceptional. Most providers carry a similar menu of offerings, so much of the marketing simply aims to repackage titles in imaginative ways. A service might promote a group of works by popular stars or directors. Or it might highlight titles that share thematic or generic qualities that seem to be popular among viewers. Often, if a blockbuster sequel is headed for theatrical release, the online service will develop a promotional campaign for previous titles in the franchise. Similarly, if a major movie or television star is about to appear in a highly promoted title, an O&M service will highlight previous work by that artist. And if a film wins an international award, video services will scramble to secure the streaming rights (since most of these films do not secure a theatrical quota slot) and/or they will feature previous work by directors and stars associated with the award-winning title.

As the number of online viewers in China increases, Hollywood companies see an opportunity to earn more revenue by distributing recent non-quota films via streaming services.[37] Yet marketing activities in this sphere are orchestrated not by the studios but by the O&M providers. For non-quota films this means the US distributors have virtually no direct impact on audience awareness, and for quota films marketing conditions remain precarious at best. If *Transformers: The Age of Extinction* is evidence of theatrical box-office potential, *Frozen* is an example of its precarity, and a film like *Blue Jasmine* (2013) is representative of the many films that never make it to the theatre, emerging only at the discretion of O&M services that perceive a self-interested rationale to market it as part of their larger universe of offerings.

The Chinese film market is growing rapidly and is, according to many industry observers, destined to become the world's largest by 2020.[38] It remains, however, an extraordinarily complicated terrain for Hollywood distributors. The challenges begin in the theatrical window, where the timing and execution of marketing campaigns is dependent on decisions made by Chinese regulators who consider the ways in which imports conform to political orthodoxies and affect the overall growth of the domestic Chinese film industry. As US films move into the O&M ancillary market, they plunge into a digital maelstrom of competing titles from film and television producers in China, East Asia and other parts of the world. It is extremely difficult to make a title stand out under such conditions, especially given the fact that most US studios have little influence over marketing activities that are largely in the hands of the major video streaming platforms. Although some innovative campaigns have been undertaken, Hollywood films are immersed in a very competitive O&M universe where their value is greatly diminished.

The constraints on international distributors and marketers are, therefore, significant, but perhaps the most difficult challenges are posed by disjunctures between the timing of marketing campaigns and the availability of Hollywood products. As we argued above, global film premieres often engender awareness among prospective viewers who must wait for the titles to appear in PRC theatres, which means their only available option is a pirated version. When the film does receive clearance for theatrical release in China, promotional campaigns again raise visibility, but high ticket prices mean that this second window of awareness may likewise encourage audiences to access pirated versions. When licensed products finally arrive online, marketing influence is again disjunctive, since the titles now confront a sea of competitors and promotional efforts are largely in the hands of O&M providers. International distributors therefore operate within the context of political and cultural constraints that contribute to the continuing prominence of unlicensed circulation.

One can, therefore, sympathise with the frustrations expressed by Hollywood executives who complain about import quotas, official favouritism and a host of other constraints. Yet it is worth noting that the Chinese government has been remarkably successful at strategically employing Hollywood blockbusters to fill the seats of its booming theatrical sector, which has in turn helped to subsidise the growth of its domestic film production capacity. Although the means have sometimes been messy, the overall goals have remained fairly clear: Chinese officials wish to exercise cultural sovereignty; domestic movie professionals want to grow their industry; and audiences want to enjoy access to a diverse range of cultural content. This is a delicate and dynamic balance of forces whereby official interests are played off against popular aspirations. Moreover, it is an equation in which piracy plays a role since it keeps pressure on both the government and the industry to innovate and open up, which they have done fitfully over the past twenty years. So, although piracy in many ways feeds off the marketing disjunctures described above, it also lubricates the very messy mechanics of change that are ushering the Chinese film industry forward.

Notes

1. The authors gratefully acknowledge research support from the Carsey-Wolf Center's Media Industries Project and the Australian Research Council.
2. US Trade Representative Report on Intellectual Property Laws in International Sphere, *USTR Special 301 Report*, 1990–4.
3. Kristin Thompson, *Exporting Entertainment: Hollywood in the World Film Market, 1907–1934* (London: BFI, 1985). John Trumpbour, 'Hollywood and the World: Export or Die', in Paul MacDonald and Janet Wasko (eds), *The Contemporary Hollywood Film Industry* (Malden, MA: Blackwell, 2008). Toby Miller, Freya Schiwy and Marta Hernandez Salvan, 'Distribution, the Forgotten Element in Transnational Cinema', *Transnational Cinemas* vol. 2 no. 2, 2012, pp. 197–215.
4. Ramon Lobato, *Shadow Economies of Cinema: Mapping Informal Film Distribution* (London: BFI, 2012). Laikwan Pang, *Creativity and Its Discontents* (Durham, NC: Duke University Press, 2012). Shujen Wang, *Framing Piracy: Globalization and Film Distribution in Greater China* (Lanham, MD: Roman & Littlefield Press, 2003).
5. Our research methodology for the section on theatrical marketing and distribution combines material from existing scholarly research, industry trade sources and Chinese film websites. Since online video platforms have received limited industrial and scholarly coverage in English, our findings are largely based on Chinese web articles, online ethnography performed by the authors between June 2013 and May 2014, and a viewer behaviour survey.
6. David Bordwell, *Planet Hong Kong 2.0* (Madison: Irvington Way Press, 2011).
7. Jessica Beaton, 'A Chinese Film is Set to Break All Chinese Box Office Records – Guess Which One', *CNN*, 6 October 2009, http://travel.cnn.com/shanghai/play/founding-republic-break-chinese-box-office-341918
8. Stephen Cremin, 'China Box Office Crosses $1.2bn in H1', *Film Business Asia*, 13 July 2012.
9. Ben Fritz and John Horn, 'Warner, China Film Clash on "Dark Knight" Debut Against "Spider-Man"', *Los Angeles Times*, 18 July 2012.
10. Etan Vlessing, 'IMAX to Simultaneously Debut "Dark Knight Rises" and "Amazing Spider-Man" in China', *The Hollywood Reporter*, 22 August 2012.

11. Angela Xiao Wu, 'Broadening the Scope of Cultural Preferences: Movie Talk and Chinese Pirate Film Consumption from the mid-1980s to 2005', *International Journal of Communication* vol. 6, 2012, pp. 501–29.

12. American Dan Mintz serves as CEO and Media Point Person. Xiao Wenge runs Finances and former Chinese gymnastic champion Wu Bing serves as Group President.

13. 'Fan Bingbing Confirmed Taking a Role in Ironman 3, Send out Greeting Messages on CCTV 6's Spring Festival Gala', *Sina Entertainment*, 7 February 2013, http://ent.sina.com.cn/m/c/2013-02-07/14363854796.shtml

14. 'Hot TV Spot: Iron-Man 3 in China', *Deadline.com*, 18 April 2013, http://deadline.com/2013/04/iron-man-3-china-commercial-video-478230/

15. Rob Cain, 'Lovers vs Fighters in China, "So Young" vs "Iron-Man 3"; and the Winner Is …', *ChinaFilmBiz*, 26 April 2013, http://chinafilmbiz.com/2013/04/26/lovers-vs-fighters-in-china-so-young-vs-iron-man-3-and-the-winner-is/

16. 'Transformers Audition Attracts 70k Chinese applicats; Stars and Amateurs on the Same Stage', *Zhengzhou Evening News*, 23 July 2013, http://media.people.com.cn/n/2013/0723/c40606-22287200.html

17. Paramount Studio Release, 2 April 2013, http://www.comingsoon.net/news/movienews.php?id=102319

18. Ying Zhu, *Two Billion Eyes: The Story of China Central Television* (New York: New Press, 2012).

19. Bingchun Meng, 'Underdetermined Globalization: Media Consumption via P2P Networks', *International Journal of Communication* vol. 6, 2012, p. 17; Elaine Jing Zhao and Michael Keane, 'Between Formal and Informal: The Shakeout in China's Online Video Industry', *Media, Culture & Society* vol. 35 no. 6, 2013, pp. 724–41; Kelly Hu, 'Competition and Collaboration: Chinese Video Websites, Subtitle Groups, State Regulation and Market', *International Journal of Cultural Studies* vol. 17 no. 5, 2014, pp. 437–51.

20. 'Set for February 5 Release, Frozen's Chinese Trailer and Poster Come Out', *Sina Entertainment*, 14 January 2014, http://ent.sina.com.cn/m/f/2014-01-14/02034080524.shtml

21. Hui Nai, 'Where Are We Going, Dad? vs Monkey King – Spring Festival Has Two Films Fighting for Box Office Revenue Through Exhibition Deals', *Mtime*, 2 February 2014, http://news.mtime.com/2014/02/02/1523662.html

22. Ibid.

23. 'Week 7: "Beijing Love Story" Well Told in Valentine's Day', *EntGroup*, 19 February 2014, http://english.entgroup.cn/views_detail.aspx?id=2235

24. Source: www.boxofficemojo.com

25. 'Week 10: Robocop Revs Up to $42mn in China', *EntGroup*, 12 March 2014, http://english.entgroup.cn/views_detail.aspx?id=2285

26. 'Week 3: Three Animations Share 60% o Weekly Revenue', *EntGroup*, 21 January 2014, http://english.entgroup.cn/views_detail.aspx?id=2172; 'Week 13: "Need for Speed" Races for Third Straight Week', *EntGroup*, 4 April 2014, http://english.entgroup.cn/views_detail.aspx?id=2346

27. China Internet Network Information Center (CCNIC), *A Report on Internet Video Use by Chinese Netizens in 2013* (Beijing: CCNIC, 2014), p. 6.

28. Analysis of most clicked shows on Youku's Chinese Internet Video Index Database performed by the authors from June 2013 to May 2014.

29. CCNIC, *A Report on Internet Video Use by Chinese Netizens in 2013*, p. 20.

30. Gavin J. Blair, '2014 to be a "Year of International Acquisition" for Chinese Online Video Giant Youku Tudou", *The Hollywood Reporter*, 3 December 2013.

31. Steven Millward, 'China Now Has 591 Million Internet Users, 460 Million Mobile Netizens', *Tech In Asia*, 17 July 2013, www.techinasia.com/cnniic-china-web-mobile-user-data-for2013/

32. 'Video Sites Retrospect and Prospect: IP and Consolidation Became Hot', *Chinabyte*, 10 December 2009, http://tech.sina.com.cn/i/2009-12-10/12023666727.shtml

33. Clifford Connan and Patrick Brzeski, 'Chinese Film, Internet Video Companies Sue Search Giant Baidu in Anti-Piracy Push', *The Hollywood Reporter*, 13 November 2013, www.hollywoodreporter.com/news/chinese-film-internet-video-companies-655605

34. Ibid., p. 17.

35. Analysis of Youku, Sohu and Tencent's video websites by the authors from June 2013 to May 2014.

36. Findings based on online ethnography performed by the authors on Youku.com, Tudou.com, film.qq.com, LeTV.com, tv.sohu.com and iqiyi.com

37. Patrick Brzeski, 'Chinese Internet Giant Tencent Licenses Disney Films for Streaming Video Service', *The Hollywood Reporter*, 9 September 2013.

38. Ernst & Young, 'Summary Report: Spotlight on China: Building a Roadmap for Success in Media and Entertainment', Ernst & Young, 2012, p. 2, http://www.ey.com/Publication/vwLUAssets/Media_and_Entertainment_-_Spotlight_on_China/$FILE/Spotlight_on_China.pdf

Film Marketing in Nollywood

A case study by Alessandro JEDLOWSKI

In the 1990s and the early 2000s, Nollywood emerged as one of the dominant entertainment industries in Africa.[1] Its history has been marked by extremely fast transformations which have affected all aspects of film production and distribution, including marketing. The industry's initial success was largely connected to the informal organisation of the industry's economy and to the application of straight-to-video distribution strategies, which appropriately responded to the challenges of the economically ravaged post-structural adjustment Nigeria.[2] Nevertheless, these same aspects had a central role in making the industry's economy particularly vulnerable to piracy and unprofessionalism, and in generating a crisis that has had a relevant impact on Nollywood over the past few years.[3] In this sense, it is possible to make a distinction between at least two different macro tendencies in what concerns film marketing in Nollywood, one corresponding roughly to the early years of the industry and to the activity of a number of producers and marketers[4] who tend to occupy today the lower end of the industry's economy, and another one which has emerged in relation to the industry's more recent economic transformations and which relates mostly to the upper end of the industry's economic structure.

Marketing in Early Nollywood

At the time of Nollywood's birth, in the early 1990s, the existing theatre, television and celluloid film industries were collapsing as a result of the dramatic local economic and political crisis that followed the application of the structural adjustment policies.[5] Nevertheless, audience demand for locally produced entertainment was high, particularly in the numerous large urban centres that characterise Nigeria. In order to reach this wide audience,[6] a set of entrepreneurs, mainly dealers in electronics and pirated copies of foreign audiovisual content, decided to exploit the popular success of well-known television and theatre actors in order to market VHS tapes of locally produced dramas. The astonishing commercial success of Living in Bondage, produced in 1992 by Igbo businessman Kenneth Nnebue,[7] established a clearly defined formula based on the combination of three main elements: 1) melodramatic narratives with strong moral and didactic contents, 2) played by local star actors (in the early years mainly coming from previous experiences in the local theatre, television or celluloid film industries, and later emerging from the video phenomenon itself)[8] and 3) distributed straight to video throughout local markets and video clubs.

Within this context, the films' production value was neither the producers' nor the audience's priority and, thanks also to the affordability of new recording and editing technologies, film budgets remained predominantly low if compared to international standards. Nigeria had long been marked by the predominance of foreign (mostly 'white' and 'western') audiovisual contents, which had perpetuated an alienating and 'self-othering' experience of media for Nigerian audiences.[9] This meant that, at least in the early years of the industry's success (early 1990s), the simple fact of being locally produced, played by local actors and based on local imageries and fantasies was, for Nollywood videos, a major added marketing value. Advertising campaigns did not play a particularly significant role in the industry's initial commercial success. In fact, in early Nollywood, they were limited to posters, street announcements and sporadic screenings of film trailers on local television stations.[10] More relevant was the role of word of mouth and of Pentecostal churches, which were often directly involved in film production and distribution,[11] and whose role in spreading the films' success was particularly relevant, even in the case of films that were not directly produced by a church but whose content was seen as relevant for evangelical purposes. From the second half of the 90s, glamorous film premieres and substantial news and media coverage also started playing a relevant role.

As the economy of Nollywood was characterised by a high level of informality, there has been a dramatic lack of reliable figures about the industry's economy.[12] This prevented producers and marketers from applying any marketing strategy based on a statistical analysis of audience consumption patterns. Within this context, most producers and marketers preferred to be on the safe side, and tended to produce films which repeated already tested narrative and aesthetic formulas, with the overall result of a constant repetition of stories and plots. This aspect, together with the high impact of piracy (initially a multiplier of the industry's popularity, but later one of its most dramatic problems),[13] progressively showed the limits of early Nollywood's production and marketing models, driving the industry to a number of important transformations.

Marketing in the 'New Nollywood'

In order to respond to the challenges of piracy, overproduction, rapid technological transformation and audience disenchantment, in the second half of the 2000s a number of Nigerian producers and marketers experimented with new marketing strategies, which included the introduction of higher budgets, international circulation via film festivals and formal distribution channels (including the internet, movie theatres and satellite television channels).[14] The introduction of these strategies resulted from the emergence of a new wave of Nigerian film professionals who decided to target transnational audiences by modifying not only the economic specificities of Nollywood's modes of operation, but also some of the key narrative and aesthetic features of Nigerian films. One of the most visible effects of these transformations has been the decrease in the production of religious films, and a proportional reduction of the influence of churches on film marketing. More conventional forms of film marketing have also began to appear, with an increase in the use of internet advertising (making-of clips, the creation of internet sites devoted to new releases, multi- and trans-media advertising campaigns) and the reliance on film stars.[15] Glamorous premieres and award ceremonies with never-ending red carpet parades, and blogs and fanzines dedicated to films stars' private lives have multiplied over the past few years. These initiatives, however, often have been targeted more towards local elites and diasporic audiences than to the lower classes of the Nigerian population which, in the early years of the industry, constituted the majority of Nollywood's viewers.[16]

Within this context, the most significant marketing transformations have emerged in relation to the way new Nollywood films' distribution windows are organised. If, in the early years, Nollywood's windowing system was mono-dimensional, with videos being released straight to video weekly in the main Nigerian film markets of Idumota (in Lagos), Onitsha and Aba (in the eastern part of Nigeria) and then further distributed by local film marketers, new Nollywood is based on a multilayered windowing system, which is closer to the one adopted by other film industries in the world, but which has the specificity of privileging diasporic audiences to local ones. New Nollywood films tend to be distributed, first, throughout diasporic markets (in the USA and Europe, and later in other African countries) and in local and international movie theatres, then via internet platforms and satellite televisions, and only lastly throughout local DVD and VCD markets. While this strategy has the overall objective of reducing the impact of piracy by privileging more formalised distribution channels and geographic areas, it has also generated a shift in the producers and distributors' marketing objectives. As the largest part of the population lives with less than $2 a day and thus has no regular access to movie theatres, the internet and satellite television, new Nollywood films can often take up to two or three years to become available to average Nigerian viewers. If, on the one hand, this ends up teasing the audience and increasing people's anticipation and curiosity for new Nollywood films, it also, on the other hand, disrupts the connection that existed between Nollywood films and popular audiences. This is the result of what can be seen as a process of 'gentrification'[17] of the Nigerian video film industry in which, at least for the upper end of the Nigerian producers' and distributors' community, diasporic and elite audiences have become the main marketing target (and the most economically relevant), and bigger corporations such as cinema chains (Silverbird and FilmHouse in Nigeria, Odeon in the UK), internet platforms (iroko.tv and ibaka.tv) and international satellite channels (Africa Magic and Nollywood.tv) have ousted local film marketers and Pentecostal churches to become the industry's key distribution players.[18]

Between early Nollywood's marketing model and new Nollywood's, a myriad of inbetween solutions have seen the light. The originality of the Nigerian video film industry lies in this large variety of options, and in their extreme fluidity and transformability. While Nollywood is, in many ways, still looking for valid solutions to make its economy viable and sustainable, the originality of its modes of operation and the rapidity of its transformations offer important analytical insights into how film production and marketing work in the sub-Saharan Africa region, a region that has long been at the margins of industrial film production, but which is today emerging as one of the most dynamic film-producing and -consuming regions of the world.

Notes

1. The use of the term 'Nollywood' has been criticised by Nigerian intellectuals and film practitioners, and it is today used mainly to refer only to the southern Nigerian video film industry, which produces films in English, in order to differentiate it from other segments of the Nigerian film industry producing videos in local languages. See Alessandro Jedlowski, 'When the Nigerian Video Film Industry Became "Nollywood": Naming, Branding and the Videos' Transnational Mobility', *Estudos Afro-Asiaticos* vol. 33 no. 1, 2, 3, 2011, pp. 225–51.
2. Cf. Jonathan Haynes and Onookome Okome, 'Evolving Popular Media: Nigerian Video Films', *Research in African Literatures* vol. 29 no. 3, 1998, pp. 106–28; Brian Larkin, 'Degraded Images, Distorted Sounds: Nigerian Video and the Infrastructure of Piracy', *Public Culture* vol. 16 no. 2, 2004, pp. 289–314; Alessandro Jedlowski, 'Small Screen Cinema: Informality and Remediation in Nollywood', *Television and New Media* vol. 13 no. 5, 2012, pp. 431–6. See also Adebayo O. Olukoshi (ed.), *The Politics of Structural Adjustment in Nigeria* (Oxford: James Currey, 1993).
3. Cf. Alessandro Jedlowski, 'From Nollywood to Nollyworld: Processes of Transnationalization in the Nigerian Video Film Industry', in Matthias Krings and Onokoome Okome (eds), *Global Nollywood: Transnational Dimensions of an African Video Film Industry* (Bloomington: Indiana University Press, 2013), pp. 25–45; Alexander Bud, 'The End of Nollywood's Guilded Age? Marketers, the State and the Struggle for Distribution',

Critical African Studies vol. 6 no. 1, 2014, pp. 91–121; Jonathan Haynes, '*Close Up*: "New Nollywood": Kunle Afolayan', *Black Camera* vol. 5 no. 2, 2014, pp. 53–73.

4. By the term 'marketer', film practitioners in Nigeria generally refer to film distributors, who have had a key role in the industry since its early years, but seem today to be losing some influence.

5. See Haynes and Okome, 'Evolving Popular Media'; Jonathan Haynes (ed.), *Nigerian Video Films* (Athens: Ohio University Press, 2000); Jedlowski, 'Small Screen Cinema'.

6. It should be remembered, incidentally, that Nigeria is one of the most populous African countries, with a population of over 170 million people.

7. Cf. Jonathan Haynes, 'Nnebue: The Anatomy of Power', *Film International* vol. 5 no. 4, 2007, pp. 30–40.

8. On what concerns the role of stars in Nollywood, see Noah Tsika, 'From Yorùbá to YouTube: Studying Nollywood's Star System', *Black Camera* vol. 5 no. 2, 2014, pp. 95–115.

9. Hamid Naficy, 'Self-Othering: A Postcolonial Discourse on Cinematic First Contacts', in Fawzia Afzal-Khan and Kalpana Seshadri-Crooks (ed.), *The Pre-Occupation of Postcolonial Studies* (Durham, NC: Duke University Press, 2000), p. 294.

10. Until recently, Nigerian local television channels used to obtain screening rights by giving Nollywood producers a few advertising slots to promote their future releases. No monetary exchange was involved in this kind of transaction.

11. Cf. Onookome Okome, '"The Message is Reaching a Lot of People": Proselytizing and Video Films of Helen Ukpabio', *Postcolonial Text* vol. 3 no. 2, 2007, http://postcolonial.org/index.php/pct/article/view/750/419 (accessed 27 August 2014); Katrien Pype, 'Religion, Migration and Media Aesthetics: Notes on the Circulation and Reception of Nigerian Films in Kinshasa', in Krings and Okome, *Global Nollywood*, pp. 199–222.

12. Jedlowski, 'Small Screen Cinema'; Ramon Lobato, *Shadow Economies of Cinema: Mapping Informal Film Distribution* (London: BFI, 2012); John McCall, 'The Capital Gap: Nollywood and the Limits of Informal Trade', *Journal of African Cinemas* vol. 4 no. 1, 2013, pp. 9–23.

13. Jedlowski, 'From Nollywood to Nollyworld'; McCall, 'The Capital Gap'.

14. Jedlowski, 'From Nollywood to Nollyworld'; Haynes, '*Close Up*'.

15. See Tsika, 'From Yorùbá to YouTube'.

16. Two examples in particular confirm this trend: the organisation of expensive and extravagant Nollywood film premieres in the Odeon cinemas in London, discussed by Jedlowski ('From Nollywood to Nollyworld', p. 35), and the specific advertising strategies adopted by the successful online Nollywood channel iroko.tv, discussed by Tsika ('From Yorùbá to YouTube', p. 102). For a discussion of early Nollywood's spectatorship see Onookome Okome, 'Nollywood: Spectatorship, Audience and the Sites of Consumption', *Postcolonial Text* vol. 3 no. 2, 2007, http://postcolonial.org/index.php/pct/article/view/763/425 (accessed 28 August 2014).

17. Tejaswini Ganti, *Producing Bollywood: Inside the Contemporary Hindi Film Industry* (Durham, NC: Duke University Press, 2012).

18. See also Jedlowski, 'Small Screen Cinema'; Jedlowski, 'From Nollywood to Nollyworld'.

Marketing High Frame Rate in *The Hobbit* Trilogy

A Spectacular Case of Promoting and Un-promoting New Cinema Technology

Miriam ROSS

The gradual shift towards digital screening technology in movie theatres during the early twenty-first century led to mainly invisible changes that standardised image quality and introduced cheaper distribution systems. Unlike digital filming and post-production technologies that were remarked upon for providing a variety of spectacular (as well as mundane) effects, digital screening technologies were normally only apparent when they failed to replicate the quality of 35mm projection. John Belton remarked on this in 2002 when he stated that 'one obvious problem with digital cinema is that it has no novelty value, at least not for film audiences'.[1] At the time he did not foresee the upsurge in 3D cinema, nor the more recent introduction of high frame rate (HFR) technology, both of which utilise digital screening systems to present significant changes to cinema's visual field.[2] Both technologies have been sold to audiences as part of the ongoing trend for innovation, novelty and constant updates to screen technology. Both have been said to offer more realistic and immersive viewing experiences, particularly with regards to the way HFR technology can provide updates to 3D viewing modes. However, more so than 3D cinema, HFR cinema has been critiqued for offering vistas that are 'too real'. When digital HFR debuted in movie theatres with the first two of Peter Jackson's Hobbit films, *The Hobbit: An Unexpected Journey* (2012) and *The Hobbit: Desolation of Smaug* (2013), critical responses varied widely between excitement at the new technology and disappointment that it offered an 'uncinematic' visual field.

In turn, HFR's uneven reception led to a paradoxical situation in which the new technology was both promoted and un-promoted. This chapter will discuss the way marketing and publicity material for these films has upheld HFR's ability to provide 'an illusion of real life', coupled with a 'truly immersive experience', at the same time as endorsing the films' non-HFR versions. In this way a complex narrative around the adoption of HFR emerges: one that does not merely see the technology's introduction as a failed attempt to produce new levels of realism, but rather an intricate interplay between new and existent technologies. Throughout this narrative a number of agents are at work: Peter Jackson and his film-making team; the publicity team at the films' studio, Warner Bros.; movie theatre chains and independent exhibitors; and a variety of bloggers and professional film journalists, each vying to come to terms with films that had been eagerly anticipated as a continuation of the visual world created in Jackson's critically acclaimed *Lord of the Rings* trilogy (2001–3).

The History of HFR

Although a film's frame rate means little to ordinary spectators, cinephiles and film technology enthusiasts know that the history of cinema has witnessed a range of frame rates, each creating their own material quality for the cinematic image. Before the twenty-four frames per second (fps) standard (which was implemented in commercial cinema during the widespread uptake of sound cinema in the 1920s), early films had variable frame rates depending on the speed at which cameras were cranked.[3] Instructions were given to projectionists in order for them to project the film at the desired speed, a speed that was not always correspondent with the filming speed.[4] For example, projecting early films at a slightly faster frame rate than the filming speed led to lighter, faster action. In this way, the film's frame rate was not bound to faithfully reproducing the temporal qualities of the events it filmed and was thus uncoupled from any direct relationship with reality in many early films. However, following the uptake of sound cinema, the norm has been to standardise the filming speed (normally 24fps) so that it corresponds with the playback speed (also 24fps), meaning that the film assumes a type of realistic replay of the film's temporal events. While 24fps produces a satisfactory temporal realism, it has long been known that an increase to filming speeds along with a concurrent increase to playback speed can reduce perceived flicker between frames and, in this way, produce a greater illusion of motion. It is within this context that experiments with higher frame rates occurred during the twentieth century; their increased filming and playback speeds operated as attempts to provide spectators with greater visual data in order to increase realism in the illusion of motion. The most well known of these experiments was Douglas Trumbull's HFR system Showscan, developed in the 1980s with the capacity for shooting and displaying moving images at 60fps.[5] Trumbull asserted that, by shooting in this way, the illusion of motion would be smoothed out.[6] The desire to improve the depiction of motion, particularly in fast-moving objects, led to other experiments with HFR technology such as the Canada National Film Board and IMAX co-production of the film *Momentum* (1992) for Expo '92 in Seville at 48fps.[7] Like many other high specification visual technologies, HFR found a place in the theme park: the Star Tours ride at Disneyland uses moving images at 60fps, as does the King Kong attraction at Universal Studios.

Nonetheless, HFR was unable to find a place in commercial movie theatres due to a familiar technological 'chicken-and-egg' scenario in which the expense of upgrading to the new technology could not be justified until sufficient content was in place while, at the same time, sufficient content could not be created until systems were in place to support its exhibition.[8] In these contexts, technology companies such as Showscan and IMAX were able to promote their new display systems during trials at specialised exhibition events but insufficient material existed in order to fully market them to general audiences. The turning point arrived when a number of different factors combined to significantly increase the availability of digital projectors in commercial movie theatres at the end of the 2000s. Although digital projection systems had been in place since *Star Wars: The Phantom Menace* (1999) was projected digitally in four theatres in the USA, and although digital prints offered significant savings to studios and distribution companies, uptake was relatively slow as exhibitors remained anxious about the high cost of installing new digital projectors.[9] However, the return of (stereoscopic) 3D cinema with initial outings from *The Polar Express* (2004) and *Chicken Little* (2005) and the huge commercial success of *Avatar* (2009) shifted the exhibition environment as exhibitors realised that they could implement a surcharge fee for 3D screenings. This acted as sufficient incentive for most major cinema chains (including those in emerging markets such as Latin America and Russia)[10] to upgrade to digital projection systems that could display 3D films as well as 2D digital films.[11] As Lisa Purse notes, 'digital technologies made 3-D's reappearance possible, but the economic imperatives of the entertainment industry made it happen'.[12]

HFR and 3D Cinema

3D cinema had an impact on the introduction of HFR to commercial movie theatres in two distinct ways. In the first instance, some of the high-end digital projectors necessary for displaying 3D moving images were capable of very fast flash rates (often 144 flashes/fps), meaning that they could display films at HFRs.[13] In this context, the technological framework for HFR display was in place, although it did often necessitate some kind of upgrade on the part of exhibitors. Second, 3D cinema itself called for a technological update. Numerous 3D film-makers found that when fast motion was captured with stereoscopic cameras strobing, ghosting and other undesirable effects occurred.[14] By filming at 48fps, these effects were greatly reduced and the smoothness in motion quality was greater than could be found in 2D cinema. This led to a ready-made narrative for marketing HFR with a two-pronged approach, one that hinted at the paradoxical strategies to be used in promoting the new technology. For audiences that were sceptical about 3D and felt that it produced uncomfortable and inferior images, HFR was a technological change to redeem stereoscopy's faults; for audiences that were in favour of the new digital 3D cinema, HFR was an added bonus that would improve an already loved system.

For the latter approach, *Avatar*'s director James Cameron provided interviews in which he built upon his history of technological development in the field of 3D cinema.[15] Having already made hyperbolic statements about the natural place for stereoscopic film-making (such as 'we see in 3-D. You look at nature, at the way nature set things up, by the Darwinian process. Everybody's got two eyes, even down into the insect world.'),[16] Cameron publicly supported Peter Jackson's experiments with HFR as an extension of his own work: 'we charged out ahead on 3D with *Avatar*, now Peter's doing it with *The Hobbit*. It takes that kind of bold move to make change.'[17] This discussion acted as a pathway to Cameron's plans for filming his *Avatar* sequels in 60fps, suggesting a continuum of ever advancing 3D technology between his and Jackson's films.

While Jackson's narrative was often supportive of and supported by Cameron's claims for how HFR could improve 3D cinema, Jackson presented a slightly different approach in which, as a first-time film-maker in 3D, he could reach out to 3D sceptics. In some interviews this involved a gentle approach to prior 3D cinema in which he acknowledged some of its problems: 'Much of what makes 3D viewing uncomfortable for *some people* is the fact that each eye is processing a lot of strobing, blur and flicker. This all but disappears in HFR 3D' (my emphasis).[18] In other interviews he set up more clearly the discontinuity between his own film-making and prior modes of 3D cinema: 'when you're shooting in 3D, both eyes are getting hit with different degrees of these artefacts [strobing, flickering, juddering], which is what gives you eye strain; that's why you get headaches watching 3D movies. 48 frames makes it much smoother.'[19] The rhetoric of the latter statement, including the use of a second person intonation, fits with the strategy Jackson has used to promote most of his films, particularly *The Lord of the Rings* trilogy, in which he posits himself as a fanboy who intimately shares the concerns and experiences of his public.[20] In doing so, Jackson has been able to negotiate the desires of his fans, both present and future, while also acting as a successful intermediary between the traditional marketing strategies of Warner Bros. (trailers, posters, production stills, red carpet events, etc.) and a highly attentive public (brought together in internet forums, blogs, Facebook sites, fan societies, etc.).[21] For *The Hobbit* trilogy, this strategy has most clearly been articulated through the release of production diaries during the filming process, most often including Peter Jackson presenting himself in a seemingly direct dialogue with his fans.[22] During this process, Peter Jackson has used his Facebook page in order to make these diaries instantly available to fans at the same time as posting brief updates to fill in fans between the release of each diary.

Building on previous strategies developed for introducing new digital technologies (the Massive software for crowd simulation in *The Lord of the Rings* trilogy;[23] motion capture processes for *King Kong* [2005][24]), Jackson's professed excitement for all things technological created public enthusiasm for his technological innovations. At the same time, although Jackson was successful during the production process in creating hype around the new technologies he was using for *The Hobbit* trilogy, he came across one of his first major challenges during the exhibition of HFR scenes at Cinemacon in April 2012.[25]

Initial Tests and Multiple Viewing Options

It is common for new media technologies to be marketed at technology trade shows such as CES (Consumer Electronics Show) and CEATEC (Combined Exhibition of Advanced Technologies) and exhibitor trade shows such as ShowEast and CineEurope. In recent years HD, 3D, surround sound systems and other new technologies for commercial and home exhibition have been introduced and promoted at these sites, normally intended to be seen by professionals working in the field. Concurrently, studios have increasingly been taking previews and early trailers to fan conventions, particularly those that have come to be associated with comic books and fantasy genres such as Comic-Con and Cinemacon. For example, Jackson previously promoted one of the films he produced, *District 9* (2009), at Comic-Con in 2009. Normally, these fan conventions are separate sites from the trade shows and have different intended audiences, the former showing content while the latter displays technology. However, the showcase of HFR scenes from *An Unexpected Journey* during Cinemacon represented the merging of sneak previews of narrative content and display technologies. Unfortunately for Jackson, critical reception, particularly that provided by the numerous bloggers at the convention, was unfavourable. For example, Devin Faraci commented that 'the 48fps footage I saw looked terrible. It looked completely non-cinematic. The sets looked like sets.'[26] Most felt that the footage was visibly poor and the HFR technology lent it a strange quality that was distinct from the visual world many had favoured in *The Lord of the Rings* trilogy. As Jackson himself pointed out, the scenes were not yet finished: colour correction was needed and the visual effects were incomplete.[27] Nonetheless, in this initial preview, the HFR technology did not visually awe the fans and bloggers in attendance in the way that had been hoped.

In what could be seen as a sign of retreat from promotion of the technology, Jackson did not screen footage in HFR when he showcased early scenes from the film at the next major convention, Comic-Con in San Diego during July 2012. Setting up a complex paradigm that has been used in subsequent press screenings for both *An Unexpected Journey* and *Desolation of Smaug*, Jackson suggested that viewership of the film could alternate between focus on the narrative content and focus on its technological display: 'I decided to screen the *Hobbit* reel at Comic-Con in 2-D and 24 frames per second, so the focus stays firmly with the content and not the technical stuff. If people want 3-D and 48fps, that choice will be there for them in December.'[28] The suggestion in the latter part of this statement that audiences might choose not to see the film in HFR represents a subtle shift from earlier statements that posited HFR as a 'must-see' replacement for older technological standards.

Jackson's shifting emphasis can be read as a reaction to negative criticism but it must also be recognised as a way of negotiating the exhibition context in which only a limited number of movie theatres were to be equipped and capable of screening the film in HFR by the December 2012 release.[29] By positing HFR as just one option among multiple ways

The Hobbit: An Unexpected Journey (2012)

of viewing *An Unexpected Journey*, Jackson allowed Warner Bros. to successfully market the seven different ways the film could be seen: 24fps 35mm/24fps digital/24fps 3D/24fps IMAX/24fps IMAX 3D/48fps 3D/48fps IMAX 3D. In an interview only a month before the film's release, Jackson stated that 'while I personally prefer watching *The Hobbit: An Unexpected Journey* in HFR 3D, I can assure you that every format will provide you with an incredible and immersive experience'.[30] His thoughts were supported by an 'HFR 3D FAQ' poster sent by the studio to movie theatre and press outlets which, at the same time as explaining the new technology, stated 'we hope you will experience HFR 3D for yourself, or enjoy *The Hobbit: An Unexpected Journey* in any format you choose, including 2D, 3D, IMAX or IMAX 3D'.[31]

Jackson also shifted away from previous statements where he had highlighted the inferior nature of 24fps. On 12 April 2011 he had stated 'we have lived with 24fps for 9 decades – not because it's the best film speed (it's not by any stretch), but because it was the cheapest speed to achieve basic acceptable results back in 1927 or whenever it was adopted'.[32] He then changed his emphasis in December 2012, when he said:

> the big thing to realize is that it's not an attempt to change the film industry. It's another choice. The projectors that can run at 48 frames can run at 24 frames – it doesn't have to be one thing or another. You can shoot a movie at 24 frames and have sequences at 48 or 60 frames within the body of the film. You can still do all the shutter-angle and strobing effects. It doesn't necessarily change how films are going to be made. It's just another choice that film-makers have got and for me, it gives that sense of reality that I love in cinema.[33]

Although these statements could be read as a contradictory attempt to increase viewership of the film while simultaneously maintaining interest in the technology he invested in,

Jackson's negotiation of the different versions of the film are not unrelated to his contemporary media environment.

John Belton has noted the way a shift towards digital technologies has encouraged viewers to accept and expect variations in their audio environments:

> The initial transition to sound (1926–1929) led to a single standard-sound on film that was met by a handful of proprietary technologies (Movietone, RCA Photophone, generic Western Electric). Digital sound is a technology of the new era of Macintosh and IBM; two standards can coexist in the digital marketplace. Consumers have adjusted/adapted to multiple standards; so long as they can run their computer programs or play back their home entertainment programs, they will tolerate multiple standards.[34]

The same logic can be applied to visual technologies where consumers are accustomed to seeing films in different formats, an issue that has recently been highly visible in movie theatres when one theatre will offer both 2D and 3D versions of the same film. During the release of *An Unexpected Journey* it was not uncommon to find movie theatres showing two or more versions of the film simultaneously. Thus, the decision not to show HFR footage at Comic-Con was not simply a case of Jackson mediating the negative press coverage that gathered after Cinemacon but was also part of a much wider tactic to assure the value and integrity of the film's multiple versions.

HFR's Digital Debut
Although this tactic was in place, the hype created around HFR during the pre-release period meant that, when the film was released, discussions about HFR were given a prevalent place. There were some enthusiastic responses to the new technology such as critic Ty Pendlebury's assertion that it produced the best 3D he had ever seen.[35] However, a large number of reviews were structured along similar lines to the press reaction to the Cinemacon footage: negative comments reiterating the critics' unhappiness with the new technology. A thorough overview of the negative reviews was conducted on Vulture.com which broke down criticism into the following fields: HFR looks too much like a video game; HFR looks too much like HD TV; HFR looks like you are watching a theatre set; HFR looks like a home movie; HFR looks like a making-of documentary.[36] Many reviews picked up on the dual function of HFR's new visual quality as both immersing and distracting. For example, Jeremy Smith said that 'An Unexpected Journey in high frame rate 3D is a deep, vicious pendulum swing between transporting and flat-out unwatchable.'[37] There were also attempts to explain scientifically why spectators would find their capacity to suspend disbelief diminished when watching HFR cinema.[38] Although these accounts were mainly initial, subjective responses without the backing of significant audience research, they did highlight an uneasy relationship between a technology that was trying to increase the presence of its filmic content in a way that replicated real-life visual processes and its break from traditional and accepted modes of cinematic visualisation. Even some of the more positive reviews, such as Stuart Muller's, suggested that multiple views were necessary in order to get used to and accept the HFR technology.[39] To some extent, Peter Jackson foresaw these responses and wrote in April 2011 that:

> Film purists will criticize the lack of blur and strobing artifacts, but all of our crew – many of whom are film purists – are now converts. You get used to this new look very quickly and it becomes a much more lifelike and comfortable viewing experience. It's similar to

the moment when vinyl records were supplanted by digital CDs. There's no doubt in my mind that we're heading towards movies being shot and projected at higher frame rates.[40]

Nonetheless, the lack of HFR content made available to the public during the wait between the first and second *Hobbit* films (no other films were released in HFR) and continuing critical scepticism of HFR meant that much less publicity material and fewer statements around HFR were released during the lead up to *Desolation of Smaug*'s December 2013 release.

While Jackson conducted far fewer discussions about HFR prior to *Desolation of Smaug*, when the film was released he did provide statements explaining that he had adjusted his use of HFR in response to negative reactions. Taking into account criticism that the images looked like HD video he said:

> what I did is work that in reverse … When I did the color timing this year, the color grading, I spent a lot of time experimenting with ways we could soften the image and make it look a bit more filmic. Not more like 35mm film necessarily, but just to take the HD quality away from it, which I think I did reasonably successfully.[41]

This process was not dissimilar to tactics used by Peter Jackson on previous films, such as *The Lord of the Rings* trilogy, where he made it clear that he was able to listen to and incorporate criticism.[42] One critic that picked up on the difference in HFR display between the two films was Todd McCarthy. He had stated of the first film that HFR technology 'while striking in some of the big spectacle scenes, predominantly looked like ultra-vivid television video, paradoxically lending the film an oddly theatrical look'.[43] With regards to the second film, he noted that 'the distractingly vivid images provided by the 48 frames per second in the first film appear to have been massaged properly this time'.[44]

Although neither Jackson's statement nor McCarthy's muted acknowledgment that HFR was no longer problematic allowed discussion of HFR to return to the same levels of positive hyperbole prior to the release of *An Unexpected Journey*, there was slowly increasing confidence among exhibitors. Even with only around 1,000 of the USA's 39,056 screens equipped to show *Desolation of Smaug* in HFR, this represented a significant increase from the 600 screens that were available for the first film.[45] IMAX also decided to increase its HFR screenings and, accompanying their decision to increase HFR screens from a hundred to 400, Regal Cinemas issued a statement saying 'with the original "Hobbit," we kept selling out of tickets for our high frame rate auditoriums … There was a huge demand from moviegoers who wanted to see the film exactly the way director Peter Jackson shot it.'[46]

Nonetheless, Jackson and the studio continued the policy they had implemented in the previous year whereby they suggested the content of the film was of primary importance and HFR was just one possible way in which to experience the film. For this reason, the HFR trailer for *Desolation of Smaug* was shown to a 'technically savvy audience' at the International Broadcasting Convention[47] but press screenings were delivered in 24fps. In similar language to his explanations for showing footage in 24fps at Comic-Con, Jackson stated 'last year people felt compelled, for obvious reasons, to write about the frame rate, as well as about the film itself. So we just said any press screenings this year, do it at 24, so at least people will just focus on the movie itself'[48] and 'that was a decision we made because we wanted people to respond to the movie as a movie'.[49] The reiteration of this paradoxical

situation, whereby critics were asked to separate the film from its technological manifestation, did not go wholly unnoticed. Peter Bradshaw noted that prior to his screening he was
given a press hand-out that repeated the importance of HFR technology but was then
shown the film in 24fps.[50] Within this context, few critics saw *Desolation of Smaug* in HFR
and few reviews were able to comment on how the HFR technology looked in comparison
to the previous film. Of the twenty-two critics surveyed by Vulture.com with regards to their
negative appraisal of the HFR aesthetic in *An Unexpected Journey*, most did not comment
on whether there was any perceivable difference in the second film. Eight critics do not
appear to have gone on to review *Desolation of Smaug*, three made it clear that they saw
the latter in 24fps and nine did not comment on its HFR aesthetic, making it unclear
whether they saw the film in HFR or not. Only two of these critics evaluated HFR technology
in *Desolation of Smaug*: the aforementioned Todd McCarthy and Richard Corliss, who
agreed that the HFR process was 'a technique less distracting than it was the first time'.[51]

Jason Gorber, one of the few critics to actively seek out an HFR screening, remarked
that, like the previous film, HFR technology took some getting used to but 'provides the
best possible showcase for the story of *The Desolation of Smaug*, and gives the viewer
the most immersive, engaging and *cinematic* entry into the world of Middle Earth'.[52] He
also addressed the historical context in which there have been numerous critical calls to
watch films in the film-maker's intended display format. For this reason companies
colourising black-and-white films have been criticised and DVD distributors have been
called upon to release films in their original aspect ratio.[53] While Jackson and Warner Bros.
have made it clear that HFR screenings are the film-maker's preferred viewing option, the
decision to screen the film to press in 24fps displays an unwillingness to engage in a
debate about the correct viewing format. In this way, their increasingly cautious approach
to marketing HFR technology allows them to negotiate the complex competing interests
of critics and fans (those in favour and those against HFR) and exhibitors (those who have
upgraded to HFR display technology and those who have not).

It would be easy to read the wavering emphasis and de-emphasis on HFR during promotional strategies for the films as attempts by Jackson and Warner Bros. to mitigate
unforeseen negative reception from critics and the public. However, it is also possible to
take into consideration a more complex narrative around the adoption of HFR that is situated in a media environment whereby multiple viewing options need to be promoted
simultaneously. This is also a media environment in which studios maintain traditional marketing strategies while directors conduct their own grassroots promotional strategies
through relationships with fans. In these contexts Jackson was unsuccessful in his
attempts to encourage industry take-up of a new technology in the same way that he had
been successful in the past with, for example, motion capture technology.

Nonetheless, the billion plus box-office revenue for each film proves that, even with the
controversies surrounding HFR technology, the films were ultimately highly profitable for
Jackson and Warner Bros. and they were, financially at least, successful in the way they
negotiated this complex terrain. In this context, HFR reveals itself as one of a long history
of cinema technologies (sound, colour, widescreen, 3D, CGI effects) that are ostensibly
introduced in order to enhance and improve audiovisual texts yet are equally part of ongoing attempts to differentiate and add value to film products in the face of widespread competition. As a signal of sophisticated marketing prowess, studios such as Warner Bros. and
experienced directors such as Peter Jackson are able to negotiate the diverse interests
and preferences of critics and audiences in order to make the introduction of a controversial new technology such as HFR lucrative.

Notes

1. John Belton, 'Digital Cinema: A False Revolution', *October* vol. 100, 2002, pp. 99–114, p. 114.
2. Both 3D and HFR technologies are available in analogue form but their widespread availability in recent years is due to the ease of reproduction and standardisation available in digital technology.
3. Kevin Brownlow, 'Silent Films: What Was the Right Speed?', *Sight & Sound* Summer, 1989, pp. 164–7.
4. Leo Douglas Graham Enticknap, *Moving Image Technology: From Zoetrope to Digital* (London: Wallflower, 2005), pp. 50–1.
5. Bill Krohn and Harley Lond, 'Showscan: A New Type of Exhibition for a Revolutionary Film Process', *Boxoffice (Archive: 1920–2000)* vol. 120 no. 2, 1984, pp. 10–11.
6. Julie Turnock, 'Removing the Pane of Glass: The Hobbit, 3D High Frame Rate Film-making, and the Rhetoric of Digital Convergence', *Film Criticism* vol. 37/38 no. 1, 2013, pp. 30–59.
7. Charles R. Acland, 'IMAX in Canadian Cinema: Geographic Transformation and Discourses of Nationhood', *Studies in Cultures, Organizations and Societies* vol. 3 no. 2, 1997, pp. 289–305; Kevin Lally, 'IMAX Unveils Big Plans for the 1990s', *The Film Journal (Archive: 1979–1996)* vol. 94 no. 5, 1991, pp. 24, 34.
8. As an example of this, Wim Wenders experimented with filming in HFR when shooting his documentary *Pina* (2011) but decided to discontinue these experiments when he realised there would be no exhibition sites capable of playing HFR. Wim Wenders, 'A Film for Pina: Keynote of the Toronto International Stereoscopic 3D Conference', *Public* vol. 47, 2013, pp. 214–33.
9. John Belton, 'Digital Cinema'.
10. '3d Update', *Variety* vol. 422 no. 13, 2011, pp. A19–A20; Anna Marie de la Fuente, 'LATIN AMERICA: Mexico and Neighbors See Opportunity to Deepen Audience through 3D Pics', *Variety* vol. 419 no. 4, 2010, p. A7.
11. Other factors also fell into place at this time such as the UK Film Council's Digital Screen Network initiative to fund the conversion to digital in art-house movie theatres on the understanding that the theatres would play independent and national films. There was also a virtual print fee agreement whereby Hollywood studios helped fund the conversion to digital projectors.
12. Lisa Purse, *Digital Imaging in Popular Cinema* (Edinburgh: Edinburgh University Press, 2013), p. 129. See also Julie Turnock, 'Removing the Pane of Glass'.
13. Although most 3D-capable digital projectors are able to display HFR films, in order to achieve the best possible image The Embassy theatre in Wellington (where *The Hobbit: An Unexpected Journey* was premiered) put in two projectors side by side. This allowed each projector to display images for one eye only but 'triple flashed' at forty-eight per second each (144 images per second). Combined, this meant 288 images per second were shown, a greater flash rate than could be achieved with just one projector
14. Barbara Flueckiger, 'Aesthetics of Stereoscopic Cinema', *Projections* vol. 6 no. 1, 2012, pp. 101–22; Wim Wenders, 'A Film for Pina'.
15. Cameron not only built specific 3D systems in order to film *Avatar*, he also heads the Pace group, a consortium involved in producing 3D camera rigs, software and other technology for stereoscopic cinema.
16. Cited in Ray Zone, *3-D Film-makers: Conversations with Creators of Stereoscopic Motion Pictures* (Oxford: Scarecrow Press, 2005).
17. James Cameron, cited in Jack Cunliffe, 'James Cameron Finally Plans to Shoot "Avatar" Sequels Next Year, Plus IMAX Posters for "The Hobbit"', *The Film Stage*, 28 November

2012, http://thefilmstage.com/news/james-cameron-finally-plans-to-shoot-avatar-sequels-next-year-plus-imax-posters-for-the-hobbit/

18. Peter Jackson cited in 'HFR 3D: Peter Jackson Explains What and Why', *Theonering.net*, 19 November 2012, www.theonering.net/torwp/2012/11/19/65492-hfr-3d-peter-jackson-explains-what-and-why/

19. Peter Jackson, cited in Ryan Lambie, 'Peter Jackson Interview: *The Hobbit*, 48FPS, Cumberbatch', *Den of Geek*, 13 December 2013, www.denofgeek.com/movies/the-hobbit/28587/peter-jackson-interview-the-hobbit-48fps-cumberbatch

20. Brian Sibley, *Peter Jackson: A Film-Maker's Journey* (London: HarperCollins Entertainment, 2006).

21. For information on how the *Lord of the Rings* Trilogy negotiated this public, see Kristin Thompson, *The Frodo Franchise: How The Lord of the Rings Became a Hollywood Blockbuster and Put New Zealand on the Map* (London: Penguin, 2007); Suzette Major, 'Cultivating a Classic: Marketing Strategies for the Lord of the Rings Films', in Harriet Margolis, Sean Cubitt, Barry King and Thierry Jutel (eds), *Studying the Event Film: The Lord of the Rings* (Manchester: Manchester University Press, 2008), pp. 47–54; Elana Shefrin, 'Lord of the Rings, Star Wars, and Participating Fandom: Mapping New Congruencies Between the Internet and Media Entertainment Culture', in Ezra E. and T. Rowden (eds), *Transnational Cinema: The Film Reader* (London: Routledge, 2006), pp. 81–96.

22. This was a similar strategy to that undertaken during the filming of *King Kong* (2005), although the first time Facebook had been used to disseminate the diaries.

23. Jackson's digital effects company, Weta, developed this software so that groups of digitally created extras would appear to move and interact in the same way as live humans and animals.

24. Tanine Allison, 'More than a Man in a Monkey Suit: Andy Serkis, Motion Capture, and Digital Realism', *Quarterly Review of Film and Video* vol. 28 no. 4, 2011, pp. 325–41.

25. Julie Turnock, 'Removing the Pane of Glass'.

26. Devin Faraci, 'CinemaCon 2012: THE HOBBIT Underwhelms at 48 Frames per Second', *Badass Digest*, 24 April 2012, http://badassdigest.com/2012/04/24/cinemacon-2012-the-hobbit-underwhelms-at-48-frames-per-secon/

27. Carolyn Giardina, 'Peter Jackson Responds to "Hobbit" Footage Critics, Explains 48-Frames Strategy', *The Hollywood Reporter*, 28 April 2012, www.hollywoodreporter.com/news/peter-jackson-responds-hobbit-footage-317755

28. Carolyn Giardina, 'Comic-Con 2012: Peter Jackson Won't Preview "The Hobbit" at 48 Frame-Per-Second Frame Rate', *The Hollywood Reporter*, 14 July 2012, www.hollywoodreporter.com/news/comic-con-2012-peter-jackson-349275

29. Following the negative press conference at Cinemacon, many exhibitors and Warner Bros. were nervous about playing the film in HFR, but in the weeks before its release a number of movie theatres increased screens available for HFR. Andrew Stewart, '"Hobbit" Tix on Sale Wed. in Five Different Versions', *Variety*, 11 June 2012, http://variety.com/2012/film/news/hobbit-tix-on-sale-wed-in-five-different-versions-1118061832/

30. 'HFR 3D'.

31. Brad Brevet, '"The Hobbit" Updates: See It in 48 FPS, New Pictures, TV Spot and Listen to Shore's Score', *Rope of Silicon*, 5 November 2012, www.ropeofsilicon.com/the-hobbit-updates-see-it-in-48-fps-new-pictures-tv-spot-and-listen-to-shores-score/

32. Peter Jackson, '48 Frames Per Second', *Facebook*, 12 April 2011, https://www.facebook.com/notes/peter-jackson/48-frames-per-second/10150222861171558

33. Edward Douglas, 'Peter Jackson on *The Hobbit* 48 FPS Controversy', *Comingsoon.net*, 12 May 2012, www.comingsoon.net/news/movienews.php?id=97749

34. John Belton, 'Digital Cinema'.

35. Ty Pendlebury and David Katzmaier, '"The Hobbit" 3D Tech Divides Our CNET Reviewers', *CNET*, 14 December 2012, http://reviews.cnet.com/8301-33199_7-57559338-221/ the-hobbit-3d-tech-divides-our-cnet-reviewers/

36. Jesse David Fox, 'What the Critics are Saying About *The Hobbit*'s High Frame Rate', *Vulture*, 15 December 2012, www.vulture.com/2012/12/critics-on-the-hobbits-high-frame-rate.html

37. Devin Faraci, 'Does ANYBODY Like 48FPS in THE HOBBIT?', *Badass Digest*, 12 April 2012, http://badassdigest.com/2012/12/04/does-anybody-like-48fps-in-the-hobbit/

38. Jen Yamato, 'The Science of High Frame Rates, Or: Why "The Hobbit" Looks Bad At 48 FPS', *Movieline*, 14 December 2012, http://movieline.com/2012/12/14/hobbit-high-frame-rate-science-48-frames-per-second/

39. Stuart Muller, 'THE HOBBIT in HFingR: An Unexpected Journey to the Glory of 48fps', *Twitch*, 14 December 2013, http://twitchfilm.com/2013/12/the-hobbit-in-hfingr-an-unexpected-journey-to-the-glory-of-48fps.html

40. Peter Jackson, '48 Frames Per Second'.

41. Peter Jackson, cited in David S. Cohen, 'Peter Jackson: High Frame Rate 3D Look Improved on "Smaug"', *Variety*, 12 November 2013, http://variety.com/2013/film/news/peter-jackson-hobbit-3d-looks-1200941962/

42. Kristin Thompson, *The Frodo Franchise*.

43. Todd McCarthy, '*The Hobbit: An Unexpected Journey*: Review', *The Hollywood Reporter*, 12 March 2012, www.hollywoodreporter.com/movie/hobbit-an-unexpected-journey/review/397416

44. Todd McCarthy, 'The Hobbit: The Desolation of Smaug: Film Review', *The Hollywood Reporter*, 12 June 2013, www.hollywoodreporter.com/movie/hobbit-desolation-smaug/review/663372

45. Gregg Kilday, 'Despite 'The Hobbit', Hollywood isn't Adopting 48 Frames per Second', *The Hollywood Reporter*, 11 March 2013, www.hollywoodreporter.com/news/hobbit-desolation-smaug-48-frames-655444. *Variety* suggested slightly different figures, that screens increased from 462 to 812, but nonetheless a significant increase: David S. Cohen, 'Peter Jackson'.

46. HFR Movies, 'Report: HFR 3D Theater Count Doubles for Desolation of Smaug', *HFR Movies*, 12 November 2013, https://web.archive.org/web/20141111023019/ http://www.hfrmovies.com/tag/peter-jackson/

47. Carolyn Giardina, 'IBC: "The Hobbit: Desolation of Smaug" Previewed in High Frame Rates and 3D', *The Hollywood Reporter*, 15 September 2013, www.hollywoodreporter.com/behind-screen/ibc-hobbit-desolation-smaug-previewed-629602

48. David S. Cohen, 'Peter Jackson'.

49. Ryan Lambie, 'Peter Jackson Interview'.

50. Peter Bradshaw, '*The Hobbit: The Desolation of Smaug* – Review', *Guardian*, 12 December 2013, sec. Film, www.theguardian.com/film/2013/dec/12/hobbit-desolation-of-smaug-review

51. Richard Corliss, '*The Hobbit: The Desolation of Smaug*: It Lives!', *Time*, 12 September 2013, http://entertainment.time.com/2013/12/09/the-hobbit-the-desolation-of-smaug-it-lives/#ixzz2tiNFLeGw

52. Jason Gorber, 'Jason Gorber's Cineruminations: THE HOBBIT and HFR, Part 2 – The Journey Continues', *Twitch*, 19 December 2013, http://twitchfilm.com/2013/12/jason-gorbers-cineruminations-hobbit-hfr-part-2.html

53. Brian Real, 'From Colorization to Orphans: The Evolution of American Public Policy on Film Preservation', *The Moving Image: The Journal of the Association of Moving Image Archivists* vol. 13 no. 1, 2013, pp. 129–50; James Kendrick, 'Aspect Ratios and Joe Six-Packs: Home Theater Enthusiasts', *The Velvet Light Trap* vol. 56, 2005, pp. 58–70.

Niche Marketing in Peru

An Interview with Claudia Zavaleta

Nolwenn MINGANT

Claudia Zavaleta is a young Chief of Marketing at Star Films, a Lima-based distribution company founded in 2002. Aman Kapoor, who owns this family business, has kept many contacts in India, his country of origin, and Bollywood films are one type of film he distributes. But his company also handles films directed at other niche audiences,[1] notably independent horror films and comedies from the USA, Mexico, Argentina, the UK, Australia and Korea.[2] Among the movies Star Films distributed in Peru are US comedy This is 40 *(2013),* Hong Kong *kung fu actioner* The Man with the Iron Fists *(2013), UK/Spain's horror film* Intruders *(2011), Thai horror film* Long kohng *(2005) and local horror movie* La Cara del Diablo *(2014).*

Is distributing Bollywood films in Peru particularly challenging?

Yes, in terms of distribution, it is quite difficult to sell Bollywood films to cinemas. They prefer blockbusters from the USA. We have our own cinema circuits, Cine Star and Movie Time, in different parts of our country. Other circuits, such as Cinemark and Cineplanet are quite exclusive. They have certain circuits for specific target audiences. Generally, Bollywood films are distributed to cinemas of lower-standard segments which are located on the periphery of Lima (what we called Conos) and some provinces of Peru.

Also, most Peruvians are not used to Bollywood stories, so there is only a small group who accepts it. However, our society is changing, economically and culturally, because of a huge migration to the capital from the interior of Peru. The elite of the capital do not dictates tastes any more. There is a new class of people, who has started to listen, for example, to Korean music and watch Bollywood films. We target this specific group.

What are the big selling points for Bollywood films?

We distribute almost exclusively Bollywood films with Shah Rukh Khan because he is the most popular actor from India in Peru, and maybe all over the world. The first Indian film we distributed was *My Name is Khan* (2010), which is one of the movies in which he stars. It was a huge hit here. Khan has a big fan base that always supports him, so we know his films are going to be successful here. We have close relations with the fan club of Khan, and we keep in touch with it every time there is a new film. For *Chennai Express* (2013), we notably used a video message Khan had recorded for the fans of Peru.[3]

Also, because our target audience prefers romantic stories from Bollywood, we try to emphasise the love element. The storyline and the role of the characters in Indian movies

Shah Rukh Khan, the most popular Bollywood star in Peru (Creative Commons/Bollywood Hungama)

are very important for our audience. Sometimes, we have to adapt the poster to highlight that element. For example, the Indian poster for *Happy New Year* (2014), which we are distributing in October, insists on the action element. We changed it to bring out the romantic element. Of course, we had to get approval from the Indian distributor.

But all Bollywood films are not easy to distribute. If we want to distribute here an action movie from India, the fans are not used to that. *Dhoom 3*, an action movie from 2013, for example, was a huge hit in India but didn't work out in Peru very well. Here, when you say Bollywood, you say dance and romance.

Furthermore, our audience is very interested in the dance element. Most people who like Bollywood movies are related to dance groups. Since there are many groups of Bollywood dancing in Lima, we organised a dance competition in 2012 to promote *Chennai Express*. It was huge and it was in all media.[4]

What about the other films you distribute?

The easiest films to sell for us are horror films. Peruvian people are so into horror films, and comedy, as well. Now, when we have a great cast in an American movie, such as John Stamos in *My Man is a Loser* (2014), we sell it on the cast. When we had a Japanese movie like *The Cult* (2013), whose actors were not well known, we sold it on the horror genre and we emphasised that element in the poster and trailer too. Otherwise, when we have a horror movie that has someone's name on the script or music composition such as *Nothing Left to Fear* (2013) that had Slash, the guitarist from Guns 'N' Roses, in the production work, we try to highlight his name everywhere. For this specific case, we had competitions to win official merchandising signed by Slash. We also video-recorded his greetings for Peru and sent them to every media.

For these kinds of films, we don't usually change the original artwork. The image on the poster is usually very well made; it has great effects, so there is no need to change it. And, anyway, we would not have enough personnel here to do it.[5]

What about films from Latin America? Is it easier to sell them in Peru, given the cultural proximity?

No. American productions are much more popular than Latin American movies. People think they are great because of the big budgets, production values and special effects. Films from Latin America are associated with film festivals and people think they are just boring dramas.

But in terms of Peruvian films, the perspective of people is changing and they are starting to accept these movies. Horror films, for example, have taken a big leap in our country. That's why we are also producing our own movies now – for example, *Mañana te cuento* (2005, 2008) and *La Cara del Diablo* (2014).

What is your biggest challenge today?
Our biggest challenge is to compete with major distributors such as New Century or UIP. Their films are distributed in all circuits and all over Peru. Also, they have big marketing campaigns, and therefore big budgets. You can see their campaigns everywhere in the streets, on TV, on the radio. We have to be much more specific when we spend money, but with the small budget we have, we manage to promote the films on radio, TV and also sell them on the internet, via Facebook and Twitter. Also we have to find partners to sell the movie, to communicate around it. That is a big challenge for us. We have a lot of horror movies and many brands don't like to get associated with horror movies. It's easier for Bollywood films or comedy movies. For *Chennai Express*, we had a partnership with Bembos, a very popular Peruvian fast-food chain. The brand communicated about our film in social media.

As a young film marketer, how would you define your job?
Film marketing aims to sell great stories to people. People like to hear stories and that's what we do in the best possible way. In order to sell movies, we have to get the audience's attention in a different way and we have to highlight elements that others don't. I think the creative element must always be present in our work, and the way you tell stories is what differentiates you from others.

Notes

1. A niche audience is a small segment of the filmgoing population with specific tastes. Niche marketing is a form of micromarketing.
2. The interview was conducted by Nolwenn Mingant on 30 September 2014. The following text is an abridged version of the interview, amended by the editors and approved by Claudia Zavaleta.
3. For Khan's popularity in Peru, see www.youtube.com/watch?v=8WY_cTFNI-A
4. An extract of the contest can be seen here: www.youtube.com/watch?v=QvjXqaRgxB8
5. The marketing team at Star Films is composed of A. Kapoor and C. Zavaleta, as well as an editor and a designer.

II
MARKETING FOR AND BY THE CONSUMER

Leaked Information and Rumours

The Buzz Effect

A case study by Joël AUGROS

Although word of mouth (WOM) was primarily oral communication – that is, casual conversations, be it face to face or by phone – as in Norman Rockwell's *The Gossips*, the term is now used for social networking as well.[1] Hollywood has long been used to relying on WOM to sell its films. A recent Nielsen report showed that 92 per cent of people 'completely' or 'somewhat' trusted 'recommendations from people [they] know' as opposed to 8 per cent who 'don't trust much or don't trust at all' other people's opinions.[2] Concerning the 'consumer opinions posted online', the proportion is 70 per cent to 30 per cent. Similarly, a 2009 report by Stradella Road showed that '80% of those surveyed said they were more likely to see a movie after hearing a positive review from other moviegoers.'[3] Hence the importance of promoting, nurturing and measuring WOM. In 2004, the Word of Mouth Marketing Association (WOMMA), for example, created the WOMUnit, 'a single unit of marketing-relevant information' passed from one consumer to another.[4]

The idea of creating WOM or buzz around a film as part of a promotion campaign has long been a standard practice for marketers. In 1920, a rumour circulated that a young virgin was wandering the streets of New York chased by a group of Turks. It was, in fact, famed publicist Harry Reichenbach's campaign for *The Virgin of Stamboul* (1920).[5] For the 'buzz' to work, the leaked information about the film must appear in newspapers, magazines and television shows not dedicated to cinema and consequently reach a larger potential audience. Although the buzz concept largely predates the development of the internet, the circulation of rumours – whether positive or negative – has grown dramatically, notably through social networks. The internet does not change the nature of the phenomenon – but it enables rumours to spread much more quickly and to reach many more people.

Hollywood has long had a strong relationship with the press. While Hollywood needs the press to sell its films, the press needs stories about stars and films to sell its papers. In order to maintain this two-way exchange, the media are rarely critical towards the US film industry. The traditional media might not be the advertising partners of the future, however. '94% of all moviegoers are now online,'[6] noted *Variety* in 2009, at a time when the MPAA members gave little attention to this media. In 2006, only 4 per cent of their marketing budget was dedicated to internet promotion. Four years later, the proportion had risen to 8 to 12 per cent, while 60 to 70 per cent was directed towards radio and television.[7] Understanding the internet and exerting some control over it has, however, proved to be a challenge for Hollywood. In 2010, *Variety* noted that 'after years of false starts – [Hollywood studios] are also finally learning to harness the internet and social networking to their advantage'.[8] This evolution can be exemplified by the studios' relationship with the website 'Ain't It Cool News'. Developed in 1996 by Harry Knowles, a film-buff from

Austin, Texas, immersed as a boy in film memorabilia sold by his parents, the site leaks preview reports and reviews the films before they are released, and, most importantly, before the marketing campaign actually begins. As early as 1999, the site had 1.5 billion visitors per day.[9] Ain't It Cool News was notably the first to share an opinion on *Titanic* (1997) as Knowles leaked the results of a test screening six months before the official release.[10] Fortunately for the studio, it was a laudatory comment.

In 1975, one could organise a sneak preview for *Jaws* in complete secrecy, but, as *Variety* noted, 'such an event nowadays would have been besieged by bloggers'.[11] Hollywood does try to preserve some control over how and when the information appears in the media. During previews organised for the press, journalists are asked 'to sign nondisclosure agreements pledging not to break review embargo dates'.[12] Controlling the circulation of information on websites is, however, more complex. Many 'gossip' sites exist, emanating either from press conglomerates, or from private individuals: Dark Horizons, Coming Attractions, Drudge Report, Mr Showbiz, E! Online ... And the studios cannot develop with these personal websites the vital give-and-take relationship that links them to the press and television.

In order to regain some degree of control, the Hollywood studios have recently striven to build a relationship with these websites' creators. Let us go back to the example of Ain't It Cool News. In 2004, *The Hollywood Reporter* noted that Knowles was mentioned as a co-producer for an adaptation of Edgar Rice Burroughs' *Princess of Mars* by Robert Rodriguez for Paramount. Although the project did not come through, Knowles has become a recurring figure in Hollywood both off-screen – at the numerous parties, private screenings and press junkets – and on-screen, with his cameo roles in *The Faculty* (1998), *My Sucky Teen Romance* (2011) and other films. Strategically, the idea is clearly to integrate the troublemaker into the Hollywood system, to make him dependent on information provided by the distributors, dependent on the material advantages offered by the studio's promotional events.[13] Nowadays, Hollywood pampers influential bloggers, just as it did in the past with the famous gossips Hedda Hopper and Louella Parsons.

Today, distributors are present on the internet in three different ways: a) through official websites, b) by hosting promotional material on third-party websites and c) through social networks and non-official websites. The use of these three types of channels is, of course, not exclusive. The choice to favour one medium over the others depends on the type of campaign and the targeted audience. The studios first create their own official websites, usually with a link to Facebook. They provide the website's content: pictures, synopses, teasers and trailers, posters ... Such sites resemble traditional press books in their format, which is modernised by the presence of more diverse and interactive elements, such as games.

The second type of internet presence is the commercial websites, such as Fandango, MovieTickets, Movies, ComingSoon and JoBlo, which provide information about films, but also offer the spectator the possibility to buy their tickets online. Information and consumption are therefore directly linked. For a minor additional cost, the distributors create specifically adapted banners and trailers for this type of site.

As for the personal websites, which are often developed by film buffs, they cannot feature such material – indeed, the studios strive to restrain them through threats of infringement of copyright and trademark. Warner applied this approach to a number of personal websites dedicated to Harry Potter. On some occasions, however, film buffs are mobilised by the studios. In clear contrast to the oppositional approach just described, personal websites were actually associated to the official campaign for *The Lord of the Rings*. The film

Viral marketing for films started in 1999, with the campaign for *The Blair Witch Project*

buffs were specifically informed when a trailer was posted on the official page. The aim of this approach is twofold: to exert some control over the opinions and rumours circulated on the film, and to have access to the fan and geek communities. Whereas the discourse of the official websites is clearly identified as emanating from the studios, the tone of the personal websites gives the impression that all the information is obtained non-officially, off the record. The presentation of the content as leaked information actually hides the marketing intent. Through their collaboration with the personal websites, the studios thus use the proliferating contacts and exchanges characteristic of the internet to convey their message. This is called electronic word of mouth (e-WOM).

The orchestrated use of e-WOM by the studios to better sell their films is known as viral marketing, a practice originating in 1999, with Artisan's campaign for *The Blair Witch Project.* For this small-budget movie,[14] Artisan chose to resort to the capillarity effect offered by teen internet forums. Rumours were circulated that the film was an authentic documentary, a tape found by accident after the shooting team mysteriously disappeared. The film's webpage featured fake interviews and fake police reports. By inventing a fictional story around the film, Artisan managed to start and fuel a debate – which is actually still ongoing. Because of the endless and heated discussions about the actual nature of the film, *The Blair Witch Project* became a must-see movie.

Other distributors have chosen to conform to the *Blair Witch* model. The major Paramount decided to follow the path of viral marketing for the J. J. Abrams production *Cloverfield* (2008), with a marketing campaign playfully blurring the lines between reality and fiction. First, an untitled trailer was released before the screenings of *Transformers* (2007). It was then circulated on the internet. This enigmatic trailer showed images of young people at a party. After hearing a loud noise, the group was seen rushing in the streets only to be faced with the head of the Statue of Liberty rolling at their feet. Fake blogs were also created and rumours circulated about the film's topic, its director and the nature of the monstrous creature. Was it an adaptation of Lovecraft? Was it an umpteenth *Godzilla*? What was this mysterious Slusho soft drink? Thanks to this campaign, the film obtained the best box office of all time for a January release. Attendance dropped, however, by 68 per cent in the second week.

Viral marketing is not necessarily divorced from real-life happenings, as the example of *Paranormal Activity* (2007) shows, a film acquired for $350,000 by DreamWorks. Distributor Paramount 'built buzz with midnight screenings in select markets and then sent fans to online site Eventful to petition for the pic to go wide when it hit 1 million requests'.[15] Interestingly, this campaign thus mixed the virtual reality of e-WOM and the physicality of the midnight screenings. A similarly mixed strategy was adopted for *District 9* (2009). The campaign skilfully associated physical promotional material (posters, ads on buses), old publicity stunts à-la-Reichenbach – such as sealing off a whole neighbourhood because of the alleged presence of aliens, and the circulation of 'information' on the internet. All these elements combined to create a story around the film before its release. A final example of this mixed strategy is *The Dark Knight* (2008). On 13 March, leaflets were distributed on the streets of Chicago encouraging voters to support the electoral campaign of Harvey Dent for District Attorney of Gotham.[16] This story was then developed on Ibelieveinharveydent.com. Another website, whysoserious.com, invited web users to become the Joker's henchmen and indicated a specific meeting place and time to participate in a treasure hunt. The campaign thus combined the traditional form of WOM (the 1920s–30s-type publicity stunt) and the most recent form of Web 2.0 marketing.

In recent years, Hollywood has thus striven to gain control of the internet to communicate about its films. By combining official and non-official internet presence, by mixing old and new marketing practices, the studios are now making the most of WOM and viral marketing to create a more intense buzz, to weave more story threads around the stories they sell.

Notes

1. Translated from French by Nolwenn Mingant.
2. Nielsen, *Global Trust in Advertising and Brand Messages*, April 2012, http://se.nielsen.com/site/documents/NielsenTrustinAdvertisingGlobalReportApril2012.pdf
3. Marc Graser, 'Internet Influences Film Audiences', *Variety*, 29 September 2009, http://variety.com/2009/digital/news/internet-influences-film-audiences-1118009343/
4. Jonathan Bing, 'Success via WOMP and Circumstance', *Variety*, 21 July 2007, http://variety.com/2005/film/news/success-via-womp-and-circumstance-1117926306/
5. Richard Korzarski, *History of the American Cinema, 3: An Evening's Entertainment: The Age of the Silent Picture 1915–1928* (Berkeley: University of California Press, 1994), p. 38.
6. Marc Graser, 'Internet Influences Film Audiences'.
7. Pamela McClintock, 'Marketing Makeover', *Variety*, 4 January 2010. Television remains the first weapon of mass persuasion, with its ability to reach speedily a large number of potential spectators.
8. Ibid.
9. *Variety*, 18 October 1999.
10. Ibid.
11. *Variety*, 12 June 2006.
12. Brian Lowry, 'Critical Divide for TV, Film', *Variety*, 30 April 2013.

13. See Jonathan Rosenbaum's *Movie Wars* (Chicago: Capella, 2000) on how the film critics benefit from perks during the press junkets.
14. Roughly $60,000.
15. *Variety*, 4 January 2010.
16. *Le Monde*, 26 March 2008.

Brave New Films, Brave New Ways

The Internet and the Future of Low- to No Budget Film Distribution and Marketing

Hayley TROWBRIDGE

The terrains of film distribution and marketing have changed (and are still changing) as part of this contemporary era of media convergence. During this transformative process numerous trends have emerged in both fields, including, among others, the implementation of digital distribution practices and marketing strategies, an increased visibility and viability of non-theatrical distribution models and the usage of non-traditional marketing avenues (e.g. social media), the entry of new companies and platforms into the distribution field (e.g. YouTube, Amazon and iTunes) and marketing arena (e.g. Twitter and Facebook), and a reinvigoration of DIY and grassroots distribution models and marketing strategies. These changes, however, should not suggest that conventional distribution and marketing methods are extinct, or that the traditional gatekeepers in these fields are obsolete. Instead, what we are witnessing is a convergence of old and new strategies, practices, methods and organisations, and it is through this coexistence and fusion of tradition and novelty that today's distribution and marketing environments are being constructed.

Innovations within distribution and marketing are not only a real game-changer for organisations operating at the top of the film industry hierarchy, but also, perhaps, more meaningfully so for those who exist at the bottom. Major film studios and DIY film-makers alike are still working out the rules of this environment.[1] The frameworks that previously governed traditional notions of distribution and marketing are being renegotiated, restructured and reorganised, but perhaps the most interesting aspect of recent innovations within these fields is that such changes are not just being played out before film consumers, but also with them. Specifically, low- to no budget film-makers and organisations are learning how to use consumers in the distribution and marketing of their films and in doing so are bypassing the traditional gatekeepers.

In previous decades the main stumbling block for independent film-makers operating within the low- to no budget and DIY realms was always distribution and, to some extent (specifically in the theatrical realm), this is still the case. Focusing specifically on the US film industry, the major studios and large independent companies have had a stranglehold on the distribution arena as they had the finances, reach and industry contacts to provide distribution in a market dominated by the theatrical release. With prints of films costing in the region of $1,500 per print (not to mention the escalating costs of advertising), the likelihood of a small-scale independent outfit or DIY film-maker having the finances available to release a film in numerous theatres across the USA was very slim. Yet, despite the dominance of mainstream fare, some 'small, offbeat, unconventional and sometimes radical independent films', as Geoff King describes, still managed to secure distribution.[2] This distribution could occur through striking a deal with a major studio, a subsidiary of one of the major studios, or a distribution company specialising in the releasing of independent or speciality films, through being 'picked up' at a festival or via opting for a limited or platform release strategy.[3]

Recently this situation has changed somewhat due to the impact of media convergence. While the theatrical realm has not been the only distribution avenue available for film-makers for quite some time — television and straight-to-video markets have represented distribution opportunities for numerous decades now — the internet has transformed the situation further. Writing about such developments, Dina Iordanova argues that the internet has created a situation in which DIY film-makers 'have at their disposal the means to access previously distant audiences … sufficient to provide the modest revenue needed to keep going'.[4] Independent outfit Brave New Films — established by film-maker Robert Greenwald — has been at the forefront of exploiting the possibilities of digital technologies. On multiple occasions, Greenwald, Brave New Films and sister company the Brave New Foundation have utilised the possibilities of the internet to bypass the traditional gatekeepers of distribution and marketing, when releasing their politically infused documentaries such as *Iraq for Sale* (2006) and *Rethink Afghanistan* (2009).[5] Specifically, theses organisations have harnessed new communication methods associated with Web 2.0 to encourage consumers to actively engage in the production, distribution, marketing and exhibition of their documentaries.[6] Using these organisations as its primary case studies, this chapter will outline some of the DIY distribution and marketing strategies currently used by independent film-makers operating in the low- to no budget film arena. The discussion surrounding this will demonstrate that such distribution and marketing strategies could offer viable methods for DIY film-makers to overcome the traditional distribution barriers through using grassroots strategies and DIY techniques to build a buzz around their films and, ultimately, connect their films with core audiences.

Media Convergence

The concept that links together the recent developments in distribution and marketing across technological, industrial and socio-cultural fields is media convergence. In his seminal study, *Convergence Culture: Where Old and New Media Collide*, Henry Jenkins asserts that contemporary media convergence should be perceived as 'the flow of content across multiple media platforms, the cooperation between multiple media industries, and the migratory behaviour of media audiences who will go to almost anywhere in search of the kinds of entertainment experiences they want'.[7] Here, he acknowledges the multidimensional nature of media convergence. For example, the flow of content is attributed to technological convergence, the dialogue between industries is a manifestation of industrial convergence and the fluidity of consumer practices is symptomatic of socio-cultural convergence. In line with this, other scholars have accounted for the multifaceted nature of media convergence. Virginia Nightingale suggests that media convergence concerns the ways in which 'technological, industrial, cultural and social changes' have impacted on the circulation of media and Tim Dwyer describes how media convergence has 'a number of distinct levels including cultural, industrial, technological or regulatory levels'.[8] Where Jenkins's writings on convergence differ from the other aforementioned studies is that he proposes that a hierarchy exists between the different expressions of media convergence. For Jenkins, media convergence is primarily a 'cultural shift' in which 'consumers are encouraged to seek out new information and make connections among dispersed media content'; the numerous technological and industrial manifestations of convergence are secondary to this.[9]

This hierarchy that Jenkins imposes is arguably artificial and using this pecking order to analyse contemporary media convergence is perhaps not the most useful approach.[10] Instead, this chapter presumes each key strand of media convergence – namely industrial, technological and socio-cultural – to be of equal importance *and* that the strands operate in a three-way dialogue with one another. Rather than a fixed hierarchy existing between the strands of convergence, this chapter adopts the stance that the expression of convergence that predominates is dependent on the perspective of enquiry. This approach is more akin to Dwyer's and Nightingale's conceptualisations of media convergence and, through using media convergence as a multifaceted methodological tool, this chapter will explore how we can understand the recent developments in the distribution and marketing of low- to no budget film.

Spreading the Word
The internet has had a major impact on the distribution and marketing practices evident in contemporary film due to its (almost) global reach and ability to facilitate the transportation of information and content instantly. Over recent years we have seen this impact embodied in the plethora of services that have emerged for the distribution of film content online, from legal film streaming services to peer-to-peer file-sharing applications that infringe on copyright law. In terms of the internet's influence on marketing, the medium has opened up new techniques for spreading marketing messages, including the use of social media platforms and user-generated content (UGC) in campaigns. Through utilising such techniques, marketers are hoping that their campaigns go viral. The concept of 'viral marketing' is, according to Tom Hutchison, essentially just another term for one of the most traditional marketing methods – word of mouth (WOM).[11] WOM pre-dates the internet and is a consumer-driven form of communication; its independence from the market means that consumers perceive it to be more credible than marketing communications driven by industry organisations.[12]

The Blair Witch Project (1999) is the often cited example for a WOM success story. For many scholars, the film's success was attributed to the ability of its offline and online marketing campaign to generate buzz and intrigue.[13] Distributed by independent outfit Artisan Entertainment, the film is estimated to have had a combined production and P&A budget of $7.1 million and yet managed to harness $248,639,099 at the worldwide box office.[14] The marketing campaign of *The Blair Witch Project* combined a mix of traditional marketing methods such as TV spots, posters and print advertisements and new possibilities offered by the growth of the internet, such as a website to accompany the film. The combination of both the online and offline materials worked together to perpetuate the myth the Blair Witch.[15] As part of the marketing campaign for *The Blair Witch Project* a pseudo-documentary – *Curse of the Blair Witch* (1999) – was televised. The documentary, much like the film's website, promoted the myth of the Blair Witch and sought to persuade people that the events that unfolded in the film were real. These marketing elements and other offline ventures such as the displaying of 'missing' posters for the student film-makers all assisted in the construction of the mock-real narrative world of the film (as well as targeting different demographics across the different platforms).

Following *The Blair Witch Project* a myriad of other film marketing campaigns began to utilise the internet, ranging from the innovative, such as the game-based website that accompanied the release of *Donnie Darko* (2001), to more mundane efforts that saw distributors launch websites for their releases that consisted of nothing more than general information about the film, cast and crew. Almost a decade after *The Blair Witch Project*'s success came the release of independently produced, supernatural horror movie *Paranormal Activity* (2007) by major studio Paramount Pictures. Produced for a mere $15,000 by the then independent outfit Blumhouse Productions, the film went on to achieve over $1.9 million at the international box office.[16] Prior to its national release, *Paranormal Activity* had been playing in a select number of locations at midnight screenings across the USA.[17] This strategy was orchestrated by online marketing executive Amy Powell, who was confident that the film could be sold primarily online.[18] The campaign asked 'moviegoers to demand via eventful.com that the movie play in their local town' and the locations that generated the most 'demands' received a screening.[19] Seeing that *Paranormal Activity* was generating significant hype, Paramount agreed that if the film received a million demands it would distribute it nationwide.[20] At the end of October 2009, *Paranormal Activity* was released nationally, having reached its target.[21] Anne Thompson suggests that the success of this film could be attributed to Powell's marketing strategy that opted for a 'grassroots movement propelling its own decisions about what to see' instead of the traditional top-down approach in which the studio tells the audience what film to see.[22] This move demonstrated the relevance of the long-held belief that positive WOM sells films. What the marketers behind the release of *Paranormal Activity* did was exploit this concept online, where consumers can spread the word at a click of a button.[23]

Despite the independent status of *The Blair Witch Project* and the independent production of *Paranormal Activity*, the theatrical distribution deals and marketing spends of both campaigns position the films outside of the low- to no budget and DIY sectors of the film industry. Therefore, these case studies do not answer the question of whether the internet and media convergence have changed the distribution and marketing practices of film-makers and companies operating in these areas; yet, according to distribution strategist Peter Broderick, it has. In an article for *indieWIRE* Broderick outlines how a set of new distribution and marketing tactics have evolved into what the author has termed the 'New World of Film Distribution'.[24] The New World's predecessor, 'The Old World of Distribution', is 'a hierarchical realm where film-makers must petition the powers that be to grant them distribution'.[25] In contrast, the 'New World' is characterised by a power-to-the-film-maker ethos and offers film-makers the opportunity to bypass the old gatekeepers of distribution and to 'reach audiences directly'.[26] The positive attributes of the 'New World' include a visible reduction in distribution costs due to the digitalisation of film and the increased viability of non-theatrical distribution routes, and the ability to 'keep control of their content' for film-makers.[27] Through using social media tools for marketing and the internet as a distribution system of content and information, film-makers are increasingly able to tap into core audiences. While attracting core audiences is not a new strategy in independent film (as Broderick himself acknowledges), the use of social media in order to directly connect with fans and niche demographics is. As Yannis Tzioumakis has outlined, the main change between the old world and the new one is, arguably, 'the relationship between film-maker and audiences'.[28] The remainder of this chapter will demonstrate how the internet and social media have played an intrinsic part in enabling outfits such as Brave New Films to not only distribute and market their films to consumers, but also to recruit consumers into the process of distribution and marketing.

Brave New Films and Some Brave New Ways

One of the recent strategies to become increasingly visible and viable over the last decade has been crowdfunding, which is the process of asking consumers to donate money towards the production of a film. It is worth noting that crowdfunding is not a recent development in independent film, as John Cassavetes' famous radio plea for funding for *Shadows* (1959) demonstrates. However, the internet as a distribution platform, social media and their ability to connect people, and dedicated fundraising sites, such as Kickstarter, have made crowdfunding a more accessible method of film financing, therefore opening it up to a much larger number of potential investees. In 2006, Greenwald used this strategy when raising funds for *Iraq for Sale*.[29] Brave New Films and Brave New Foundation again used this technique for their other projects such as *Rethink Afghanistan* – a feature-length documentary that was released (for free) in short segments online.[30]

Crowdfunding is also currently being used to fund distribution costs in a bid to make theatrical distribution more attainable. Documentary film-maker Nick Broomfield raised over $30,000 towards the distribution costs of a North American release of *Sarah Palin: You Betcha!* (2011).[31] These crowdfunding methods, whether used for production or distribution costs, can be a useful way of accumulating a database of contacts to which the films in question (and future projects) can be marketed. As journalist Rhodri Marsden suggests, crowdfunding changes the relationship between producer and consumer.[32] Through involving audience members in the financing of the films, old boundaries between media producer and media consumer are again being eroded. This process is symptomatic of the current 'convergence culture' and is a result of both technological and socio-cultural developments.[33] Specifically, it relates to what Jenkins has termed 'participatory culture' – a subsector of 'convergence culture' in which consumers actively engage in the production and circulation of content.[34]

Brave New Films' participatory strategies, however, extend beyond the crowdfunding model. Indeed, when distributing *Uncovered: The Whole Truth about the Iraq War* (2003), Greenwald bypassed theatrical distribution and instead used social networking sites such as MoveOn.org and MeetUp.com to organise house parties to which a DVD copy of the film would be sent and then screened to an audience.[35] Distributing the film in this way, Greenwald was able to cut down on P&A costs and, as Chuck Tryon accounts, the film-maker was able to use social media to facilitate simultaneous screenings of the documentary at 'over 2,600 locations'.[36] This number of screens is the equivalent of a saturation release in the theatrical realm and, despite the fact that the number of screens playing the film was not repeated to such a volume every night over a number of weeks, this method of distribution can still be considered to be successful in terms of its accomplishment of connecting a niche-market film to a sizeable audience.

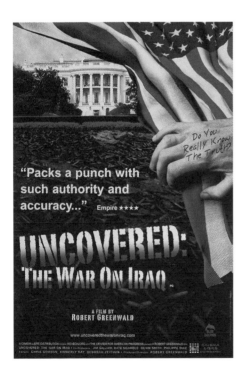

Uncovered: The Whole Truth about the Iraq War
(2003): using social media to cut down P&A costs

This practice falls into the wider remit of crowdsourcing, which is the 'outsourcing to the public, jobs typically performed by employees'.[37] Through this, Greenwald is advocating that consumers take on the role of distributors and exhibitors of his films. Brave New Films' website has a page dedicated to signing members of the public as 'distribution advocates' whose activities can range from using social networking sites to promote films, to hosting screenings.[38] The individual website for *Rethink Afghanistan* also has a facility that allows consumers to search for 'grassroots screening' events in their area.[39] As stated earlier, the feature-length documentary was released online, in short sections. The strategy could have been influenced by what Matt Hills has referred to as an on-demand access to content and mobility of mediated communication.[40] The sections were hosted by YouTube and embedded into the documentary's website. As the sections are available online, Greenwald has made them available on-demand and people did not need to wait for a screening to be organised in their local area. Additionally, people nowadays consume media on-the-go, which is facilitated by technological developments that have made media hardware more mobile. Therefore, the short sections are well suited to this form of media consumption. A feature film may be too long to watch on your smartphone on the commute to work, but a ten-minute section of *Rethink Afghanistan* would be ideal.

Tryon suggests that the aforementioned Greenwald films fall into the category of the 'transmedia documentary', which are 'a set of nonfiction films that use the participatory culture of the web to enhance the possibilities for both a vibrant public sphere cultivated around important political issues and an activist culture invested in social and political change'.[41] These types of films are also linked by their use of alternative distribution methods such as 'streaming video, digital downloads, or social media tools that facilitate public or semi-public screenings'.[42] These strategies however, are not just confined to the documentary realm, but can also be found in fiction film. As Broderick (2008) outlines, 'mumblecore' film-makers Arin Crumley and Susan Buice promoted *Four Eyed Monsters* (2005) through podcasts and made it available to view for free on social media outlets, but made money from the film through a shared ad revenue deal and eventually negotiated a television and home video distribution deal with the Independent Film Channel (IFC).[43]

While technological convergence may be facilitating the distribution methods covered in this chapter (via the digitalisation of media content), it is also the increasingly visible and viable DIY culture of media production, distribution and exhibition in which the roles of the consumer and producer converge that is driving such distribution strategies. Without consumers of such media content financing, marketing, distributing and exhibiting it, crowdsourcing strategies would become redundant and these films would not receive the scale of distribution that they have had. Additionally, at an industrial level, new platforms and organisations entering into the fields of distribution and marketing, such as MeetUp.com, Facebook, Twitter and YouTube, have brought about changes to traditional practices.

In *Spreadable Media: Creating Value and Meaning in a Networked Culture*, Henry Jenkins, Sam Ford and Joshua Green suggest that when an artist hands over some of the control of the circulation of their work to consumers (as Greenwald has done) it helps their work to spread.[44] Media products that 'circulate' are examples of the concept of what the authors refer to in the aforementioned study as 'spreadable media'.[45] They perceive distribution, on the one hand, as representing a process 'where the movement of media content is largely — or totally — controlled by the commercial interests producing and selling it', whereas circulation, on the other hand, 'refers to an emerging hybrid model, where a mix of top-down and bottom-up forces determine how material is shared across and among cultures in far more participatory (and messier) ways'.[46] The concept of circulation has been growing in momentum over recent years, particularly within the field of media and cultural studies, and is now emerging within film studies discourses. Iordanova has suggested that the traditional window releasing system will become just one of many ways in which film migrates across different countries and the outcome of this will be 'a new film circulation environment' that has a 'plethora of circuits and, possibly, revenue streams'.[47]

Referring back to Greenwald's distribution strategies behind *Rethink Afghanistan* we can see how circulation works. While Greenwald's company could control who they distributed the DVD copies to for the grassroots screenings, the decision to make the documentary also available online meant that the online circulation of this content was out of their control. Additionally, the campaign attached to the film and the invitation for people to get involved in activism via social networking sites and so on also further exemplifies how 'spreadable media' and 'circulation' are useful concepts when discussing strategies such as the ones adopted by Greenwald and Brave New Films. However, the term 'circulation' also has its critics. Ramon Lobato suggests that while it is useful to situate discussions of film distribution closer to notions of circulation, it is important not to overlook the importance of agency in this process – something the author feels some discussions of circulation do.[48]

Offering an alternative terming to this semantic discussion, Mark Pesce refers to such forms of distribution as 'network digital distribution' and enthusiastically suggests that these strategies could mean that film-makers could bypass traditional gatekeepers who have a 'stranglehold' of the market.[49] This concept is one that is quite useful as it retains the agency of the term 'distribution', while simultaneously recognising the networked way in which content now circulates and flows. Regardless of how they are termed, whether such models of 'network digital distribution' can be rolled out across a wide spectrum of films within the independent film landscape remains to be seen. For the cases discussed here, however, it has been relatively successful and appears to be a sustainable model for low-budget, independent film production. Film-makers such as Greenwald, Buice and Crumley have used the internet and social media to construct a direct channel of communication with their consumers, ultimately creating a viable means of marketing and connecting their films to a global audience. If consumers of independent film continue to back such distribution and marketing methods, perhaps a sustainable model of low- to no budget independent film production, distribution and exhibition could emerge.

Notes

1. I am characterising DIY film-makers here along economic lines as being those film-makers without the financial backing of a major studio or a large or mid-scale independent company. These film-makers produce their films through their own financing channels – loans, credit cards, friends, families, sponsors etc. and also produce their films on very small budgets, usually borrowing equipment, props, costumes etc. and offering payment on a deferred basis.
2. Geoff King, *American Independent Cinema* (New York: I.B.Tauris, 2005), p. 51.
3. A limited release strategy can be a more affordable option for independent film-makers as it targets key cities and once the film has finished playing in one location it is moved onto a new location; therefore, as Finola Kerrigan notes 'physical prints can be moved after a film has closed in a particular area and the revenue earned can be reinvested in localised publicity campaigns as the film moves around'. Similarly, a platform release sees a film open in a few key locations, then as positive word of mouth spreads and the box-office takings accumulate the release is widened. Finola Kerrigan, *Film Marketing* (Burlington: Elsevier, 2010), pp. 161–2.

4. Dina Iordanova, 'Digital Disruption: Technological Innovation and Global Film Circulation', in Dina Iordanova and Stuart Cunningham (eds), *Digital Disruption: Cinema Moves On-line* (St Andrews: St Andrews Film Studies, 2012), p. 7.

5. Brave New Films is a US-based new media organisation that uses film to educate, influence and inform people about social and political issues and was founded by Robert Greenwald, who is also president of sister organisation, Brave New Foundation, that aims to 'champion social injustice by using a model of media, education, and grassroots volunteer involvement that inspires, empowers, motivates and teaches civic participation and makes a difference' (www.bravenewfoundation.org/about). The two organisations are intrinsically linked as the Foundation uses Brave New Films' media products in their campaigns.

6. It is important to note, as Dave Chaffey does, that Web 2.0 does not equate to 'a new web standard or a "paradigm − ... shift"', but instead it is 'an evolution of technologies and communications approaches which have grown in importance since 2004–2005'. Dave Chaffey, 'E-Marketing', in M. J. Baker and S. Hart (eds), *The Marketing Handbook* (Amsterdam: Elsevier/Butterworth-Heinemann, 2008, 6th edn), p. 504.

7. Henry Jenkins, *Convergence Culture: When Old and New Media Collide* (New York: New York University Press, 2006), p. 2.

8. Virginia Nightingale, 'New Media Worlds? Challenges for Convergence', in Virginia Nightingale and Tim Dwyer (eds), *New Media Worlds: Challenges for Convergence* (Melbourne: Oxford University Press, 2007), p. 20; Tim Dwyer, *Media Convergence* (Maidenhead: McGraw-Hill and Open University Press, 2010), p. 5.

9. Jenkins, *Convergence Culture*, p. 3.

10. In assuming a hierarchy between the different strands of media convergence it is possible to overlook how the strands relate to and impact on one another. Additionally, if Jenkins's hierarchy were to be adopted in this chapter it would mean that the technological development and industrial rearrangements occurring within film distribution would be deemed less important than the socio-cultural changes and this assumption would paint a misleading picture of the current state of no to low-budget/DIY film distribution.

11. Tom Hutchison, 'New Media Marketing', in Paul Allen, Tom Hutchison and Amy Macy (eds), *Record Label Marketing* (Burlington, MA: Focal Press, 2010), pp. 319.

12. Jo Brown, Amanda J. Broderick and Nick Lee, 'Word of Mouth Communication with Communities: Conceptualising the Online Social Network', *Journal of Interactive Marketing* vol. 21 no. 3, 2007, p. 4.

13. Paul Booth, 'Intermediality in Film and Internet: Donnie Darko and Issues of Narrative Substantiality', *Journal of Narrative Theory* vol. 38 no. 3, 2008, pp. 398–414; William M. Kunz, *Culture Conglomerates: Consolidation in the Motion Picture and Television Industries* (Washington, DC: Rowman & Littlefield, 2007); Al Lieberman and Patricia Esgate, *The Entertainment Marketing Revolution: Bringing the Moguls, the Media and the Magic to the World* (New Jersey: Financial Times/Prentice Hall, 2002); Claire Molloy, *Memento* (Edinburgh: Edinburgh University Press, 2010); and Chuck Tryon, 'Video from the Void: Video Spectatorship, Domestic Film Cultures, and Contemporary Horror Film', *Journal of Film and Video* vol. 61 no. 3, 2009, pp. 40–51.

14. Source: www.boxofficemojo.com

15. The campaign tried to establish the fictional film as a documentary produced by student film-makers who set out to investigate the legend of the Blair Witch. As part of this pseudo-real investigation the students visit the alleged 'home' of the Blair Witch and are never seen again; the video footage that they had recorded during their search is all that was recovered.

16. Source: Boxofficemojo.com. When Blumhouse Productions produced *Paranormal Activity* the company would be considered as an independent outfit within the discourse of independence, but in 2011 it was announced that the company had signed a three-year 'first look' agreement with major studio Universal Pictures, bringing its independent status into question. Justin Kroll, 'U Inks 3-year Deal with "Paranormal" Producer: Blumhouse Productions First-look Deal Brings A-list Horror Shingle to U', *Variety.com*, 29 June 2011, www.variety.com/article/VR1118039322

17. Pamela McClintock, 'New Focus for Film Marketing: Internet, Mobile Grab more Studio Spending', *Variety.com*, 30 December 2009, www.variety.com/article/VR1118013209

18. Amy Powell, cited in Anne Thompson,'With Paranormal Activity, Paramount Sets New Marketing Model', *indieWIRE*, 15 October 2009, http://blogs.indiewire.com/thompsononhollywood/with_paranormal_activity_paramount_sets_new_marketing_model

19. Ibid.

20. Ibid.

21. Source: www.boxofficemojo.com. The film had a seventeen-week theatrical run that saw it open in just twelve theatres in its opening week, yet playing in over 2,700 theatres at its widest release. The eventual saturation release given to *Paranormal Activity* by Paramount Pictures was towards the lower end of their 2009 theatrical releases; however, it was the widest release given to a horror film that year by the distributor and the other films that were released on more screens were event films or contained big-name actors.

22. Thompson,'With Paranormal Activity, Paramount Sets New Marketing Model'.

23. Ibid.

24. Peter Broderick, 'Welcome to the New World of Distribution', *indieWIRE*, 15–16 September 2008, www.peterbroderick.com/writing/writing/welcometothenewworld.html

25. Ibid.

26. Ibid.

27. Ibid.

28. Yannis Tzioumakis, 'Reclaiming Independence: American Independent Cinema Distribution and Exhibition Practices beyond Indiewood', *Mise au point* (online), paragraph 7, 26 June 2012, www.map.revues.org/585

29. Kirsner Scott, 'Filmmakers Hope for Online Funds', *Variety.com*, 30 March 2007, www.variety.com/2007/film/news/filmmakers-hope-for-online-funds-1117962289/

30. See www.bravenewfilms.org/videos/rethinkafghanistan/

31. Addie Morfoot, 'Can Crowdfunding Pay? "You Betcha!"', *Variety.com*, 3 September 2011, www.variety.com/article/VR1118042148

32. Rhodri Marsden, 'Crowdfunding: Raising Money from Strangers', *The Independent Online*, 2 February 2011, www.independent.co.uk/life-style/gadgets-and-tech/features/crowdfunding-raising-money-from-strangers-2201277.html

33. Jenkins, *Convergence Culture*, 2006.

34. Ibid., p. 331.

35. Chuck Tryon, *Reinventing Cinema: Movies in the Age of Media Convergence* (New Brunswick, NJ: Rutgers University Press, 2009), p. 98.

36. Ibid., p. 100.

37. Kristina Dell, 'Crowdfunding', *Time International*, 15 September 2008 vol. 172 no. 11, 2008, pp. 39–40.

38. See www.bravenewfilms.org/dosomething/distribution.php

39. See www.bravenewfilms.org/videos/rethinkafghanistan/

40. Matt Hills, 'Participatory Culture: Mobility, Interactivity and Identity', in Glen Creeber and Royston Martin (eds), *Digital Cultures: Understanding New Media* (electronic book) (Berkshire: Open University Press, 2009), pp. 107–21.

41. Chuck Tryon, 'Digital Distribution, Participatory Culture, and the Transmedia Documentary', *Jump Cut: A Review of Contemporary Media* vol. 53, 2011, http://www.ejumpcut.org/archive/jc53.2011/TryonWebDoc/

42. Ibid.

43. Broderick, 'Welcome To The New World of Distribution'. 'Mumblecore' is a term used in film journalism and numerous academic writings to account for a loose category of films that emerged within the 2000s that focused on the everyday activities of post-collegiates. Popular culture journalist Dennis Lim outlines the features of films dubbed 'mumblecore' as being the inclusion of non-professional actors, semi-improvised dialogue and a focus on personal relationships rather than explicit plot points and action. Dennis Lim, 'A Generation Finds Its Mumble', *The New York Times*, 19 August 2007, www.nytimes.com/2007/08/19/movies/19lim.html?pagewanted=all&_r=0

44. Henry Jenkins, Sam Ford and Joshua Green, *Spreadable Media: Creating Value and Meaning in a Networked Culture* (New York: New York University Press, 2013).

45. Ibid.

46. Ibid., p. 1.

47. Iordanova, *Digital Disruption*, p. 1.

48. Ramon Lobato, *Shadow Economies of Cinema: Mapping Informal Film Distribution* (London: BFI, 2012), p. 2.

49. Pesce, cited in Tryon, *Reinventing Cinema*, p. 94.

Between Storytelling and Marketing, the SocialSamba Model

An Interview with Aaron Williams

Nolwenn MINGANT

In 2010, social technology expert Aaron Williams and entrepreneur Matthew Shilts founded a new type of internet experience: a 'scripted social networking' website which they named SocialSamba.[1] Both thought that being able to befriend James Bond or Homer Simpson on Facebook and interact with them would be a lot more exciting that having just posts from friends and family on one's wall. This is how they created a new type of internet experience. The SocialSamba website offers its visitors interactive 'choose-your-own-adventure' storylines. When visitors register into a story, they become protagonists of that story, interact with the main characters and make choices to orient the plot. As this interview shows, the internet offers many interactive opportunities. The goal of SocialSamba, which was nominated for an Emmy Award for Outstanding Creative Achievement in Interactive Media – Original Interactive Television Programming in 2012, is 'to create a new way of storytelling'.[2]

How did you create the SocialSamba.com storytelling experience?
Our first customer was USA Network here in the USA, with a television show called *Covered Affairs*,[3] a sort of spy thriller. It quickly became clear that in order to create a connection with a character, we couldn't just use Facebook and Twitter out of the box, use them the way they're created today. First, Facebook and Twitter are designed to be in real time. It's OK to get one post here or one post there, but to follow a story, especially one that goes over multiple days, was next to impossible. The second thing was that Facebook and Twitter are good at creating followers. In other words, I can be a voyeur of the characters, but it's actually difficult to create a real connection between me and these characters. If I'm going to take the time to befriend James Bond, I really want to feel like I befriended James Bond. I want him to call me by my name; I want to be able to participate in his adventures. I don't want to just watch him do it.

So what we realised is that we could solve all of these problems by creating a platform where storytellers can script out the entire experience with a set of characters and then we will play it back for each fan whenever they want it. What that means is we get the best of both worlds. You get a very deep connection because you get your own personalised experience with these characters and, at the same time, you can experience it whenever you want. So we could create these stories and put them into a bookshelf of stories, if you will, and then fans can come and take them down and befriend the characters and experience their lives whenever they want to engage.

Then we created this technology which enabled that to happen and we launched our first story with USA Network in the summer of 2011.

And it was a huge success for USA Network. We were really impressed with the depth of engagement that we got and how often fans were coming back to engage. We were watching Twitter and seeing them talk about the new relationship that they could have with the characters, one in which the characters really treated them like a friend. It was really exciting.

The format of the stories follows the choose-your-own-adventure book type. Who writes the content for the scripted storyline?

The original creators, and I think that's really important. Social Samba is a technology company. We provide a platform. We're all technologists and we don't have any writers on the staff. When we work with these companies, they're the ones that create this great content and stories, which is what they're good at. Sometimes they will bring in additional support from a third party, transmedia producers like 30 Ninjas and Starlight Runner that manage the whole production for them. But the key to our success has been that we get the creators and writers of the shows involved in creating the content.

How long does a story remain available on the site after the original programme has stopped being aired?

We rate our service on the number of readers that come in on the platform to experience it. So for all of our customers, we're happy to let them continue to have the story online as long as they will pay when somebody comes in to read the story. All our customers so far have been happy to let the story up and running on their Facebook page or on their website. They're seeing a lot of value from having these stories available for the fans.

Did you, from the start, consider that this was a new marketing model?

We saw very early on the potential from the marketing side because the first things we heard from a lot of these companies was 'We have a Facebook page, we have billions of fans, and we have no idea of what to do with those billions of fans.' And they were posting content through their Facebook timeline trying desperately to get fans to respond. But the engagement rate was usually 0.1 per cent or 0.5 per cent if they were doing a great job. So those engagement rates were just terrible and these guys, especially on the marketing side, knew that if they had a tool, like ours, with fourteen minutes on average per visit, getting fans to come back three times and really talk with their characters and their brands, that would have huge value. So I think we saw that pretty early on, but I have to say we got most excited when we saw the actual creators of the show excited about the ability to tell an interactive story and be able to see how the fans engage and participate in that conversation with the characters. We certainly see the value both in terms of this being a great storytelling medium and at the same time a significant tool for the marketers. When we give these fans great content, they love sharing it with their friends, they love inviting them to come in and participate as well.

Would you say it is a form of viral marketing?

We certainly see ourselves as being a technique of viral marketing. We don't do it as overtly as some of the other viral marketing techniques, but what we do is we just give the fans great content, give them an easy way to share it with their friends and they take advantage of that. On average we have fans sharing two pieces of content per story they read back to their friends. When you get that level of sharing, it's not hard for these stories to go viral when you see more people coming in from referral than you see people coming in from some of the pages of the TV channels.

Most of the stories are about TV shows. Are you more interested in these types of stories?
No, we're agnostic in terms of where the storytellers come from. We worked in TV primarily because that's my background. But we also did two movies with Warner Bros.: *Dolphin Tale* (2011), a family movie, and *Joyful Noise* (2011), a gospel choir movie. It follows the same idea in terms of the opportunity to come in and engage with the characters. The only slight difference was that, for a TV show, you get to know the characters really well, and so primarily the reason you come to experience the story is because you know the characters and you can't get enough of engaging with them. But for a movie, usually you don't know the characters when you visit the platform, so we have to use a little bit more of gamification – that is, to make it a little bit more of a game to come in and experience the story with the characters. In the case of *Joyful Noise*, for instance, we made the experience feel like you were auditioning for the choir. You would come in and friend the cast of the movie and they would ask you a bunch of questions and talk to you about being in the choir and see if you personally were worthy of joining their choir and they would play clips from the movie and ask you what kind of music you like. That whole story then has a sort of goal, you're trying to convince them to let you into the choir and if you did that we'd put you in a sweepstake to win a Kindle Fire. That had a real kind of outcome as well in terms of being able to reward people for getting the right outcome in the story. If you didn't, of course, we invited you to come back and do the story again.

Beyond offering scripted experience, SocialSamba is now also encouraging fans to write their own storylines.
Yes, in May 2012, we launched a fan fiction platform called SagaWriter. So if you go to SocialSamba.com, you can now see stories created by fans, not professionals any more. We're encouraging anyone to come in and use our platform and create more stories. And in that case, we're seeing actually more movie stories than TV stories. For movie franchises, for example *Hunger Games* (2012), we have a handful of really good parodies that have been created on our site by fans and then shared to their friends. And we're really excited about that opportunity because we know that brand owners are not able to produce enough content to feed the insatiable appetite of the fans. So if you give them an outlet where they can come in and create some of the content and share it with the other fans, then you certainly have a quantity of content that gets really interesting and can help to feed that appetite. Also, in September 2012, we launched a new project with Turner for a science-fiction TV show they have called *Falling Skies*.[4] The creators of the show are going to write three episodes or stories in our platform and then publish that out to the fans and that third episode is ending on a cliffhanger, they're not going to know exactly what the ending is. And they're going to invite fans to come in and write the ending – that is, to write the fourth episode. What you end up with is three episodes of great content created by the writers of the show and then a quantity of content of hundreds, maybe even thousands, of fourth episodes, created by the fans and shared with each other. And then the creators of the show pick one of those fourth episodes and name it the official fourth episode and then move on and create episodes 5, 6 and 7. We call this model co-creation, where the creators of the show are doing their part to create most of the content but they're opening it up to fans to create the quantity of content that's going to keep all the

fans engaged over a longer period of time. This social storytelling is really going to grow over the next couple of years.

What proportion of users who read the stories then start to write their own?
About 1 per cent. For us, that's a fantastic number. We also added a Facebook button on every story, so with one click you can publish your story out to your Facebook page. Fans can come in and experience that story directly from your page. We've seen the real significance of the sprinkling of our content now around the web. Hundreds of Facebook pages have included tags now with stories running on them. So it's not even about going to SocialSamba.com any more. It's how we can find all the different channels where our stories can get experienced, where fans can share them in the most logical place for them.

The website seems to favour certain genres and types of programmes, notably anime and fantasy. What about the demographics of the fans?
On the SocialSamba website, we haven't done any specific targeted marketing towards any one group or another. We let it grow organically and see what the fans are creating. We have very healthy communities around zombies and anime and *Hunger Games* and *Pokémon*. We didn't pick those four genres to be the top genres, they just happened to be. But I think you can even see across those groups, there's a diversity of demographics. We have some stories that are very popular with twenty-five- to forty-five-year-old men. We have some stories like the *Teen Wolf* (2011–) story from MTV that are very popular with thirteen- to fifteen-year-old girls. I actually don't think this storytelling medium is more applicable to one demographic or another. I think it's more about doing a good job of telling a story.

   For example, the movie *Dolphin Tale* was, for us, targeted at two demographics: tweens and young kids, and parents who would want to see a family story. When we created the experience, we assumed we would mostly get these parents, so we really wrote the story targeted at them. But we were really surprised in the first week to see how often people were posting back, either through Twitter or through Facebook and saying 'I'm loving this story and I'm reading it with my three kids.' That kind of experience surprised us. There was that sort of co-play between parents and kids. And also, Facebook these days is everybody, just like TV is everybody. So as long as you create a good story and match it to your demographic and what they would expect, you can actually reach any demographic inside Facebook.

How do you envisage the future?

When we first talked in 2012, Aaron Williams was excited about developing opportunities with brand and the immersive possibilities of augmented reality. We asked him the question again in 2014.

There have been a couple of important changes to the social storytelling landscape since we last talked. First, brands have seen the response from fans (and the engagement rate), and have jumped in to create branded stories and conversations. These are typically not the long, character-driven narratives that our entertainment customers create, and can be as simple as thanking every new fan that follows a brand on Twitter. And, second, the participation from these brands has awoken Twitter and Facebook. There is far more investment and innovation happening by the major platforms, and more consolidation happening as start-ups join larger companies and push to scale. The market is maturing, and that's very healthy.

Notes

1. www.socialsamba.com/front (website no longer active).
2. The interview was conducted by Nolwenn Mingant on 24 September 2012. The following text is an abridged version of the interview, amended by the editors and approved by Aaron Williams.
3. *Covered Affairs* (2010–12) follows the story of a young female CIA trainee.
4. *Falling Skies* (2011–13) is a TV series about survivors of an Alien invasion.

Promoting in Six Seconds

New Advertising Strategies Using the Video Social Network Vine in Spain

A case study by Javier LOZANO DELMAR and
José Antonio MUÑIZ-VELÁZQUEZ

Nowadays, with the concept of Web 2.0, viewers participate in the conception and creation of advertising and promotional campaigns, becoming involved in the process. Along with the integration of the concept of entertainment in advertising (advertainment, branded content, etc.), new advertising formats whose goal is to lure and entice the viewer are emerging. With this in mind, the aim of this chapter is to provide an enlightening overview of the new digital promotion strategies that are currently being developed in the field of film marketing. What we propose with this case study is to explore new film promotion strategies through the use of the social network Vine in Spain. This work will focus on two main advertising campaigns, which have perfectly combined entertainment, advertising and user-generated content (UGC).

Vine was launched on 24 January 2013 and, before its release, Twitter had already acquired it. As was posted on Twitter's blog on 24 January: 'Today, we're introducing Vine: a mobile service that lets you capture and share short looping videos. Like Tweets, the brevity of videos on Vine (6 seconds or less) inspires creativity.'[1] According to Twitter: 'we introduced Vine because we wanted to make it easier for people to create and share videos from a device we almost always have with us: our phone.'[2] For Vine's general manager and co-founder, Colin Kroll, 'Video is the new frontier.'[3] With Vine's arrival, Twitter users were able to publish videos directly from the 140-character social network. Vine's language was also adapted to Twitter's by using hashtags, trending topics or 'revines', the counterparts of retweets.

In the summer of 2013, Vine reached 40 million users worldwide.[4] According to Global Web Index,[5] Vine was the fastest-growing application in 2013, expanding its estimated audience by 403 per cent. However, Vine still has the smallest worldwide reach (just 3 per cent of mobile users). As stated in Nielsen's annual report about US Digital Consumers (2014):

> Facebook remains the largest social network used in both the Web and mobile: consumers are embracing other social platforms such as LinkedIn (up 37% among users), Pinterest (triple unique users on smartphone apps), and Instagram (nearly double the number of unique users in 2013).[6]

In Spain, Vine also remains one of the least-known social networks. A 2014 study on social media shows that only 10 per cent of the interviewees recognised Vine,[7] as opposed to 99 per cent for Facebook, 92 per cent for Twitter and 88 per cent for YouTube. According to the same study, whose aim is to understand the behaviour of internet users, 'the social networks most used or visited are Facebook (94 per cent) and YouTube (68 per cent)'.

Vine represents only 2 per cent of social network use. Nevertheless, it should be noted that in the past year Vine has been used as a centre of various Spanish film promotional campaigns focused on the use of consumer-generated advertising (CGA).

Advertising with Vine

Dunkin' Donuts became the first company to utilise Vine in a television advertising campaign on 9 September 2013.[8] Many brands (Lowe, Samsung, Doritos, etc.) have created a social network profile to extend their message or design creative advertising strategies to promote some of their products. One such case was the advertising campaign produced by Airbnb, the website that allows users to find and book accommodation around the world. As indicated on the website of the campaign itself:

> Airbnb is a pioneer of social innovation and built on the belief that great stories come from connection and collaboration. It was only natural that we came up with an idea based on those principles. The result was 'Hollywood & Vines', a first-of-its-kind short film directed via Twitter and shot entirely on Vine.[9]

The final short was edited using nearly a hundred submissions on Vine, which were created by social network users. Airbnb's objective was to create 'a story of travel, adventure, and finding your place in the world'.[10] Thus, Airbnb used the social micro-video network to invite users to create the brand's TV commercial.

This advertising campaign reflects the change in the advertising industry in the last few years. Advertising is starting to focus on 'prosumers' who participate and interact with brands and products. As Nielsen Spain stated in a 2011 study about consumption:

> the buying and consumption habits have changed, and manufacturers and distributors face a new consumer. We must go from a loyal consumer to a fan consumer, one who admires the brand and has positive thoughts and feelings for it. Because to the fan consumer, the brand is more than just a name, and is easily differentiated from other brands.[11]

In fact, (fan) consumers are the new advertisers and they are transforming the advertising industry.[12] The rise of new mobile digital devices and social networks allows a democratisation of technology (creating and editing images, video, music, etc.) and a variety of accessible tools for this hyperactive and hyperconnected new prosumer. Regarding film consumption, viewers are not just consuming content but, at the same time, are becoming prosumers and generating all kinds of content through new forms of expression such as mash-ups, memes and, of course, ads. This is what happened with the Airbnb campaign, which was based on UGC practices, inviting this avid prosumer to adopt the role of the advertiser, and, therefore, create their own ads for the product. This particular type of UGC is called consumer-generated advertising (CGA).[13] As it has been noted in recent research, CGA helps persuasion, increases trustworthiness and, therefore, advertising effectiveness.[14] It is a change of perspective. Now, the role of film marketing should be to design a unique experience that brings the viewing and consumption experience beyond the screen.[15]

Consumer-generated Advertising Using Vine

For the Spanish theatrical release of *Carrie* (2013), distributor Sony Pictures launched one of the first marketing campaigns in Spain designed to advertise a film using Vine. The campaign, which was produced by OMD Spain, was a contest that encouraged CGA. Through the website CarrieVine.es and the Sony Pictures Spain Vine account,[16] users were invited to create their own video simulating a telekinesis effect, just like the protagonist's superpowers in the film. The video had to be recorded using Vine and posted on Twitter using the hashtag #CarrieVine. A Vine promo was launched with a slogan inviting users to participate in the campaign: 'There are more people than me, and they can do the same things that I do.'[17] The best Vines would win a mobile phone and a tablet. All Vines were collected on the website and are still available on Vine under the hashtag #CarrieVine.

With this communication strategy, Sony Pictures supplemented conventional advertising material for the film (such as trailers, posters, etc.) through a social media action inviting the viewer to build their own micro-film (UGC) which also worked as advertising material (CGA) for the movie. In these Vines, viewers were transformed into the protagonists of their own micro-film which plays with the main narrative elements from Carrie's world. Although this is still an isolated case in Spanish film promotion, Vine used the same strategy as Airbnb, placing the prosumer at the centre of the strategy, and using the technological possibilities of new mobile devices and the ability to make a message 'contagious' by releasing it through a social network.

Another instance is the subscription TV channel Canal +, which decided to release the first episode of *Game of Thrones*' (2011–) fourth season in a movie theatre. This channel premiered the TV show as an actual film and, therefore, with a promotional campaign in theatres. Canal + hatched the idea of a promotional campaign including a Vine Booth that allowed viewers to create Vines/selfies 360° at the movie theatre. This Vine Booth had already been used at other events such as the Golden Globes event in 2014, where celebrities were invited to create and publish their own selfies 360°.[18] On this occasion, Canal + invited the viewers of the series to portray themselves as different characters from the show and to post their 360° selfies on the Canal + Series Vine account.[19] As Berni Melero,[20] head of Multimedia Communication in Canal +, said, the goal of the campaign was to design an entertainment experience about *Game of Thrones*, where viewers were the centre of the action:

> Canal + is the first company in the world that has Vine Booth serving the fans. Up till now this machine had only been used by celebrities. We had queues of people who wanted to have his Vine taken, wearing exclusive outfits from *Game of Thrones*. We generated a good feeling among those who participated and extended a bit more the entertainment experience of *Game of Thrones*.[21]

It is interesting to look at how other distributors have used Vine as a simple video platform without fully exploring the social implications of the network. For instance, to promote the release of *The Wolverine* (2013), director James Mangold posted on Vine and Twitter what he called a 'tweaser' (Vine + Twitter + Teaser), a micro-movie trailer.[22] We can see similar uses within the official Vine account for *X-Men: Days of Future Past* (2014)[23] or the profile used by HBO to promote *Game of Thrones*,[24] where the users are shown key moments of previous episodes and glimpses of upcoming episodes, which were launched before the premiere of the new season. *Sabotage* (2014) also released several micro-movie trailers in six seconds.[25] Buddha Jones, the agency responsible for these Vine trailers, won the 'Best Vine' brand new category at the Fifteenth Annual Golden Trailer Awards. *Muppets Most Wanted* (2014) launched a series of Vine promos advertising the movie and also Toyota Highlander.[26]

In these cases, Vines are used as micro-movie trailers, reducing their narrative and advertising appeal to the shortest possible expression. These Vines work as teasers of the teaser, but they are still coming attractions, anticipating new footage from the upcoming film and attracting viewers through the conventional formula of showing film content. Furthermore, they are created and launched by the film's distributor, where consumers remain passive viewers and are unable to participate or engage with any of the content.

Some other films go further and use Vine for showing behind-the-camera scenes, new footage or on-set clips, such as *Chef* (2014),[27] through the Vine personal account of the film's director. This is also very common in TV promotion, as can be seen, for instance, in the promotional campaign for the new series *The Flash* (2014).[28] In these cases, Vine works as a platform to deliver extra content, which is updated.

However, Canal + and Sony Pictures Spain chose to care for their viewers and to place the prosumer in the middle of a communicative campaign where they can participate and interact with film and television content. Thus, the main content creator is not the channel, nor the distributor, but the said viewers through their own mobile phones and the Vine social network. On television, many TV shows are allowing viewers to become an important part of the series – *Hannibal* (2013–) is just one example. In this show, fans constantly generate online content and, therefore, are establishing a community built around the series. Fannibals[29] are the actual advertisers of *Hannibal*.

Film marketing should design advertising strategies that embrace new social networks as a modern way for the viewer's expression. The purpose of using Vine in film marketing should not only be to entice viewers to see the movie by delivering new footage – which belongs to the past – but also to invite them to be part of a consumer experience, where they are the protagonists. As Melero said, it is all about generating an entertainment experience with viewers.[30] Spectators are the new advertisers and UGC (in any form) is the new film marketing.

Notes

1. https://blog.twitter.com/2013/vine-a-new-way-to-share-video
2. https://blog.twitter.com/our-first-birthday-a-year-on-vine-0
3. http://techcrunch.com/2014/01/23/one-year-in-vines-battle-has-just-begun/
4. https://twitter.com/vineapp/statuses/369911739782946816
5. Global Web Index (2013), 'Q3 GWI Launch: Video and Images Dominate Mobile App Growth', http://blog.globalwebindex.net/mobile-app-usage
6. Nielsen US, *The Digital Consumer*, February 2014, p. 16.
7. Interactive Advertising Bureau, 'V Estudio Annual de Redes Sociales', 2014, www.iabspain.net/wp-content/uploads/downloads/2014/04/V-Estudio-Anual-de-Redes-Sociales-versi%C3%B3n-reducida.pdf
8. '25 Things You Should Know about Vine', http://www.searchenginejournal.com/25-things-know-vine/87383/
9. http://hollywoodandvines.com/
10. Ibid.
11. Nielsen España, *Del consumidor fiel, al consumidor fan*, 2011, http://es.nielsen.com/site/documents/BNConsumidorNov-2011 (link no longer live).
12. Javier Lozano Delmar, Victor Hernández-Santaolalla and Marina Ramos, 'Fandom Generated Content: An Approach to the Concept of Fanadvertising', *Participations, Journal of Audience & Reception Studies* vol. 10 no. 1, 2013, pp. 351–6.

13. Rob Walker, 'Firefox Flicks', *The New York Times*, 28 May 2006, www.nytimes.com/2006/05/28/magazine/28wwln_consumed.html

14. Benjamin Lawrence, Susan Fournier and Frédéric Brunel, 'When Companies Don't Make the Ad: A Multimethod Inquiry Into the Differential Effectiveness of Consumer-Generated Advertising', *Journal of Advertising* vol. 42 no. 4, 2013, pp. 292–307. Debra V. Thompson and Prashant Malaviya, 'Consumer-Generated Ads: Does Awareness of Advertising Co-Creation Help or Hurt Persuasion?', *Journal of Marketing* vol. 77, 2013, pp. 33–47.

15. Javier Lozano Delmar, 'Nuevas formas publicitarias digitales en *Juego de Tronos*. La publicidad mediante experiencias', in Javier Lozano Delmar, Irene Raya and Francisco Javier López Rodríguez (eds), *Reyes, espadas, cuervos y dragones. Estudio del fenómeno televisivo* Juego de Tronos (Madrid: Fragua, 2013), pp. 509–36.

16. https://vine.co/v/hUphuwleWhV

17. https://vine.co/v/hUp5JtwrLKr

18. https://vine.co/goldenglobes

19. https://vine.co/canalplusseries

20. Interview with Berni Melero, head of Multimedia Communication in Canal + and responsible for Vine communication campaigns.

21. Another example of the use of Vine Booth in Spanish film promotion was during the theatrical premiere of *The Amazing Spider-Man 2* (2014). In this case, Vine Booth was used only by celebrities during a private premiere. You can see the results here: https://vine.co/u/1066124313725407232

22. https://twitter.com/mang0ld/status/316221584950038528

23. https://vine.co/xmenmovies

24. https://vine.co/GameofThrones

25. https://vine.co/sabotagemovie

26. https://vine.co/tags/ToyotaHighlander

27. https://vine.co/v/hmD2aaPZYwD

28. https://vine.co/CW_TheFlash

29. *Hannibal* TV show fandom denomination.

30. Interview with Melero.

Piracy and Promotion

Understanding the Double-edged Power of Crowds

Ramon LOBATO

Film distribution in the internet era is characterised by a deep-seated contradiction. Distributors want their films to go viral, to generate buzz, to be discussed on blogs, to be tweeted about and to compete passionately for the attention of their potential audience. At the same time, however, distributors must exercise control over this viral activity. They invite the public to share some – but not all – of the text. Marketing materials (trailers, stills, plot points, gossip) will ideally circulate widely, but the full experience must be retained exclusively for those who pay for the movie ticket, DVD or video-on-demand (VoD) service. The goal is to stimulate consumer desire for a film without fully satisfying it, leaving a productive excess – a surplus emotional investment – that leads to paid consumption.

The obvious contradiction in this scenario is that internet marketing is linked in a number of ways with piracy. Creating awareness means creating demand, and demand cannot easily be contained in the formal spaces of trailers, teasers and marketing paratexts. Audiences whose interest has been aroused online want to see the whole movie through the same digital channels that initially brought it to their attention: from this perspective, the next stop after IMDb will be, in many cases, The Pirate Bay or another piracy platform. Current distribution practice is, therefore, a balancing act. Studio marketing and promotional staff nurture the 'good' crowd activities, the kinds that build brand awareness around agreed-upon themes. Brand protection and anti-piracy staff elsewhere in the organisation work furiously to curtail 'bad' behaviours: the piracy that soaks up potential audiences, or pre-release leaks that can lead to bad word of mouth and kill a film's chances at the box office. But these two phenomena are, in fact, different sides of the same coin.

Thinking of piracy and promotion in this way, as intertwined aspects of film markets, is the most appropriate starting point for research on digital distribution. Yet the current discussion on this topic is still marked by the same kinds of partisan divisions that run through the copyright policy debate. Intellectual property defenders fume about content theft, while free culture advocates and brand consultants talk up the marketing benefits of viral buzz, arguing that obscurity, rather than piracy, is the film-maker's real enemy.

An easy mistake to make when engaging with the piracy/promotion question is to side with one camp or the other, the copyright protectionists or the free culture enthusiasts, as though these were the only positions available. But this is not an either/or scenario. Neither side has a monopoly on truth, precisely because the effect of piracy will vary significantly from one film to another. The now-familiar arguments about the 'good' or 'bad' effects of piracy (useful publicity versus damaging substitution) are not truth claims so much as they are references to particular kinds of economic effects that may actually coexist, along with a range of other middle-range effects. There are no inviolable rules here. We need to think more concretely about particular situations in which piracy may be more or less damaging, or more or less useful, to producers.

This allows a range of interesting questions to be asked. Under what circumstances does piracy align with promotion and, ultimately, sales? Under what circumstances does it undermine them? What are the variables in play, in terms of distribution strategy, audiences and market conditions? Finally (and this is a question of particular significance for cinema scholars), where do elements like genre and audience fit into this picture? What kinds of movies are more likely to do well in a copyright-weak environment and which ones are likely to suffer?

Recent research in media economics, communication studies and film studies sheds light on some of these variables. In this chapter, I want to bring some strands of this literature together into a loose typology of different scenarios, illustrating the uneven effects that piracy can have. The aim is to develop a more differentiated conception of piracy's effects on film-makers, one that treads a middle path between the alarmist predictions of copyright maximalists and the utopian dreams of internet libertarians.

A Meso-level Theory of the Piracy/Promotion Relationship

The fields of media economics and film, media and communication studies have produced many studies of the impact of piracy on film distribution. However, these bodies of knowledge are rarely put into dialogue; they are separated by an epistemic gulf that makes translation between the fields difficult. To bridge this gulf, we need a meso-level theory of the piracy/promotion relationship – an approach that is responsive both to macro market trends and to the specific characteristics of particular audiences, texts and networks. This section traces the outlines of such a theory.

Let us begin with the economic literature and what it tells us about the piracy/promotion relationship. Economists have conducted a great deal of research on digital piracy over the last two decades, partly because the open nature of peer-to-peer networks offers appealing, ready-made datasets that lend themselves to quantitative analysis. When correlated with industry sales figures, such data offer a bounty of possibilities for empirical studies.[1] Much of this literature is devoted to the question of substitution effects (whether piracy has a negative effect on sales), bundling and pricing issues and, to a lesser extent, questions of consumer surplus and welfare. However, a vein of this literature explicitly considers the promotional aspects of piracy, exploring ways that piracy can affect consumer awareness and willingness to pay for motion pictures. Smith and Telang argued that broadband internet access (notwithstanding the piracy problem that comes with it) is generally positive for DVD sales in the USA, noting promotional effects and expanded consumer choice.[2] Waldfogel similarly foregrounds new avenues for product discovery in his analysis of the piracy/promotion relationship in TV distribution.[3] In a simulation-based study of the marketing/downloading nexus, Croxson concludes that 'To the extent that piracy raises consumption (some consume who otherwise never would), consumption fuels hype, and hype in turn boosts future demand, a seller may tolerate illegal copies, even at some risk to current sales.'[4]

Studies such as these come to different conclusions about the impact of piracy on paid consumption, but they usefully draw our attention to some of the 'middle-range' phenomena that lie between piracy and promotion, such as sampling behaviour by consumers (the try-before-you-buy effect) and the role of network effects in shaping consumer demand. If we take these studies seriously, it becomes rather difficult to think of piracy as a singular phenomenon.

The economic literature on the piracy/promotion relationship is limited in the sense that it cannot tell us very much about how this relationship works at ground level, and how it may affect diverse films, film-makers and audience segments. Economic studies – even those that take consumption of individual products/texts as their unit of analysis – tend to operate at fairly high levels of abstraction. The large-scale datasets considered most rigorous by economists (Nielsen Videoscan and box-office figures) are useful for tracking broad shifts in national or international markets but cannot easily be correlated in a way that tells us much about factors like genre, audience, or taste. In other words, they reveal little about how the piracy/promotion relation works in practice. Such studies tend to fail the common-sense test of media scholars, who understand that teenage audiences for superhero movies act in very different ways from nature documentary viewers; that casual moviegoers have different kinds of consumption patterns and ethical dispositions from hardcore genre fans; and that the experience of watching certain kinds of movies can diminish greatly (or not at all) when watched at home on a small screen as opposed to a cinema screen.

Qualitative research on the piracy/promotion nexus in film and media studies supplies some of these missing puzzle pieces by showing the variability of distribution and consumption scenarios. Film and communication scholars generally take individual texts, genres and audiences as their starting point, and then examine the diverse manifestations of piracy on those objects. A well-known example is Henry Jenkins's book *Convergence Culture*, which featured a section 'When Piracy Becomes Promotion' about the emergence of anime markets in the USA in the home video era.[5] Piracy was a central element in Jenkins's story because it had a market-nurturing effect: anime bootlegs built an audience that would not have otherwise existed, since at the time there was no real legal market to speak of (Japanese distributors at that time were not engaged with the US market, leaving bootleggers and fans as the only distributors of note). Fan clubs played a vital role here as mediators and market-makers for the future anime industry, and effectively functioned as a promotional apparatus for an industry-in-waiting. Jenkins concluded that 'the clubs were not trying to profit from anime distribution but rather to expand the market'.

Research on the piracy/promotion nexus in film and media studies is generally informed by scepticism of intellectual property rhetoric and a commitment to ideas of textual diversity, accessibility and fan engagement. Consequently, the stated or unstated aim of much of this research has been to critique anti-piracy overreach by showing the unpredictable – and sometimes revenue-positive – effects that different kinds of pirate circulation can have. However, a weakness of this approach is that it focuses on exceptional rather than typical market situations: the counter-intuitive examples when piracy does something we would not expect it to. Hence, the feel-good story of fan-fuelled anime distribution is privileged over more sombre examples of revenue leakage that could be found elsewhere.

Placing qualitative research side-by-side with the quantitative economic literature is difficult, as each body of work has a distinct methodology, analytical orientation and ontological position. But doing so can be useful because it brings the claims and assumptions of these perspectives (and the resulting knowledge gaps) into focus. Economists succeed in tracing patterns across national and international markets and identifying rules and logics, while telling us little or nothing about the kinds of texts that are likely to do well or poorly from pirate publicity. Conversely, media researchers – who specialise in case studies and singular examples – can tell us quite a bit about what piracy means for particular texts, but struggle to scale this up into wider rules or observations.

What middle path can be navigated between these different traditions of research? One possibility is to identify some meso-level patterns, moving us away from industry-wide/market-wide arguments on the one hand, and micro-level examples on the other, towards some mid-range arguments about the common scenarios and consequences of piracy as regards particular kinds of movie cultures and particular distribution models. Such an approach would have the advantage of being able to connect observable macro trends (the domain of economic analysis) with textual and audience characteristics (the domain of qualities, aesthetics, affects and engagements), allowing a distinction to be made between different kinds of piracy situations, involving different kinds of texts, with different kinds of outcomes for producers and audiences. In this way we can start to distinguish common scenarios in which the free publicity of crowds may be a resource that film-makers can exploit, and other scenarios in which film-makers will prefer to leave that genie in its bottle.

When is Pirate Promotion Useful?
The various arguments advanced so far can now be formed into a tentative hypothesis. Piracy *can* coexist with promotion, performing a revenue-enhancing function that boosts rather than cannibalises sales, but only under particular conditions, where certain kinds of variables come into play. Some of these variables are market-related, concerning supply and demand; others relate to texts and textual qualities. Let us consider each category in turn.

Market variables
The positive stories of piracy-as-publicity usually stem from cases of market failure, censorship, inappropriate pricing, or ineffective distribution. When no legal distribution channels exist – or when they are inaccessible to consumers – piracy has no negative effect on sales. Indeed, it is likely to operate as a kind of de facto market that can build taste and viewing cultures over time. This is what Julian Thomas and I have elsewhere described as a 'market-priming' or 'incubating' function.[6]

Recent scholarship has produced some fascinating insights into this variety of piracy. Jonathan Gray has studied the reception of Hollywood cinema in Malawi, where the major studios do not bother competing, and pirate distributors – who import discs *en masse* from factories in China, via South Africa – are the only available distribution chain for Hollywood movies.[7] Barbara Klinger has written of the way that *Titanic* (1997) circulated in Afghanistan, where cinema was strictly banned in Taliban-controlled areas, leaving basically all cinema circulation as pirate circulation.[8] In these instances piracy cannot help but function as a form of promotion, creating what Miller *et al.* call 'cultures of anticipation' for particular kinds of cinema, and potentially softening up audiences for a time when legal alternatives are available.[9] Such effects are not exclusive to Hollywood. Consider the case of Indian cinema, an enormous cultural industry whose foreign distribution arm (and a great deal of its domestic distribution system) is informal in nature. In many countries with Indian diasporas distribution has been largely through piracy, and many markets have been considered too small or chaotic for legal distributors to bother with.[10] Government restrictions also played a part. In Pakistan, for example, Indian films were banned between 1965 and 2006, and then again in 2013, meaning that for much of the recent past the entire Indian cinema market in Pakistan has been a pirate market. There is no question that piracy did much of the work of extending Indian cinema's reach into these spaces.

Translation is another variable to consider. Poor availability of subtitled or dubbed texts in many national markets functions as a natural market barrier, leading to increased reliance on informal and pirate alternatives. Many minor language markets (Romania or Hungary, for example) do not have access to the full array of translated texts that larger media markets are used to. Pirates and 'fansubbers' regularly fill this market gap.

In these specific scenarios, when legal markets are constrained by structural or political factors, piracy can serve a promotional function without cannibalising revenues. There cannot be losses when there is no infrastructure for profit.

Textual and audience variables

Another way to clarify the variable effects of the piracy/promotion relationship is to look at the problem from a textual perspective, asking what kinds of texts are most likely to do well under conditions of widespread piracy, and when pirate popularity is likely to translate back into formal sales. This requires a way of explaining the link between textual content and consumer action.

In a recent study Jenkins, Ford and Green consider the textual drivers of digital sharing.[11] Providing a detailed typology of what they call 'spreadable' texts, the authors identify some textual characteristics that lend themselves to wide dissemination through social media, streaming and viral networks. They identify a number of commodity characteristics (easy availability, portability, reusability and relevance to multiple audiences), as well as a textual checklist of qualities (including humour, parody, open-endedness, mystery, controversy and timeliness), suggesting that texts with these features are likely to spread better than those without them. Their argument refers mostly to short-form web content, rather than feature films. While it is difficult to extend many of these categories to feature-length movies, beyond their marketing paratexts, the taxonomy is a useful first step in considering the textual qualities of 'spreadable' feature films.

So, what textual 'rules' might apply for features? Is the pirate/sharing/viral economy simply an echo chamber of the box office, or does it have its own specificities and quirks? Do pirates like the same movies as everybody else?

Opinion here varies depending on which part of the pirate economy you are looking at. Canclini has argued that street-level pirate markets in Latin America simply reproduce the hits and ignore the niche content.[12] Other studies of popular pirate marketplaces, such as Quiapo in Manila, have shown some of the long-tail aspects of pirate markets, which give rise to distinct and specific taste formations – particular kinds of cult and niche cinephilia – that differ from those found in legal markets.[13] Private torrent communities like Karagarga, with their extraordinarily complex taste hierarchies, offer another example.[14] The diverse taste cultures of these networks are extremely interesting for film scholars, though an economist might, perhaps, find the phenomenon unsurprising, concluding that the diversity of any pirate market is likely to be a function of its scale, as well as the characteristics of its user/client base. In other words, the bigger and more complex the pirate market, the more variation can be found there.

Superbrands and Sleeper Hits

Let us conduct a small experiment to test these ideas. In recent years the website TorrentFreak, an informal but respected authority on pirate practices, has been compiling a list of the most downloaded movies each year. Based on data from a number of Bit Torrent trackers, this ranking offers us a reasonable sense of what kinds of movies are most popular in the global hive-mind of the torrents.[15] The TorrentFreak list typically mirrors

Project X: the most downloaded film of 2012

the global box-office tables, suggesting that pirate activity tends to follow the precedents set by established forms of film marketing, and underscoring the earlier point about the co-constitutive nature of piracy and film marketing. But, occasionally, a smaller film with a passionate peer-to-peer (P2P) audience makes the cut, raising interesting questions about the relationship between marketing, piracy and taste.

In 2012 TorrentFreak announced that the year's most downloaded movie was music video director Nima Nourizadeh's debut feature *Project X*. The sensationalist story of a Pasadena house party that spirals wildly out of control, *Project X* is shot in lurid shaky-cam, stars a cast of unknown and non-professional actors and features abundant sex, drugs, slow-mo booty shots and drug use. Reviews ranged from lukewarm to excoriating (*The Telegraph* called it 'flamboyantly loathsome on every imaginable level'[16]), but the film went on to be a massive hit on Bit Torrent, becoming the most widely downloaded movie of the year, edging out big-budget behemoths like *Mission Impossible – Ghost Protocol* (2011), *The Dark Knight Rises* (2012) and *The Avengers* (2012).

Project X, which was produced by Joel Silver (*Lethal Weapon* [1987]) and backed by Warner Bros., has a production backstory that mirrors its viral mode of circulation. Inspired by a real-life party in Australia that became a huge street riot after the Facebook invite was circulated too widely (the host was Corey Delaney, a hoodie-wearing working-class teen who became a minor celebrity in that country for a short period), *Project X* represents an unusual harmonisation of form, content and distribution. At every level, the film embodied a viral circulatory logic: a Facebook invite leads to a violent crowd; the crowd attract news helicopters; the news coverage leads to more viral coverage, then a movie deal; then the movie itself goes viral. Piracy was central to the movie's cultural impact, and has garnered the director legitimate industry attention that suggests a promising Hollywood career. His latest project is the Kristen Stewart vehicle *American Ultra* (2015).

Project X is a rare example of a pirate 'sleeper hit', a film of modest profile and mid-level budget ($12 million), that achieved great success in both formal and informal markets. Its pirate popularity has been useful for the film's brand, cementing its status as a global teen movie in a way that formal distribution alone would not have been able to. But this is an exception rather than the rule. Few sleeper hits make it big on Bit Torrent without prior visibility at the box office. Certainly, to my recollection, no truly independent film has ever made it to the Top 10 torrents. To be a hit in the pirate economy, you generally need a strong box-office opening. In a film like *Project X*, which confounds this rule, we can see both the possibilities and the limits of viral promotion.

Project X's textual features should also be taken into account. Its massive pirate popularity was partly due to its recognisable genre identity (the frat party/Spring Break movie) but also to its R-rating (which blocked most of the film's natural audience from being able to see it at the movies, increasing demand for pirate copies). The film also had a 'spreadable' aspect, in that its narrative was structured as a series of small gags and incidents; it's the kind of film that can be watched, and enjoyed, in brief chunks, requiring less time commitment and, therefore, lending itself to digital over theatrical distribution. Taking into account these qualities, the runaway popularity of *Project X* on Bit Torrent seems less a random accident and more a confluence of specific regulatory/market factors (classification) and textual characteristics (genre).

When market and textual variables come together in this way, sleeper hits can emerge through pirate promotion alone. But such conditions are very rare. Few film-makers will be able to strike it lucky on this basis alone. The case of direct-to-torrent releases is worth noting here. In recent years, a number of film-makers have experimented with releasing their movies on Bit Torrent, either in tandem with a conventional release window or as their sole distribution strategy. Some of these have done relatively well this way. One example is the Australian horror film *The Tunnel* (2011), which premiered on pay-TV and then was made available for free on Bit Torrent. Its pay-TV deal mitigated the risk of taking a punt on free distribution, and its strong genre identity and target market aligned well with torrent users. Other straight-to-torrent movies with very clearly defined audiences can also benefit from pirate publicity alone (witness the theological sci-fi title *The Man From Earth* [2007], a modest torrent hit). However, there are very few examples of films that break out from the extreme long tail and due to pirate promotion alone. As noted previously, pirate promotion generally needs to be combined with some other kind of release platform and publicity engine.

This reveals a gap between the discourse around the purported democracy of P2P platforms and the reality of film promotion. Most media texts that try a torrent-first distribution model remain stuck in the far reaches of the long tail forever (illustrated clearly by the content in The Pirate Bay's PromoBay section – a strange mix of B-grade music videos and short films). These various examples suggest that the marketing potential of pirate circulation is real, but severely constrained by external factors. Pirate promotion can augment a traditional marketing campaign, but it cannot substitute for it.

Reading across these examples, we could conclude that genre appears to be a crucial factor in determining what kinds of films may achieve widespread buzz due to pirate promotion. Generally speaking, genre films (especially sci-fi, teen and horror) are at an advantage because they have a pre-existing audience base that is prone to over-invest time and money in their consumption, and may be happy to go and see the same film several times, or buy the same film in multiple formats, even after viewing the downloaded copy. In the case of horror and exploitation cinemas, there is also a degree of cultural capital to be attained by the notion of difficult to attain or even forbidden texts. It is, therefore, more likely that obvious disparities between the level of 'legal' and 'pirate' publicity and circulation will be visible in genre-film markets compared to other markets.

The Value Question

The final issue to consider when analysing the piracy/promotion relationship is the question of value. What constitutes value for different film-makers? What kind of reception do film-makers want for their movies – and where does piracy fit into this picture? On this count, as with everything else discussed in this chapter, there is a great deal of variation from case to case.

All cultural production has an economic dimension, and all producers want to reach some kind of an audience, even if it is a very small one. But value is not always commensurate with revenues. Intangible values like prestige, adoration and social capital can matter just as much to some film-makers as revenues do, and this is also sometimes the case for film producers. Economic value is coexistent with other kinds of value: symbolic, social and reputational. Cultural producers are diversely motivated individuals.

The sociology of culture offers a vast field of literature that explores this issue, but for a pithy formulation we could turn instead to the independent film consultant Jon Reiss (2011), the author of numerous books on indie distribution and marketing.[17] Reiss offers the following typology of film-makers' motivations:

1. Fortune (money)
2. Audience
3. Traditional career launch (get your next film made in the studio or indie financing model)
4. Change the world
5. New goal: a long-term connection with a sustainable fan base.

This list gives us a sense of the motivational differences among film-makers. What I want to foreground here is that piracy, and the promotion that may or may not come with it, can mean a variety of things depending on what you value as a film-maker. Revenue-motivated film-makers are understandably wary of piracy. In contrast, reputationally motivated film-makers – especially first-time film-makers for whom the first feature often functions as a loss-leader calling card, opening up the way to the second – are keen for any kind of exposure, and may see piracy as a means to an end. Industry stakeholders, such as funding bodies and national institutions, also have different value systems. National funding bodies that view cinema as a kind of cultural diplomacy for the nation/region will likely take a different view of pirate promotion from a production company that wants only to make its money back.

Note the fifth of Reiss's categories – a long-term connection with a sustainable fan base. This is a way of thinking about the audience that is increasingly widespread, especially among indie film-makers, reflecting the take-up of branding discourse throughout film marketing. Piracy has an ambivalent, but potentially positive character in this paradigm, precisely because the emphasis is on growing audiences and building a brand first, and generating revenues later. Hence, we should not necessarily assume that indie film-makers seeking to build 'brandpower' will have the same attitudes to piracy as big-name studio directors. Conversely, we should not necessarily assume that indie producers always think their films will do well in the pirate economy jackpot or that they are any less invested in intellectual property protection than more established directors.[18]

Different industry structures, conditions and discourses produce different understandings of value for the people in those industries. This helps to explain film-makers' variable attitudes to piracy. If content is king, then protection is paramount. But if the brand is king, then protection assumes secondary importance to circulation. The 'meaning' of piracy shifts in each case, depending on where different film-makers and film institutions are positioned on this merry-go-round of value claims.

This brings us back to our initial point. To understand piracy in any meaningful way, it is advisable to stop thinking about it as a coherent 'thing', or a fixed type of consumer behaviour, and instead view it as a bundle of functions and effects that manifest differently across time and space. To the extent that we can even speak of them, piracy's effects are variable and context-dependent.

At the same time, there are patterns to be seen amid this chaos. This chapter has examined a few of these patterns, focusing on common interactions between pirate distribution, promotion, text, genre, market and audience that can be seen in current film culture. As argued, the key to a meaningful analysis of the piracy/promotion relationship is to disaggregate the functions and effects of piracy so that we can understand its dynamics at a more granular level. There is much more work to be done, but such a path is likely to lead to a better understanding of the issues facing today's film-makers, distributors and audiences, and also – potentially – towards a more sophisticated copyright debate than the one we currently have.

Acknowledgment
Many thanks to Alexandra Heller-Nicholas for her invaluable contributions to this chapter.

Notes
1. For up-to-date reviews, see: Joel Waldfogel, 'Copyright Research in the Digital Age: Moving from Piracy to the Supply of New Products', *American Economic Review* vol. 102 no. 3, 2012, pp. 337–42; Paul Belleflamme and Martin Peitz, 'Digital Piracy: Theory', in *Oxford Handbook of the Digital Economy* (Oxford: Oxford University Press, 2012), pp. 489–530; Michael D. Smith and Rahul Telang, 'Assessing the Academic Literature Regarding the Impact of Media Piracy on Sales', *Social Science Research Network*, 19 August 2012, http://ssrn.com/abstract=2132153
2. Michael D. Smith and Rahul Telang, 'Piracy or Promotion? The Impact of Broadband Internet Penetration on DVD Sales', *Information Economics and Policy* vol. 22 no. 4, 2010, pp. 289–98.
3. Joel Waldfogel, '*Lost* on the Web: Does Web Distribution Stimulate or Depress Television Viewing?', *Information Economics & Policy* vol. 21 no. 2, 2009, pp. 158–68.
4. Karen Croxson, 'Promotional Piracy', *Oxonomics* vol. 2 no. 1–2, 2007, p. 14.
5. Henry Jenkins, *Convergence Culture: Where Old and New Media Collide* (New York: New York University Press, 2006).
6. Ramon Lobato and Julian Thomas, *The Informal Media Economy* (Cambridge: Polity, 2015).
7. Jonathan Gray, 'Mobility Through Piracy, or How Steven Seagal Got to Malawi', *Popular Communication* vol. 9 no. 2, 2011, pp. 99–113.
8. Barbara Klinger, 'Contraband Cinema: Piracy, Titanic, and Central Asia', *Cinema Journal* vol. 49 no. 2, 2010, pp. 106–24.
9. Toby Miller, Nitin Govil, John McMurria and Richard Maxwell, *Global Hollywood* (London: BFI, 2001), p. 116.

10. Manas Ray, 'Bollywood Down Under: Fiji–Indian Cultural History and Popular Assertion', in S. Cunningham and J. Sinclair (eds), *Floating Lives: The Media and Asian Diasporas* (St Lucia: University of Queensland Press, 2000), pp. 136–79; Adrian Athique, 'The Global Dynamics of Indian Media Piracy: Export Markets, Playback Media and the Informal Economy', *Media, Culture and Society* vol. 30 no. 5, 2008, pp. 699–717.

11. Henry Jenkins, Sam Ford and Joshua Green, *Spreadable Media: Creating Value and Meaning in a Networked Culture* (New York: New York University Press, 2013).

12. Nestor Garcia Canclini, 'Latin American Cinema as Industry and as Culture: Its Trasnational Relocation', keynote speech presented at the Transnational Cinema in Globalising Societies Conference, Puebla, Mexico, 30 September 2008.

13. Ekky Imanjaya, 'The Other Side of Indonesia: New Order's Indonesian Exploitation Cinema as Cult Films', *Colloquy* vol. 18, 2009, pp. 143–59; Jasmine Nadua Trice, 'The Quiapo Cinémathèque: Transnational DVDs and Alternative Modernities in the Heart of Manila', *International Journal of Cultural Studies* vol. 13 no. 5, 2010, pp. 531–50.

14. Abigail de Kosnik, 'The Long Life of Art and Exploitation Distribution: A Case Study of a Private Torrent Tracker', paper at Society for Cinema and Media Studies conference, Seattle, 19-23 March 2014.

15. The most-downloaded list is published each year in December on the TorrentFreak website. For the 2012 list, see Ernesto, 'Project X Most Pirated Movie of the Year', *TorrentFreak*, 27 December 2012, https://torrentfreak.com/project-x-most-pirated-movie-of-2012-121227/

16. Robbie Collin, review of 'Project X', *The Telegraph*, 1 March 2012, www.telegraph.co.uk/culture/film/filmreviews/9116418/Project-X-review.html

17. Jon Reiss, 'A New Path to Engage Film Audiences and Create Careers: An Introduction', in Jon Reiss and Sherri Chandler (eds), *Selling Your Film Without Selling Your Soul: Case Studies in Hybrid, DIY and P2P Independent Distribution* (Los Angeles: The Film Collaborative, 2011). For sociological treatments, see: Pierre Bourdieu, *The Field of Cultural Production* (New York: Columbia University Press, 1993); David Hesmondhalgh, *The Cultural Industries* (New York: Sage, 2002); David Hesmondhalgh and Sarah Baker, *Creative Labour: Media Work in Three Cultural Industries* (Abingdon: Routledge, 2011).

18. As suggested recently by a popular manifesto from director Ti West: 'Why Piracy Hurts Indie Film (and It's Not All About The Money)', *Indiewire*, 6 May 2014, www.indiewire.com/article/ti-west-on-why-piracy-hurts-indie-film

Marketing *Bait* (2012)

Using SMART Data to Identify *e-guanxi* Among China's 'Internet Aborigines'

Brian YECIES, Jie YANG, Matthew BERRYMAN and Kai SOH

The emergent field of digital humanities is an interdisciplinary arena for studying the evolution of the arts and humanities in an increasingly interconnected and globalised world. Collecting, analysing and visualising big data are driving this area forward – particularly for collaborative teams of film and media studies scholars and IT experts seeking to understand the dynamic role that social networks are playing in the mediasphere. For online and mobile video-on-demand (VoD) giants such as Sohu, Youku, Sina Video, Tencent Video and LeTV, 'big data' – including sentiment analysis, generated from millions of user interactions and transactions – informs daily (and sometimes hourly) decisions about the production, distribution and exhibition of media and associated promotional advertising content. Amid this ocean of data, which extends far beyond conspicuous user ratings, electronic word-of-mouth (e-WOM) communication plays a crucial role because of its power to influence followers and their social networks – in similar ways that *guanxi* or the personal networks of influence that pervade Chinese society function in the real world.

The Douban (www.douban.com) social networking service (SNS) is a well-known Chinese-language website that offers cinema fans across China a major space for building what we term '*e-guanxi*' through the sharing and evaluation of information and opinions about films released in cinemas – as well as accessed on VoD platforms, purchased in illegal DVD shops, or downloaded illegally via peer file-sharing platforms. Yet, despite Douban's popularity among China's 'internet aborigines' – a label that describes mainstream cinemagoers and fans in their twenties who spend a large proportion of their waking hours using online and mobile internet and Web 2.0 applications – there has been little research on the potential social benefits and commercial applications of Chinese-language e-WOM as a tool for developing and utilising *e-guanxi* in the world of film fandom and marketing.[1] For scholars seeking to open up conversations in the digital humanities, as well as audiovisual and digital content industry firms and practitioners interested in the Chinese market, this situation presents an opportunity for gaining deeper insights into the world's largest media audience as we move into the 'Asian Century'.[2]

Fishing for *e-guanxi*

In this chapter, we present a case study of e-WOM promotion of the action-disaster-horror-thriller film *Bait* (2012) to understand how geographically dispersed Chinese-speaking fans – representatives of the largest media audience in the world – are using Douban to effectively expand the online cultures of social and commercial film promotion. To achieve this aim, and to discover information that goes beyond simple browsing of the Douban database, we undertook the beginning stages of sentiment analysis of all 4,348 valid user comments regarding *Bait*.[3] That is, we conducted word segmentation and dependency analysis on this dataset in order to track the transformative stages undergone by e-WOM in relation to this film. Sentiment analysis (aka opinion mining) uses a combination of machine (system) learning and cloud computing data analysis tools for collecting and distinguishing opinions and attitudes from a source. The basic stages of sentiment analysis include: harvesting data, analysing data and visualising data. Our dataset for this study comprised comments that users posted on the *Bait* topic page (the comments were also stored elsewhere on the individual user's profile page). With each new posting, the searchable library of user-generated content expands, enabling other users (followers) to also leave additional comments. Our aim was to investigate the local reception of a particular foreign film that contains inserted 'China-specific content' – an increasingly common strategy in the case of Hollywood blockbusters destined for Chinese audiences.

Bait is the first official Australian–Singapore co-production. It was shot in 3D, and exhibited in both 2D and 3D on cinema screens in twenty-eight countries between September 2012 and August 2013. The film's Chinese distributors, Yunnan Film Group and Enlight Media, produced a special localised version for the Chinese market, which the first author saw in October 2012 in one of Beijing's numerous multiplex cinemas. We hope that our preliminary development of a novel content-harvesting tool for collecting and analysing quantitative and qualitative data relating to film audiences, and our investigations into the make-up of *e-guanxi*, will offer a template to supplement traditional film marketing and cinema studies research methods.

Bait presents a group of people trapped in a supermarket after a tsunami has devastated a small beach town in Queensland, Australia. A ravenous great white shark stalks the survivors in the supermarket's flooded aisles and underground parking garage. The film was shot on location in Queensland, Coolangatta on the Gold Coast, Surfers Paradise and Warner Roadshow Studios, which over the last twenty years or so have been responsible for hundreds of highly successful international television series and film productions (primarily in the US market). Director Kimble Rendall and a small army of screenwriters including Shayne Armstrong, Shane Krause, John Kim and Russell Mulachy, as well as most of the cast (including Xavier Samuel, Sharni Vinson, Phoebe Tonkin, Julian McMahon, Cariba Heine, Alex Russell, Lincoln Lewis and Dan Wyllie) are all Australians. The cast also included Singaporean actors Adrian Pang and Qi Yuwu, the latter of whom is a Chinese actor based in Singapore.[4] In the international version made for Australia, Singapore and most other countries except China, the dialogue fondly mentions 'Singapore' several times, while the version made for the Chinese market replaces these references with 'Beijing'. The Chinese version also includes an extra two and a half minutes featuring a trendy nightclub in Beijing's Sanlitun district and starring famous Chinese actor Ashton Chen (aka Shi Xiaolong).[5]

We have focused on *Bait* not only because it is the first official co-production between Australia and Singapore, but also because it earned a total of A$27 million in China, reportedly recouping a major share (around 85 per cent) of its total production budget in this single market. Opening on 12 October 2012, *Bait* played in 3D on more than 1,700 screens in China for a thirty-one-day period.[6] At the time, *Bait* had relatively little competition from other local and foreign films released in cinemas.[7] Needless to say, its performance in China unleashed a tidal wave of excitement throughout the Australian film industry, garnering headlines such as: 'Shark Flick Boost to Aussie Film Industry', 'China Eats Up Bait 3D', 'Sinking Our Teeth into China' and 'Great White Makes Waves in Chinese Cinemas' – a euphoric response to the possibility of breaking into the massive and highly lucrative Chinese market.[8]

Since its inception in early 2005 – only a month after YouTube was launched in the USA – Douban has become one of China's biggest online social library systems and platforms for facilitating user-generated interactions and reviews of creative and cultural contents – films, television programmes, books, music and radio programmes, as well as cultural events in selected Chinese cities and other international centres. Both registered and unregistered users can use the tools on this hybridised Amazon-IMDb-Myspace-Facebook Web 2.0 SNS site to create and share a library of personal details, search for information and to make recommendations to their followers as well as casual readers. The result is the generation of vast quantities of participatory and collaborative e-WOM, not to mention increasing users' motivation to engage with the media being discussed. According to the Douban website, Douban attracts more than 100 million unique visitors each month and has amassed over 65 million registered users. It is currently accessed by over 30 per cent of Chinese internet users, making the site a major magnet for the new waves of film marketing experienced by film fans across China.

Like Twitter, Douban is known as a 'follower network', meaning that users can share information and spread messages and ratings of media texts among geographically dispersed followers and/or follow others.[9] Depending on the level of trust among followers, members' user-generated reviews – or what is generally known as e-WOM – enables users to judge the quality and rating of particular media or products. However, at face value, the rating system used by Chinese film fans, at least on the Douban site, appears to be less efficacious as a measure of audience approval than ratings used on English-language sites by western film fans – for example, on IMDb or Metacritic. Chinese users on Douban – that is, members of a 'collectivist society' – have been observed showing increased alignment with their fellow netizens in terms of film ratings. In other words, they value group harmony over the expression of individual opinions that are extremely different from the group.[10] As a result, we may ask what are some of the other ways of measuring or gauging audience opinions of a film? And, how is it possible to automate this analytical process? As discussed below, several innovative methods have been developed to calculate users' opinions of films on Douban, approaches that reveal some of the nuances inherent in film marketing and promotion via WOM across social networks.

As a concept, WOM is considered by industry professionals and theorists alike as a powerful communication tool and social networking channel for spreading awareness of a product or service in both offline and online worlds. WOM appears most efficacious when consumers actively create and/or distribute information about or recommendations of products or services to other consumers.[11] This process creates a sense of grassroots legitimacy because the message is – ostensibly, at least – initiated by a member of one's own peer or interest group rather than by the manufacturer of the product or service. With the proliferation of the internet and mobile media, marketers have increasingly used e-WOM as a key strategic tool to develop and strengthen trust between consumers and products, brands and services. Simultaneously, via online platforms and mobile applications social media networks have radically changed the ways in which information is shared and spread beyond traditional offline WOM – that is, face-to-face conversations.[12] This tool has also given rise to the creation of new communities that make play of their power to motivate the decisions and actions of members who actively seek and accept advice online.[13]

Today, e-WOM is a critical factor in a film's commercial success. A sentiment analysis of comments made on forty films on a Yahoo Movies message board reveals that WOM is most active during the pre-release period and the opening week of a film.[14] While somewhat predictable, it is known that the power of WOM can fade quickly.[15] This is precisely why distributors have long attempted to release domestic and international films at strategic times, while also using WOM as an important marketing tool to create awareness and 'buzz' around a film during the pre-release phase and its opening weekend.[16] Used as a stand-alone prediction tool, WOM has been shown to accurately gauge box-office statistics during a film's opening week and offer a rough estimate of its period of popularity among audiences, but is not a good predictor of box-office revenues after the opening week. While previous studies show that high production values, critical response and 'star power' often do no more than create public awareness of a new release, our study shows that, in China, star power also creates a sense of expectation or 'buzz' around a film. For example, most of the Chinese news reports for *Bait* focused on the actor Ashton Chen rather than on the film itself. Of all the personal names mentioned in the dataset, Chen's name appears most frequently – with a majority of users citing him as the primary reason for watching the film.

With these and other factors in mind, the value of using data quarried from Douban to achieve a better quantitative and qualitative understanding of Chinese audience tastes becomes apparent. This approach can, in turn, inform strategies not only for producing and promoting films featuring particular actors, plot elements and locations, etc., but also for modifying or localising stories for specific markets, regions and target audiences. Documenting online follower/following relationships and the circumstances that create their vectors of influence – what we might call *e-guanxi* – is an ambitious undertaking. It involves the collection (or harvesting) of big data – that is, massive amounts of data created by users over time and over a wide geographical catchment – so big that it requires machine (system) learning and cloud computing data analysis tools for processing. The first step towards identifying and understanding *e-guanxi* is to undertake sentiment analyses among a core group of users and branch out from there – that is, to collect and analyse data harvested from a single cohort and then expand the investigation to include other films on which this group has commented, then track others who are following them and so on. We are using *Bait* as our starting point in this process.

The SMART Data Analysis Platform

To strengthen the connections between cinema studies and the field of film marketing more specifically with digital humanities, this pilot project utilises the expertise of a team of IT specialists from the SMART Infrastructure Facility at the University of Wollongong, a national centre for infrastructure solutions. SMART stands for 'Simulation, Modelling, Analysis, Research and Teaching'. Specifically, we employ a range of machine learning algorithms and cloud computing techniques for data analysis, as well as the translation of conceptual models into implementation programs and code prototyping. In plain English, the SMART team employs advanced IT skills to develop a novel and more efficient technique for investigating big data connected to audience analysis than those available to researchers using traditional qualitative and quantitative survey and analysis instruments. While the Douban dataset for *Bait* is not exactly 'big data', the complex systems modelling and analysis techniques employed in this exploratory study constitute a working prototype for analysing films and case studies involving much larger volumes, variety and velocities typically associated with sources of big data.

With this in mind, we have developed a general platform for social media data processing, which we have termed 'SmartLearning'. The platform consists of three components:

1. Harvesting, which collects the data from various sources and saves them to a database;
2. Analytics, which supports the processing or modification of existing data using sophisticated algorithms such as:

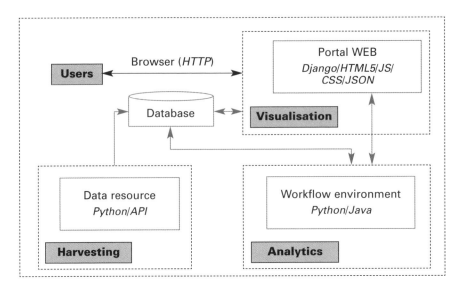

Figure 1: Flowchart of the data-processing platform (SmartLearning)

a. supervised/unsupervised machine learning techniques to assist with classification, clustering and prediction;
b. natural language processing techniques to assist with sentiment analysis.[17]
3. Visualisation, which enables interactivity with the data using the graphic user interface.

The next step is to apply the SmartLearning platform to Douban for data collection, analysis and visualisation. To make the various types of data considered in this study compatible with each other, the following data structure has been employed (see Figure 2).

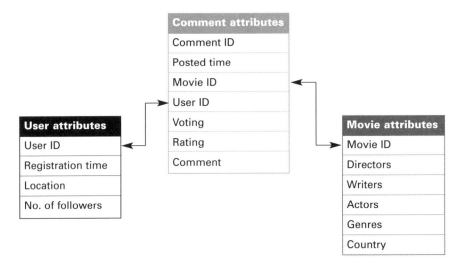

Figure 2: Data structure for analysing users, comments and films discussed on Douban

In our study, we identified three categories of data to be considered: user, comment and movie. The user ID is the key attribute used to link one user to a specific comment, while the movie ID is used for identifying the particular film to which the comment applies. Note that for each film considered, a given user can leave only a single comment. This is because the website retains a user's most recent comment while removing previous comments by the same user.

Analysis of Results: Timing, Location and Opinion Mean Everything

A majority of the users studied (3,012) posted their comments in October 2012, the time of the near-simultaneous release date of *Bait* on 1,700 screens across China. At this time, the total number of screens in Australia was 1,997, compared to a total of 13,118 in China – a figure that has since risen to about 25,000.[18] After one month – corresponding to the end of the film's cinema run in China – the number of comments had fallen to 519, a significant drop in the e-WOM surrounding the film's release. Hence, the primary period of interest for this study was the one-month period between 13 September 2012 – the first appearance of *Bait* on P2P file-sharing networks – and 14 November – marking the release of *Bait* on commercial DVD, just three days after its thirty-one-day cinema run in China.[19]

In our study, authors of comments were identifiable at the provincial level, including the municipalities of Beijing, Tianjin, Shanghai and Chongqing (treated as provinces). Unsurprisingly, most users were located in developed cities and provinces such as Beijing, Shanghai, Guangdong, Jiangsu, Zhejiang, Hubei, Hunan, Fujian, Chongqing, Sichuan and Shandong (all results scaled for total Douban population). Generally speaking, in these centres the user experience is enhanced by greater access to faster internet speeds and more advanced public infrastructure for mobile telephony. Thus, the data illustrates increased participation from a greater number of users from these areas. More significantly, when we examined the dataset we found key regional variants among comments made by registered users in each of these areas (see Figure 4 below). Users without a specific area indicated in their profile are labelled as 'empty' herein.

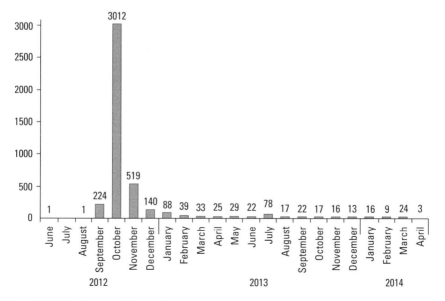

Figure 3: Number of comments by month

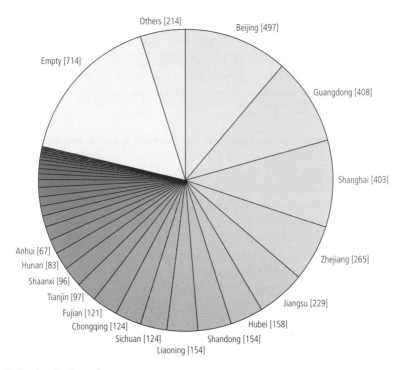

Figure 4: Geo-location from all users

To interpret the collected data – that is, to identify and extract subjective information from the source material and turn it into usable data – a two-stage framework was implemented to facilitate sentiment analysis: word segmentation and dependency analysis, or identifying the particular positive and negative terms linked to the key words being segmented.

First, the basic procedure for the word segmentation stage involved dividing complete sentences into smaller syntactical and semantic components. However, one of the major differences between English- and Chinese-based language processing is the way in which such segments are indicated. For instance, while in English a space is usually used to separate words, Chinese has a significantly different structure in which word division is either non-existent or works in different ways. Thus, any procedure adopted for segmenting Chinese words must consider the specific language habits of Chinese users. A primary 'dictionary' was required to perform this function, and devising such a tool was one of the most challenging aspects of the methodology we adopted.

In addition, for our study we introduced five sub-dictionaries for *Bait*: actor (including actress), director, main character, location and story (see Table 1), each designed to elicit information about a particular aspect of the movie. As a result, word segmentation was carried out on the basis of these five sub-dictionaries in addition to the primary dictionary. Not only was each dictionary used for word segmentation, but they also functioned as sorting mechanisms through which to identify and categorise various user opinions. In adopting this approach, our analysis of the dataset constitutes a major advance on previous studies, which rely either on data available in English-language sources (which present fewer problems than a Chinese-language dataset) or are restricted to a single, and thus limited, dictionary of Chinese terms.

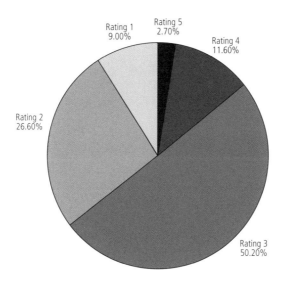

Figure 5: Distribution of ratings for each comment for *Bait*[20]

Table 1: Multiple sub-dictionaries used for word segmentation in *Bait*

Actor	英雄, hero, 女主角, 男主角, 男配角, 演员, 山姆, 沙妮, 泽维尔, 戚玉武, 玉武, 释小龙, 小龙
Director	导演, 金波•兰道
Main character	狗狗, 狗, 鲨鱼, 鱼, 大白鲨
Location	澳大利亚, 澳洲, 中国, 北京, 海滩, 酒吧, 新加坡, 海
Story	特效, 场景, 台词, 剧情, 逻辑, 3D, 故事, 质量, 节奏, 成本, 制作, 情节, 视觉

The above table illustrates our approach to the task of word segmentation and dependency grammar analysis. Figure 6, below, depicts how the dependency analysis was conducted. Each sentence is represented as a dependency tree, in which each tree node denotes a single language unit. The relationship between these units is represented by the dependency arcs that connect 'parent' with 'offspring' terms. As an example, the dependency tree used to analyse the user comment '故事讲得很清楚, 人物长的都不赖并且个性都很鲜明 ('well-told story, attractive people with strong personality traits') is shown in Figure 6. The words or phrases isolated within each box represent the word segmentation stage, while arrows represent dependencies of words towards each other.

Second, at the dependency analysis stage, our model revealed syntactical structures or hidden relationships among particular words (see Table 2 below). The dependency analysis process has enabled us to identify how individuals and aggregates of individuals describe a special term. In turn, we are able to mine the sentiment or opinions from the audience's comments. Given space limitations, we list the top ten keywords extracted from the dependency analysis and show the results in the following table.

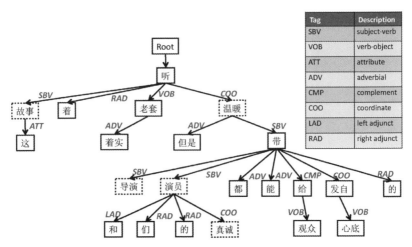

Tag	Description
SBV	subject-verb
VOB	verb-object
ATT	attribute
ADV	adverbial
CMP	complement
COO	coordinate
LAD	left adjunct
RAD	right adjunct

Figure 6: Dependency analysis for a single user comment

All of the keywords shown in Table 2 are used as the modifiers to describe items from the five sub-dictionaries. A few observations can be made. Audiences mention aspects of the story the most, while 'director' (and the name of the director, Kimble Rendall) is the least mentioned factor. There are 457 keywords used for discussions concerning the story (including special effects or production costs/budget), compared to only twenty of those for 'director'. The results reveal the appeal of these five factors in the following order: story, main characters, actor, location, followed, last, by director. Surprisingly, as seen in Table 3, audiences posted limited opinions about the primary locations featured in the film: Australia, Gold Coast, beach and Queensland. (Anecdotally, this contrasts to the number of times that 'Australia' was heard by the first author among general discussions on the streets of Beijing in October 2012, when *Bait 3D* was screening.) Unsurprisingly, the shark (one of the main characters) is more eye-catching to this cohort; comments abound regarding the 大 (big) shark, how it 游 (swims) around and 咬 (bites) and 吃 (eats) people. Others mentioned the shark in a different way, reflecting on its fake (假) appearance. At the same time, the results reflect the important presence of the 'actor', suggesting that the inclusion of Ashton Chen was a primary driver for watching this film.

Furthermore, among the keywords extracted in the dependency analysis there are more negative than positive or neutral terms. For instance, 小 (low/small) cost/budget is the most frequently mentioned keyword relating to the story. Although some positive words were detected, such as 不错 (not bad, which carries a more positive connotation in Chinese terms than 'not bad' in English), 惊悚 (scary), 刺激 (exciting), a majority considered the movie as 烂 (bad), 假 (fake), or 无聊 (boring). In terms of the actor, some neutral keywords are found, such as 看到 (see), 看 (see), 出现 (turn out), 找到 (find), 出来 (turn out), which occupy nearly 45.4 per cent of the results. Yet, one of the major points of contention for members of the Chinese audience was they were displeased about Ashton Chen's limited presence in the film and, by extension, unhappy about the misleading nature of *Bait*'s promotional trailers, which featured more of Chen than the international trailers.

As we hypothesised, our findings indicate that e-WOM related to *Bait* traversed the social network pathways (that is, follower/followee) created by registered users in particular ways that corresponded to the film's release history, as well as its appearance on P2P

Table 2: Dependency analysis for *Bait* (results categorised according to five sub-dictionaries)

	Actor	Director	Main character	Location	Story
	说好的 (where is) 42	拍 (cast) 9	吃 (eat) 72	合拍 (joint cast) 6	小 (low/small) 112
	看到 (see) 32	省钱 (saving money) 2	大 (big) 60	投资 (invest) 4	一般 (average) 78
	打酱油 (pointless) 29	可以 (fine) 2	好 (good) 36	好 (good) 4	不错 (not bad) 67
	看 (see) 20	不好意思 (sorry) 1	假 (fake) 31	耀眼 (shining) 2	简单 (simple) 47
	帅 (handsome) 20	不如 (worse) 1	小 (small) 23	老 (old) 2	低 (cheap/low) 37
	出现 (turn out) 18	不错 (good) 1	饱 (full) 12	小 (small) 2	烂 (bad) 36
	找到 (find) 12	仔细 (careful) 1	冲 (rush) 12	牵强 (farfetched) 2	假 (fake) 30
	不错 (good) 10	保守 (conservative) 1	可爱 (cute) 20	牺牲 (sacrifice) 2	无聊 (boring) 27
	出来 (turn out) 7	吓唬 (scare) 1	咬 (bite) 11	生活 (life) 2	惊悚 (scary) 12
	喜欢 (like) 6	仁慈 (mercy) 1	游 (swim) 11	跳舞 (dance) 2	刺激 (exciting) 11
Total	196	20	288	28	457

file-sharing networks and in local 'illegal' DVD shops. In other words, as Figure 3 illustrates, in this instance e-WOM built in intensity over time. The chronological pattern revealed by the e-WOM was consistent across the cities and provinces where users were located – a trend reflected in the various dictionaries used to analyse sentiment in the user comments.

Our preliminary findings confirm previous studies that show that, in Chinese SNS, users place more trust in the people they follow than is the case with Americans participating in US-based SNS. According to one recent study, the relationships that Chinese social media users maintain through e-WOM are more influential than those experienced by their counterparts in the USA.[21] To us, this reveals the trailhead leading to *e-guanxi*. Given this trend,

Table 3: Additional regional variants among comments made by registered users

	上海 Shanghai	北京 Beijing	四川 Sichuan	山东 Shandong	广东 Guangdong	江苏 Jiangsu	浙江 Zhejiang	湖北 Hubei	湖南 Hunan	福建 Fujian	重庆 Chongqing	TOTAL
					Province + number of times							
3D		17	8			8		6				39
中国 (China)	16	30	4	12	21	15			8	9	11	126
停车场 (car park)												0
剧情 (story)	36	38	10	7	38	21	29	17	8	10	15	229
劫匪 (robbers)												0
华人 (Chinese)												0
吓人 (scary)												0
垃圾 (rubbish)								7				7
大白鲨 (great white shark)	15	17		6		10		6		5	7	66
鲨鱼 (shark)	92	73	18	38	89	31	59	37	11	23	28	499
女主 (female lead)						8						8
释小龙 (Ashton Chen)	48	46	17	19	36	35	34	19	10	15	17	296
镜头 (lens)	20	18	4	8	19	12	10	5	6	5	7	114
酱油 (pointless)											9	9
美国 (America)												0
电影院 (cinema)	19	19		7	21	8	13	11	6	10		114
电影 (movie)	45	71	12	18	43	24	23	16	13	14	13	292
烂片 (bad film)	14		4		16		9		4	6		53
灾难 (disaster)									3			3
灾难片 (disaster film)	19	23		7		10						59
澳洲 (Australia)												0
海滩 (beach)												0
男主 (male lead)	20					9						29
Total per province	344	352	77	122	283	191	177	124	69	97	107	1943

and given how Douban users actively engage in e-WOM by offering, searching for and sharing opinions, it is no surprise that the Chinese bloggers we studied had a marked degree of influence on the opinions and attitudes of fellow cinema fans. We hope that our findings will expand industry understandings of how 'residual' (i.e. post-theatrical release) WOM functions to augment the key commercial vehicles – chiefly advertisements and promotional trailers (aka previews) in cinemas and traditional media channels – for promoting a given film and motivating audiences to access it on one platform or another. Our findings are relevant to Chinese and foreign film producers alike because at least one third of all internet users in China use some form of SNS, with nearly half this figure active on a daily basis.[22] Openness and sharing are among the salient characteristics of the SNS generation, and Douban – where 92.5 per cent of users are aged between eighteen and thirty-five – is a key online platform, offering users a space to broadcast their views to a potentially vast number of attentive listeners.[23] In 2014, among China's 'internet aborigines' e-WOM has become a critical element in the film marketing mix, creating a new and ever-changing synergy of the 'broadcasting power of the internet' and social media.[24]

In a major industry report published in 2013 by Screen Australia on collaborative projects with Asian partners, *Bait 3D* is mentioned several times as a successful co-production that exceeded expectations.[25] The report, which was produced by the Australian government's chief agency for strengthening innovation, cultural relevance and the commerciality of the Australian film industry, offers a promising new pathway for collaboration with Chinese film-makers and fresh opportunities to connect with audiences in China. Yet, while having much of value to offer, the report has nothing to say about *Bait*'s reception by Asian audiences, let alone how they view Australian films or international productions with additional Chinese content more generally. In a small way, we hope that our study has made a start towards addressing this gap.

Today, a plethora of open-access big data sources are enabling academic film studies researchers, as well as government funding bodies for national film industries, to outstrip conventional audience studies and augment the often secretive investigations carried out by the US Motion Picture Association (MPA) and film studio conglomerates on global film markets. Up until now, and partly because they are relatively easy to identify and code, box-office revenues and consumption patterns among a range of demographic groups have been the primary focus of such research. Before online social media sources such as Douban became available, film audience research was dominated by industry bodies such as the MPA, as well as international research organisations such as Nielsen or its smaller equivalent in Australia, Roy Morgan Research. Historically, a blend of commercial marketing and WOM has provided the chief source of motivation for audiences and their drive towards (or away from) specific films.[26] In the pre-social media era, audience opinion played a limited role in this process because of the challenges involved in categorising and analysing this type of data. Today, sentiment analysis is changing everything.

The approach employed by the present study offers film-makers and industry players an opportunity to discover the particular elements – whether or not they are inserted as China-specific content – that are drawing audiences towards (or away from) certain films. Accordingly, such data can be used to inform multiple strategies for producing *and* marketing certain films in certain places – to achieve an unprecedented level of localisation on all fronts.

There is no doubt that the contemporary global media industry has experienced a fundamental shift as a result of embracing new production, distribution and exhibition methods in the digital era. Within this dynamic arena, collaborative research teams such as that established at the University of Wollongong are pioneering advances in the digital human-ities by addressing a growing need for sentiment analysis solutions based on large amounts of user data. In turn, investigations such as ours are being used to reshape the ways in which public media products are produced. Identifying *e-guanxi* is no easy task, and this chapter only begins to scratch the surface of doing so. Yet, given the fundamental role and importance of *guanxi* in Chinese society, it is unsurprising that a parallel phenom-enon should exist in the online world. Sentiment analysis of film data among Douban users has value precisely because it reveals the opinions of the masses – here, the filmgoing demographic. We have barely scratched the surface of what can be learned about the cul-tural habits of young Chinese by analysing the quantitative and qualitative data generated by fans (registered users) on Douban.

In short, we hope that our findings will offer an alternative method of analysing e-WOM content among China's internet aborigines, while also demonstrating the potential for fur-ther development in this area. Our next step will be to drill deeper into the dataset in order to observe significant shifts in the timing of particular aspects addressed in each posting – insofar as they reflect either a positive or negative opinion (i.e. the polarity of the partic-ular 'sentiment' expressed). In so doing, we aim to demonstrate that Douban's registered film commentators possess a measurable degree of influence on those who follow them online, and what the interconnecting roles of sentiment, timing and location tell us about the transformation of e-WOM as a function of film marketing on social networks. With a model for identifying these trends established, and with the *Bait* dataset as a baseline, we can now compare and contrast our findings with the social media promotion of further popular and successful foreign films – defined in terms of total gross box-office revenues that have surpassed the $100 million milestone since 2011 – that have generated truly big data among Chinese film fans. Such films include: *Iron Man 3* (2013), *X-Men: Days of Future Past* (2014) and *Transformers 4: Age of Extinction* (2014), which each contained specific Chinese elements such as popular actors – for example, Fan Bingbing or Li Bingbing – and/or the insertion of 'local content' for the Chinese market. Over time and with the collection of bigger data, we hope to identify additional meaningful patterns in Chinese-language e-WOM traffic by utilising the natural language processing techniques outlined here.

Acknowledgment

This chapter draws on research currently being conducted in association with an Australian Research Council Discovery project, *Willing Collaborators: Negotiating Change in East Asian Media Production* DP 140101643.

Notes

1. The phrase 'internet aborigines' appeared in an interview with Zhang Zhao, CEO of Le Vision Pictures (the film production division of Leshi Internet Information and Technology Corp.) and co-producer of the box-office hit *Tiny Times 3.0* (2014). See Liu Wei, 8 May 2014, 'Film Company Utilizes Marketing Techniques', *China Daily*, www.chinadaily.com.cn/culture/2014-05/08/content_17493073.htm

2. Australian in the Asian Century Implementation Task Force, *Australia in the Asian Century: White Paper Canberra*, Commonwealth of Australia, 2012.

3. The total number of comments for *Bait* on Douban (as of 29 August 2014) was 4,788; however, 440 comments have been discounted as they were either generated by fake users or were deemed to be commercial or paid advertisements. Among the valid

comments, a further 425 were disregarded because their authors failed to give the film a rating, an essential variable in our analysis.

4. In making *Bait*, Australian companies Arclight Films, Pictures in Paradise and Story Bridge Films partnered with Singaporean companies Blackmagic Design and Widescreen Media, which produced the 3D technology and VFX and colour-grading/post-production services, respectively. Singaporeans Alex Oh and Joe Ng wrote the musical score.

5. At the time of writing, a YouTube video containing six minutes of deleted scenes focuses heavily on Chen, making him appear more of a central character in the localised version. He toasts to the Gold Coast with actress Sharni Vinson and her Chinese friends in the Sanlitun nightclub. In an action-adventure sequence involving Chen as part of a search and rescue team, he saves a mother and child from a burning building, surviving an explosion and then rappelling off a roof. Chen rides a motorcycle to meet his girlfriend and gives her a necklace in front of the blue Beijing (Olympics) National Aquatics Center (aka the Water Cube). Finally, after playing volleyball at the search and rescue team's base, Chen and colleagues are collected, debriefed and sent to Australia on an emergency tsunami rescue mission. Chen and his Chinese rescue team save two Chinese women trapped in the rubble caused by the disaster. See www.youtube.com/watch?v=-IJ6VDpd9cQ

6. Screen Australia, 'Media Release 2012: Bait 3D Opens Number One at the Chinese Box Office', Screen Australia, 16 October 2012, http://www.screenaustralia.gov.au/news_and_events/2012/mr_121016_Bait3D.aspx; mUmBRELLA, 'Bait 3D makes $20m at Chinese Box Office', 26 October 2012, http://mumbrella.com.au/bait-3d-makes-20m-at-chinese-box-office-123125

7. For the week between 29 October and 4 November, the other films to make the top ten box office in China were (in ranking order): *The Bourne Legacy* (2012, USA); *Tai Chi Hero* (2012, China, aka *Tai Chi 2*), *Total Recall* (2012), *Derrière les murs* (2011, France, aka *Behind the Walls 3D*); *Haunting Love* (2012, China), *The Twilight Saga: Breaking Dawn – Part 1* (2011, USA); *The Tree in the Rain* (2012, China); *Taken 2* (2012, France); and *All for Love* (2012, China). See 'Mainland Box Office Chart for Week 44, 2012 – Chinese Films', www.chinesefilms.cn/141/2012/11/09/122s12839.htm

8. Screen staff, 'China Box Office Monthly Round-up: Bait 3D Makes Surprise Attack', *Screen Daily*, 12 November 2012, www.screendaily.com/china-box-office-monthly-round-up-bait-3d-makes-surprise-attack/5048999.article; J. Pearlman, 'Shark Flick Boost to Aussie Film Industry', *Straits Times*, 6 March 2011; Anon, 'China Eats Up Bait 3D', *The Gold Coast Bulletin*, 17 October 2012.

9. J. Zhao, J. Lui, Don Towsley, X. Guan and Y. Zhou, 'Empirical Analysis of the Evolution of Follower Network: A Case Study on Douban', *IEEE INFOCOM WKSHPS*, 2011, pp. 924–9.

10. N. S. Koh, N. Hu and E. K. Clemons, 'Do Online Reviews Reflect a Product's True Perceived Quality? An Investigation of Online Movie Reviews Across Culture', *Electronic Commerce Research and Applications* vol. 9 no. 5, 2010, p. 374.

11. See A. J. Kimmeland and P. J. Kitchen, 'Word of Mouth and Social Media', *Journal of Marketing Communications* vol. 20 no. 1–2, 2014, pp. 2–4; and E. Keller, 'Unleashing the Power of Word of Mouth: Creating Brand Advocacy to Drive Growth', *Journal of Advertising* vol. 47 no. 4, 2007, pp. 448–52.

12. M. Laroche, Z.Yang, G. H. G. McDougall and I. Bergon, 'Internet versus Bricks-and-mortar Retailers: An Investigation into Intangibility and its Consequences', *Journal of Retailing* vol. 81 no. 4, 2005, pp. 251–67.

13. A. Toder-Alon, F. F. Brunel and S. Fournier, 'Word-of-mouth Rhetorics In Social Media Talk', *Journal of Marketing Communications* vol. 20 no. 1–2, 2014, pp. 42–64.

14. Y. Liu, 'Word of Mouth for Movies: Its Dynamics and Impacts on Box Office Revenue', *Journal of Marketing* vol. 70 no. 3, 2006, pp. 74–89.

15. H. Roschk and S. Großе, 'Talk About Films: Word-of-mouth Behaviour and the Network of Success Determinants of Motion Pictures', *Journal of Promotion Management* vol. 19 no. 3, 2013, pp. 229–16.

16. A. Elberse and J. Eliashberg, 'Demand and Supply Dynamics for Sequentially Released Products in International Markets: The Case of Motion Pictures', *Marketing Science* vol. 22 no. 3, 2003, pp. 329–54.

17. Natural language processing is commonly associated with algorithms today. It involves the training and ability of a computer and/or an application to process and understand human language – a process by which evaluations and predictions can be made.

18. See Stephen Cremin, 'Peter Loehr on the China Opportunity', *Film Business Asia*, 15 September 2014, www.filmbiz.asia/news/peter-loehr-on-the-china-opportunity; Cinema, 'Audiovisual Markets: Research', Screen Australia, 2014, http://www.screenaustralia.gov.au/research/statistics/cinemahistoryoverview.aspx; and Statista, 'Number of Cinema Screens in China from 2007 to 2013', Statista: The Statistic Portal, 2014, www.statista.com/statistics/279111/number-of-cinema-screens-in-china/

19. Other key dates for *Bait* included: 5 September (first cinema screenings, which took place in Italy); 9 September (released in USA); 20 September (released in Australia and Malaysia); 27 September (released in Russia, and also appearance of *Bait* in 'illegal' DVD shops in China); and 25 October (released in Singapore).

20. From data collected up until 1 March 2014. This pie chart shows the distribution of ratings for each comment for *Bait*. The total number of valid ratings surveyed is 3,923, among which 50.2 per cent rated the movie at 3 out of 5. The average rating is 2.401.

21. S. C. Chu and S. M. Choi, 'Electronic Word-of-mouth in Social Networking Sites: A Cross-cultural Study of United States and China', *Journal of Global Marketing* vol. 24 no. 3, 2011, pp. 263–81.

22. CCNIC, 'Statistic Report on Internet Development in China' (Beijing: CCCNIC, 2014).

23. See L. Yu, S. Asur and B. A. Huberman, 'What Trends in Chinese Social Media', arXiv.org – Cornell University Library no. 1107.3522 (2011), p. 1; and H. Bakhshi and P. Schneider, 'Found in Translation: Understanding Chinese Demand for British Content', Nesta, 1 August 2013, www.nesta.org.uk/blog/found-translation-understanding-chinese-demand-british-content

24. See 'Beyond the Box Office: Understanding Audiences in a Multi-screen World', Screen Australia, 2011, viewed 13 May 2014, www.screenaustralia.gov.au/research/beyond_box_office.aspx

25. Screen Australia, *Common Ground: Opportunities for Australian Screen Partnership in Asia* (Canberra: Screen Australia, 2013).

26. Film Victoria, *Australian Feature Films, Fictional Television and Documentaries: The Results from our Roy Morgan Research* (Melbourne: Film Victoria Australia, 2010).

From Marketing to Performing the Market

The Emerging Role of Digital Data in the Independent Film Business

Michael FRANKLIN, Dimitrinka STOYANOVA RUSSELL and Barbara TOWNLEY

The global film industry has been radically disrupted by digital technology.[1] This research deals with the impacts of disruption in the non-studio, or independent film industry in the UK. Accounting for inflation, between 2002 and 2012 film revenues from physical formats fell by £908 million in the UK,[2] a decrease widely attributed to piracy and new consumption patterns of digital entertainment. In the same period video on demand (VoD) revenues increased only £164 million, while an average of twelve new feature films were released theatrically every week.[3] In response to increasing financial pressure on films to find their audience, innovative producers are leveraging digital marketing and distribution technologies to develop new ways of creating market awareness and delivering films. Electronic home video, including VoD, is projected to become the main contributor to global filmed entertainment revenue by 2017.[4] One implication is the move by film producers to capitalise more directly on international rights exploitation in some territories by circumventing traditional intermediaries via direct distribution services. Documentaries are at the forefront of this change because of two general characteristics. Compared to fiction films, documentaries tend to have lower budgets and, therefore, fewer ties to market financiers and affiliated historical distribution arrangements. Documentaries also enjoy more easily defined and located initial audiences to target due to their specific subject matter.

Digital marketing and distribution technologies, together labelled engagement tools, change the way the market is made for individual films. For example, producers are able to use spreadable[5] film trailers throughout a film's life cycle to develop interest, capture data and exploit intellectual property rights internationally. The generation of public awareness and conversion of such attention into practical support such as crowd distribution and, eventually, revenues is predicated on the use of social media measures and consumption data including 'Likes'[6], 'Shares'[7] and 'Views'.[8] These can be conceptualised together as digital engagement metrics (DEMs) by looking at the agency they exhibit in coordinating activity. Such figures, also called social media 'buzz' or online word of mouth (e-WOM), are presented both in public and in generally unseen or 'black-boxed' private network arrangements for evaluation and mediation. This chapter shows they can be considered 'performative utterances' that take an active role in shaping the market.[9]

Drawing on participant observation of film marketing campaigns over an extended period, 2011–14,[10] this research traces two feature documentaries to provide insight into emergent, co-constitutive technological, economic and organisational developments in film marketing. Specifically, the chapter provides original empirical evidence of how new tools function as 'socially distributed points of sale', building network relationships between market actors such as companies and audiences. We interpret the conjoined marketing and distribution initiatives as transformations in the performance of market making.

Literature Review: Market Devices and Digital Engagement Data in Film

The film industry has been studied from a variety of perspectives. The inherently quantitative format of digital data makes positivistic interrogations a popular approach for those investigating DEMs and film. Studies have quantified the predictive power on box office of aggregated blog references,[11] Wikipedia editing,[12] Tweet rates[13] and spread of quality-related Tweets.[14] Such e-WOM activity involves feedback effects[15] and research has determined that a large social multiplier exists.[16] This literature is helpful in understanding the overarching connections between some digital engagements and financial returns. However, such approaches do not capture how such information is interpreted, formatted and applied within the industry. Therefore, the agency of such metrics in reshaping and partially performing the market is under-appreciated.

It is useful to adopt a complementary account, and theorise the materials, role and effect of networks, agencies and processes at work as a social construction. This approach is connected to the literature of market devices[17] that builds on multifaceted notions of market making.[18] Recent marketing studies shed light on the importance of performativity, representation, calculation and materiality.[19] Drawing on concepts from Actor Network Theory (ANT), economic sociology and social studies of finance, the combined role of market tools and ideas as enacted in marketing operations has come to the fore. This scholarship calls for sensitivity to 'the hybrid combinations of devices, individuals and organisations that potentially partake in marketing', also collectively called an 'assemblage'.[20] An important process these elements are taken to co-produce is performativity. This term describes the way ideas about markets (theories and models) and marketing tools combine to shape markets they describe.[21] Performativity and representation go hand in hand, and often rely on specific materialities to bridge or translate practices appearing as ideas and images into individual market exchanges.[22] For example, in social studies of finance, MacKenzie explores calculative formulae sheets as schedules for action and a prescriptive model to be enacted, or putting in motion the world they describe.[23]

Social media data are noted to have performative characteristics – 'they can generate user affects, enact more activities and thus multiply themselves' – and rely on a 'medium-specific infrastructure' that simultaneously measures action as well.[24] The editable, interactive and distributed characteristics of digital objects mean they can be rearranged and disseminated.[25] The mass sharing of traceable digital objects produces metrics that enable quantified management processes in market construction. As multifaceted rankings, marketing metrics are not passive, but constitutive of the world, influencing the organisation of actors within the domain they create.[26] In the literature on creative industries, Baym[27] explores the unseen, evaluative, constructive role of digital metrics in the music industry domain. Vonderau[28] analyses Warner Bros.' notion of 'connected viewing', a controlled and narrowly defined scenario for internet distribution as a 'productive' organisational instrument. Both Facebook Likes and connected viewing are used to enrol other market actors, describe and make the market in a certain way.

Methods: Participant Observation for Longitudinal Case Study

The view that markets are assembled – that is, not totally reducible to either rational actor models or institutional embeddedness – prompts a broadly constructivist methodology. The study adopts a longitudinal case study approach[29] to understand how digital data are taking a new role in film marketing. Two case films were purposively selected on the basis that they are produced by a company that specifically raised investment to try new digital business models and hired a new member of staff to pursue them. Therefore, the films are illustrative and, in some respects, revelatory in that the phenomena have not previously been studied.[30]

Participant observation was sustained across the years 2011–14, resulting in the building of trust and, thereby, unfettered access to the film projects.[31] Fieldwork included observing fifteen meetings or co-working practices as film marketing and distribution campaigns were planned and executed by the producers, executive producers and company directors. Observations lasted between one and six hours each and provided direct observational and open-ended non-structured interview data from extended informal conversations. These were analysed in conjunction with over eighty pages of email conversations. These emails discussed the detail of over eighty-five documents, including recoupment charts, budgets, finance plans, marketing plans, investment applications, press releases, PowerPoints, business plans and quantitative engagement results from online services, social media and film distribution services. Iterative comparison and thematic interrogation of the multiple types of data was undertaken to develop a corroborated insight into the role of DEMs in market assembly practices.

Case Orientation: Motivation and Set-up for Innovation in Documentary Production

In 2011 the Scottish Documentary Institute (SDI) successfully applied to a National Film Fund for £100,000 to support their Virtuous Circle (VC) initiative (formerly called the 'Micro Major Model'). The VC project is led by a specific member of staff called the producer of marketing and distribution (PMD). The motivation to apply digital disintermediation strategies for sustainability was conceived in response to the industrial challenges of digital disruption and historical characteristics specific to documentary that make its organisational process particularly unattractive and uncertain. Rather than a package of script, talent and budget that can be assessed by financiers like a fiction film, a documentary is driven by subject footage: 'By the time the narrative is discovered, 60–70% of the film is in the can and only then ready to be pitched to broadcasters and sales agents.'[32] As a result 'documentary is funded in a piece meal fashion stretching development money for as long as possible'.[33] This means production companies must effectively cashflow 'early stage production' without knowing that the film will generate a fee.

SDI's approach to combat these problems rests on a number of interrelated creative and analytic capacities that restructure activity across all SDI's film-making endeavours: 'Central to this concept is that a virtuous circle derives from the positive reinforcement of outreach > engagement > retention (of audience) & direct relationships with stakeholders and audiences.'[34] SDI activity implements social media tools to: research, enter and develop online networks already interested in a film's subject; attach these networks to the film through traceable digital connections; and exploit multiple types of engagement. The anticipated results are: a larger online audience to generate increased total revenues; a database of engaged fans to recycle between SDI films; the input of valuable resources such as donations throughout the extended lives of every film; and the capacity for direct distribution of finished films so as to obtain a larger than normal proportion of revenues. This activity requires continuous digital stewardship to manage the feedback loop.

In order to set the scene, the timeline in Table 1 provides a summary of events and concerns the films *I Am Breathing* (2013), the story of a young father's last year with motor neurone disease and *Future my Love* (2013), an exploration of a radically different economic and social model.

Table 1: Summary of market action events for *I Am Breathing* and *Future My Love*

Date	Market action
2011	
February–May	SDI develops VC in conjunction with National Film Fund. Processes for linking digital audience engagement to financial goals are mapped out.
April–May	National Film Fund assessment and award of funding, works with SDI to set up monitoring and delivery systems.
June–July	Hiring of PMD.
August–December	Development of detailed benchmark for current documentary practices using past film. Preparation for sale, technology testing, audience engagement of first film on SDI portfolio, generation of different data categories.
October–December	Contracting, embedding measurement of digital variables in market assemblage.
2012	
January–December	Digital engagement activities including website design and builds, creation of www.nationbuilder.com (a website and client database service) databases, Facebook pages, Twitter accounts, negotiations on international rights sales, e.g. to foreign distributors, TV broadcasters, festival presentations of films, development and production of unreleased films.
June	Edinburgh Festival premiere of *Future My Love.*
October	SDI use nationbuilder contacts for industry enrolment, e.g. targeting TV commissioning editors.
2013	
January–April	SDI refinances the VC with new investment funds, concentrating on the film *I Am Breathing.* Development of new digital technology with Distrify to enable innovative film sharing and social impact options including gifting and charity donations. Both films play at Hotdocs, North America's largest documentary festival. Distributor Kinosmith buys Canadian rights to both films.
June	Edinburgh Festival premiere of *I Am Breathing* with digitally enabled global screening day. VoD tool allows downloads for community distribution offline. Over 170 screenings in thirty-five countries around the world, some with Skype intros from team. Twitter and Facebook campaign of audiences submitting photos of billboard posters.
August	Email petition to get *I Am Breathing* theatrically released, 2,000-signature target reached within days, 250 community and festival screenings.

Table 1 (*continued*)

Date	Market action
August–October	UK theatrical release of *I Am Breathing*, Twitter campaign started in 2010 with first co-production deal news, continuously engaging audiences, using subject-specific hashtags #MND #ALS in the newsfeed as well as film project development information.
September	Application of VC principles across to SDI's portfolio. US release of *I Am Breathing* in Los Angeles and New York.
October	DVD and digital release of *I Am Breathing* with inbuilt donation mechanism and online community hosting functionality.
August	Theatrical release (UK) leads to DVD and VoD release of *I Am Breathing*.
November	Theatrical release of *Future My Love* (UK) *I Am Breathing* directors win BAFTA Scotland Award.
2014	
March	'Pay it Forward' initiative enables film gifting and sharing for *I Am Breathing*. Free *Future My Love* film vouchers launched on Zeitgeist day (part of a global sustainability movement with 30,000 Twitter followers and 151,000 Facebook Likes).

Discussion

So how do digital data play a role in performing the independent film market? The case speaks to two broad types of activity in which digital engagement tools, their metrics and associations display aspects of performativity. In these processes marketing is a fully complicit part of a cohesive whole that constitutes the market making of a given film.

The first set of actions concern the industry-focused construction of a market assemblage fundamentally reoriented to a digital action schedule. This involves the enrolment of traditional actors, such as investors, into SDI's conception of the market. The second component of the role of digital data in this context is the instantiation of new evaluation processes and the construction of new network relationships. Public audiences are enrolled as market actors in a non-traditional configuration: as co-distributors.

Such transformations rely upon the successful establishment of 'interessement'[35] between the network of individuals, companies and materials bringing the project to fruition. This is a process of co-definition, in which, through mutual adjustment or translation, the actors negotiate and set their identity and lock their position relative to each other for a certain time.[36] This enrolment is often mediated by material tools[37] and related to valuation procedures.[38] In this case digital engagement technology plays the key role. Public audiences are transformed into market actors as marketers and distributors through extended socio-technical work, including information dissemination and community building.

Hybridisation of established frameworks to enrol market actors

Key to the successful realisation of a market for any independent film is the enrolment of multiple actors with different specialisms. This involves the building and maintenance of coordinating concepts, entangling the requisite partners and the creation of maps or plans of action. SDI achieved this through a number of different tools. Traditional market attachment devices were supplemented by the construction of measurement and reporting tools that enabled the investor, the National Film Fund, to evaluate performance in a way both intelligible to themselves internally and in conversation with SDI.

This framework was labelled the 'Master Sheet' and its format was developed along the lines of conventional film business devices such as a 'recoupment waterfall', so as to associate metrics like 'email sign-ups' and 'views', with revenue figures. The document is written using common film language (deferrals, net profit, 50 per cent profit sharing), is easily circulated via email, readily altered for internal calculations and annotated for negotiation points. The Master Sheet is an Excel spreadsheet compendium of film finance plans, recoupment charts, sales data and marketing analytics. Each VC film has a column and the sheet is split up into three horizontal sections: 'inputs', 'outputs' and 'audience and following'. Financial data describing the life cycle of the film – development, production and marketing and distribution – are set out in segments. Part one, the inputs section, shows the sources of finance for the films' development, production and marketing. As a corollary these figures also indicate the ownership of intellectual property and the relative recoupment positions of market actors. Part two shows whether rights have been pre-sold to distributors or TV companies and is continually updated to depict the 'outputs' or outcomes of such deals. The film's exploitation in monetary terms includes figures for each distribution window – for example, theatrical and VoD, as well as other sources of income such as community workshops.

Part three of the Master Sheet collates the most important DEMs that SDI links to the financial performance above. Market-making activity, operationalised through tools such as nationbuilder, forms the daily work of the PMD and such data often pulls the team around it, becoming very influential. The SDI team make associations between digital and non-digital figures and calculate results that enable them to take creative decisions, allocate resources and construct the market for each film. For example, because DEMs are understood as evidence of consumer demand their relative performance on a geographic and distribution window basis informs SDI's evaluation of where to target their promotional activity, and likely avenues for rights sales and influences deal term considerations. When such indicators are available early in the film's life and cross-referenced with offline marketing activities, SDI can ensure the film is available in all appropriate territories using internet distribution. SDI can act like a traditional sales agent, or generate revenue through 'rights retention by self distribution'.[39]

When the networked marketing components, such as trailers, blogs and dispersed audiences, are partially decontextualised as aggregated totals, they simultaneously function as currency to demonstrate value to foreign broadcasters and film investors. Public-facing metrics such as Likes, Follows and Views are valorising and valuation mechanisms in that they produce and assess value. By liking a Facebook page, you judge it but also add to its total valuation score, which often alters the way others perceive it. A page with a few hundred Likes is viewed negatively and not worthy of one's time, a few thousand legitimises the media or brand represented as professional and serious. Such visible data are adjusted and reframed alongside private 'black-boxed' analytics data in the Master Sheet, forming a hybridised tool for market attachment. As Facebook Likes are reinscribed into other syntactic forms – first into analytics software, then into data tables – they help to qualify a film as a market object. The film becomes finely distinguished by its many heterogeneous characteristics summarised in neat rows: its cost, its distribution in international markets and its social fanbase become understood as interrelated. DEMs provide a language; they perform a shortcut at an interface to make coordination and communication possible.[40]

SDI's materialisation of associations between digital engagement and financial returns allows for shared calculations of value to be made across company boundaries, despite revolving around unfamiliar and uncertain information. The content and purpose of the Sheet was enshrined in legal contracts attached to economic transactions between investor and producer. This has the effect of solidifying the meaning, role and anticipated effects of the digital aspects of SDI's project. By financing SDI's VC initiative, the National Film Fund agreed with SDI's conception that the creative and analytic capacities of digital tools are inherently linked.

New technology and reconfigured market actor roles

While in aggregate DEMs have a market-shaping role by facilitating investment and distribution plans, explained above, technological intervention also has a much more visible performative aspect. Both films enjoyed extended engagement campaigns utilising social media, blogs, websites, email marketing and offline festival promotion. At the heart of this activity was the use of the Distrify player, an embeddable, shareable video player that is both film trailer and VoD platform. It is a marketing and sales tool that implicates the social networks that host it as co-distributors. Initially placed on the films' websites and Facebook pages and then spread far wider, the player can generate a large amount of data. The following screen shot displays both the trailer window and illustrates the connected statistics.

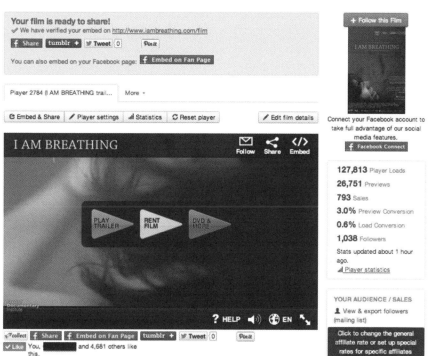

Screenshot 1: Distrify VOD player and analytics data for *I Am Breathing* (courtesy of Distrify)

This player gives three central options in its arrow icons: 'Play Trailer', 'Rent Film' and 'More'. The first two options are self-explanatory and generate many of the figures on the right-hand side of the screen. A ratio describing how many users have watched the trailer and then gone on to purchase the film – 'preview conversion' – is one example of a causal connection between marketing activity and financial return. This is a key DEM used by SDI in managing their audience engagement activity. The player is connectable to Facebook, Twitter, Pinterest and Tumblr; SDI is able to trace the source of users into the player. This enables cross-referencing of social media marketing with conversions to purchase. The sales can be segmented by time, geography and type. This fine-grained analytical toolset enables SDI to make connections between all aspects of their audience engagement strategy and market results.

The options to Follow, Share and Embed in the top right of the player window are also important. The sharing function notifies the user's own social network that they have engaged with the film, but also shares the player and thus the opportunity to rent, buy or share the film itself, rather than solely information about it. The embed option in the top far right of the player allows the user to host the film on their own website or blog, thereby widening the distribution infrastructure of the film. All of these options attach the user to the market assemblage of the film in a quantifiable way. The network of users who are enrolled and assume agency in economic transactions is traced, fed back into the producer's calculative framework and impacts a subsequent transaction. For example, spikes in player loads (the top line of the first graph) and sales in the graph below on the global screening day and UK festival premiere for the film in June 2013 were associated with significant increases in digital engagement.

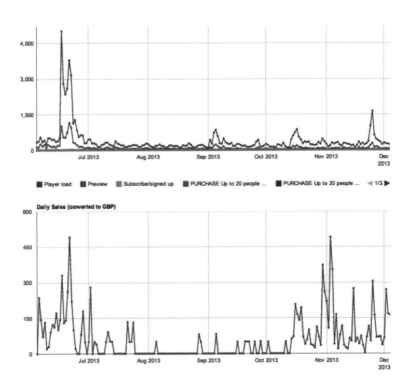

Screenshot 2: Distrify analytics data for *I Am Breathing*

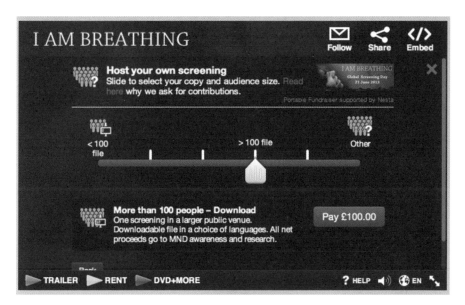

Screenshot 3: Distrify VOD player displaying community distribution tool for *I Am Breathing* (courtesy of Distrify)

Through their user experience design and connectivity to other web services, the players can combine with users to perform a conjoined promotion and distribution role. This constitutes an innovative reconfiguration of the film market, which was further developed via a specifically targeted technological interface to facilitate community screenings for *I Am Breathing*. In the following illustration the shareable trailer player shows a sliding scale that indicates how large an audience can be reached through each digital format and with what economic transaction. Built into the facility to host a screening and become part of the theatrical distribution network are also the marketing tools to promote it.

The technology for *Future my Love* was also redeveloped to fit a particular social purpose. One example is the development of a 'Pay it Forward' tool: a film gifting option set up to enable users to send on the film to friends to watch for free. This was conceived to align the marketing and distribution structure to the subject matter, which concerns alternative non-monetary societies.

The user interface for each film was subtly altered at different periods of the release. An arrow linking to cinema listings gave way to 'DVD', then to options for gifting, or for *I Am Breathing*, to donate to the MND Association. The social contexts and material elements of the digital devices simultaneously shape each other.[41] This impacts their further circulation and adoption, which feed back into organisational decisions. The quote below illustrates the design for engagement and reorganised schedule enabled by new digital methods, upon which further market-shaping activities are based:

Over the months leading up to the launch … the PMD together with tech consultant and graphic designer have been able to plan, design, and implement … a comprehensive website with many options for engagement (word-spreading, feedback, requesting screeners, hosting screenings). Traditionally, these interactive aspects were not tackled prior to completion of a documentary, or even months [after].[42]

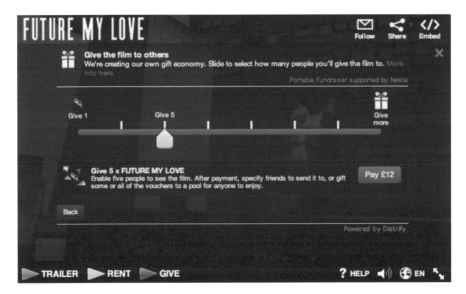

Screenshot 4: Distrify VOD player displaying 'Pay it Forward' toolset for *Future My Love* (courtesy of Distrify)

Digital interactions between film producers, film content and audiences that create networks of marketing awareness and potential channels of distribution are inseparable from the DEMs that both describe and mobilise the market. Understanding this emerging film marketing trend in terms of a performative socio-technical assemblage helps to contextualise film in the digitally disrupted era in relation to how other creative goods are produced. As Entwistle and Slater[43] interpret a fashion model's look, a film also emerges from, and is sustained by, an extended apparatus of interconnected arrangements, including calculative frameworks. In this case the arrangements are reliant upon and enacted through their digital materiality. DEMs are constructed as having value in regard to both social impact[44] and financial returns and this adds to the importance of a broadened understanding of marketing as part of market making in the current film industry.

This chapter shows how new digital engagement tools, through the connective and calculative capacity of their metrics, reconfigure the market for SDI's documentaries and should prompt a broader view of what constitutes film marketing. Through the mobilisation of ideas, materials, technology and networks of market actors, DEMs help to construct the market for a given film. This leads to film-makers taking on new roles as data managers and audiences to obtain new agency as marketers and distributors. These innovations are predicated on the manipulability and quantifiable nature of digital technology. SDI is able to spread the means of distributing their films as an engagement strategy in itself. This creates communities and calls them to action while SDI continually adapts the technical and creative material to the specific subject and life stage of their films. This is an increasingly complex process with multiple layers of valuation. An audience member may view a trailer, recommend the film to Facebook friends and even co-distribute a film on VoD by embedding a player on their webpage; this visible, conscious market action is traced digitally. These traces are quantified as DEMs, aggregated, fitted into frameworks and used as currency in further arrangements for market construction.

Notes

1. This work is produced with the great support of ESRC Capacity Building Cluster: Capitalising on Creativity, RES 187-24-0014, and the help and insight of Noe Mendelle, Sonja Henrici and Ben Kempas of the Scottish Documentary Institute.

2. British Film Institute (BFI), *Statistical Yearbook 2013*, http://www.bfi.org.uk/sites/bfi.org.uk/files/downloads/bfi-statistical-yearbook-2013.pdf, p. 162.

3. Ibid., p. 14.

4. 'Digital Home Entertainment to Exceed Physical by 2016, Study Finds', *Variety.com*, 3 June 2014, http://variety.com/2014/digital/news/digital-home-entertainment-to-exceed-physical-by-2016-study-finds-1201207708/

5. Henry Jenkins, Sam Ford and Josh Green, *Spreadable Media: Creating Value and Meaning in a Networked Culture* (New York: New York University Press, 2013). The authors define content and technology that is easily shareable online as spreadable, as opposed to using biological metaphors such as virality.

6. 'Likes' are a metric generated from the Facebook social media platform and available throughout the web as part of that network's social graph (see https://developers.facebook.com/docs/plugins/like-button). The clicking of the Like button is a somewhat public statement of evaluation by the user regarding the piece of content to which the button is attached.

7. 'Shares' are also a count, reflecting the use of a 'social button', which, in relation to Facebook pushes the chosen content out to the user's social network (see https://developers.facebook.com/docs/plugins/share-button).

8. 'Views' are a common metric describing the amount of times a video has been watched, the popularity of the term can be ascribed to YouTube. See https://support.google.com/youtube/answer/1714329?hl=en

9. Michel Callon, 'What does it Mean to Say that Economics is Performative?', in Donald Mackenzie, Fabian Muniesa and Lucia Sui (eds), *Do Economists make Markets?* (Princeton, NJ: Princeton University Press, 2007), p. 317.

10. The first author worked as a representative of a public investor in numerous of the producer's projects.

11. Eldar Sadikov, Aditya Parameswaran and Petros Venetis, 'Blogs as Predictors of Movie Success', Proceedings of the Third International ICWSM Conference, March 2009.

12. Márton Mestyán, Taha Yasseri and Ja nos Kertész, 'Early Prediction of Movie Box Office Success Based on Wikipedia Activity Big Data', *PLoS ONE* vol. 8 no. 8, 2012.

13. Sitaram Asur and Bernard Huberman, 'Predicting the Future with Social Media', IEEE/WIC/ACM International Conference, August 2010.

14. Thorsten Hennig-Thurau, Caroline Wiertz and Fabian Feldhaus, 'Exploring the "Twitter Effect": An Investigation of the Impact of Microblogging Word of Mouth on Consumers' Early Adoption of New Products', *Cass Knowledge Paper – Film, Media, and Entertainment Research Centre*, 2012.

15. Wenjing, Duan, Gu Bin and Andrew Whinston, 'The Dynamics of Online Word-of-mouth and Product Sales – An Empirical Investigation of the Movie Industry', *Journal of Retailing* vol. 84 no. 2, 2008, pp. 233–42.

16. Enrico Moretti, 'Social Learning and Peer Effects in Consumption: Evidence from Movie Sales', *The Review of Economic Studies* vol. 78 no. 1, 2011, pp. 356–93.

17. Michel Callon, Yuval Millo and Fabian Muniesa, 'An Introduction to Market Devices', in Michel Callon, Yuval Millo and Fabian Muniesa (eds), *Market Devices* (Oxford: Blackwell, 2007).

18. Luis Araujo, 'Markets, Market-making and Marketing', *Marketing Theory* vol. 7 no. 3, 2007, pp. 211–26.
19. Johan Hagberg and Hans Kjellberg, 'Who Performs Marketing? Dimensions of Agential Variation in Market Practice', *Industrial Marketing Management* vol. 39 no. 6, 2010, pp. 1028–37.
20. Ibid., p. 1029.
21. Callon, 'What does it Mean to Say that Economics is Performative?', p. 317.
22. Hans Kjellberg and Claes-Fredrik Helgesson, 'Multiple Versions of Markets: Multiplicity and Performativity in Market Practice', *Industrial Marketing Management* vol. 35 no. 7, 2006, pp. 839–55.
23. Donald MacKenzie, 'Is Economics Performative? Option Theory and the Construction of Derivatives Market', *Journal of the History of Economic Thought* vol. 28 no. 1, 2006, pp. 29–55.
24. Carolin Gerlitz and Anne Helmond, 'The Like Economy: Social Buttons and the Data-intensive Web', *New Media & Society*, vol. 15 no. 8 (2013), p. 1360.
25. Jannis Kallinikos, Paul Leonardi and Bonnie Nardi, 'The Challenge of Materiality: Origins, Scope, and Prospects', in Paul Leonardi, Bonnie Nardi and Jannis Kallinikos (eds), *Materiality and Organizing: Social Interaction in a Technological World* (Oxford: Oxford University Press, 2012).
26. Ibid., p. 12.
27. Nancy Baym, 'Data Not Seen: The Uses and Shortcomings of Social Media Metrics', *First Monday* vol. 18 no. 10, 2013, http://firstmonday.org/ojs/index.php/fm/article/view/4873/3752
28. Patrick Vonderau, 'Beyond Piracy: Understanding Digital Markets', in Jennifer Holt and Kevin Sanson (eds), C*onnected Viewing: Selling, Sharing, and Streaming Media in the Digital Era* (New York/London: Routledge, 2013).
29. Robert Yin, 'The Case Study Crisis: Some Answers', *Administrative Science Quarterly* vol. 26 no. 7, 1981, pp. 58–65.
30. Alan Bryman and Emma Bell, *Business Research Methods* (New York: Oxford University Press, 2007).
31. Danny Jorgensen, 'Participant Observation: A Methodology for Human Studies', *Applied Social Research Methods Series* (London: Sage, 1989).
32. Micro Major Investment Proposal, 25 February 2011.
33. VC Investment Assessment Form, 14 March 2011.
34. Micro Major Investment Proposal, 25 February 2011.
35. Michel Callon, 'Some Elements of a Sociology of Translation: Domestication of the Scallops and the Fishermen of Saint Brieuc Bay', in Mario Biagioli (ed.), *The Science Studies Reader* (London: Routledge, 1999), pp. 67–84.
36. Ibid.
37. David Stark and Verena Paravel, 'PowerPoint in Public Digital Technologies and the New Morphology of Demonstration', *Theory, Culture & Society* vol. 25 no. 5, 2008, pp. 30–55.
38. Callon, Millo and Muniesa, *Market Devices*.
39. SDI proposal for Micro-Major Project, 25 February 2011.
40. Mahmood Zargar, 'Managing Knowledge Boundaries in Bioinformatics Research Units', Conference of the European Group for Organisational Studies, 4 July 2013.
41. Madeline Akrich, Michel Callon and Bruno Latour, 'The Key to Success in Innovation: Part 1 The Art of Interessement', *International Journal of Innovation Management* vol. 6 no. 2, 2002.

42. VC Project Update, August 2012.

43. Joanne Entwistle and Don Slater, 'Reassembling the Cultural: Fashion Models, Brands and the Meaning of "Culture" after ANT', *Journal of Cultural Economy* vol. 7 no. 2, 2013, p. 9.

44. Jana Diesner, Susie Pak, Jinesok Kim, Kiumars Soltani and Amirhossein Aleyasen, 'A Computational Assessment of the Impact of Social Justice Documentaries', iConference, March 2014.

POSTSCRIPT
THE INVISIBLE SIDE OF BUSINESS: B-TO-B MARKETING

Marketing the 'Avatar Revolution', or How to Sell Digital Technology to Exhibitors

Kira KITSOPANIDOU

Hailed by critics and industry insiders as a technological and cinematic breakthrough, James Cameron's epic movie *Avatar* offers an illustration of how Hollywood blockbusters are 'discursively supported and constructed'[1] as movies that will break all records and set new benchmarks.[2] Mainstream and corporate media repeatedly emphasised that News Corporation spent millions around the world to sell the 'Avatar revolution'.[3] Far from being a mere 'gimmick', however, the 'revolution' was larger than the film itself.[4] As Charles Acland has shown in his analysis of *Avatar* as 'technological tentpole':

> Avatar is celebrated and promoted to stand out as a flagship work beckoning the next wave of industrial and consumer technologies and entertainments. With Avatar, we have 3-D filming processes, 3-D exhibition, digital exhibition and 3-D home entertainment all counting on the film's appeal for their own advancement.[5]

In 2011, Vince Pace and Cameron formed the Cameron–Pace Group (CPG) with the specific purpose to 'make 3D ubiquitous over the next five to 10 years on all platforms' and applicable to all industries of entertainment, be it games, broadcast or film. [6] Building the *Avatar* brand was essential in promoting 3D technology and entertainment across global markets and different media platforms. Using the concept of 'conversion marketing',[7] a high strategic marketing that aims to get consumers to take specific actions, the purpose of this chapter is to describe how, through a carefully designed campaign, the movie became a powerful selling vehicle of state-of-the art technology to theatres internationally, also promoting 3D technology's penetration in the home.

Exhibition, the Digital Revolution and 3D Economics before *Avatar*

Before *Avatar*'s release, the 'digital revolution' encountered strong resistance from the exhibition sector. As for 3D, there have been several revivals since the 1920s, the golden age for 3D movie presentation being the early 1950s. The novelty, however, faded each time and 3D never overcame its status as a gimmick. In 2005, digital projection was relatively new and there were only a handful of digital installations in the world. Between 2006 and 2008, the worldwide market for digital projectors more than doubled, with most of the growth stemming from the US market, which accounted for two-thirds of all digital installations. However, digital screens' share of the global theatre market remained modest throughout 2007 and 2008. In 2008, the digital deployment made some progress in the international market, with the European market doubling the number of its screens. In the USA, progress was slowed down considerably due to the stock market crash of October 2008. The worldwide economic downturn and the freezing of the credit markets also put most wide-scale conversion initiatives on hold in Europe and Asia.

With the digital take-off speed being slower than foreseen, Hollywood studios – the main beneficiaries of the economies of scale achieved by digital distribution – needed to build an argument that would spur the need for digital projection and convince sceptical exhibitors to upgrade to digital, even during economic hardship. That argument was 3D presentation. The 3D renaissance was ignited by the release of *Polar Express* in IMAX 3D in December 2003. However, until 2005 only IMAX theatres were able to show 3D movies. The release of *Chicken Little*, the first digital 3D animation feature in 2005, followed by *Monster House* in mid-2006 and *Meet the Robinsons* in early 2007 revived interest in the 3D format.

At the 2005 NATO/Showest official convention of theatre owners, the most technophile of the American mainstream film directors, such as George Lucas, James Cameron, Robert Zemeckis and Robert Rodriguez, were mobilised to convince the exhibitors to switch over to digital projection, touting digital 3D as the next big innovation. Among the first to embrace digital 3D as the new standard were the animation studios. Jeffrey Katzenberg, founder and CEO of DreamWorks Animation, became its highest-profile ambassador when he announced, in March 2007, that the entire DreamWorks Animation production would be released exclusively in 3D digital, starting in 2009 with the release of *Monsters vs Aliens*. But despite the fact that box-office takes for 3D versions of movies were three to four times higher than 2D versions, the 3D digital market was slowed down by the scarcity of 3D films and screens. The boom so confidently announced at NATO/Showest had not yet materialised.

Early in 2009, there were roughly 1,250 digital 3D screens out of 5,620 digital screens in the USA, even fewer in the international market.[8] For the release of *Monsters vs Aliens*, Katzenberg travelled for eighteen months around the country and all over the world, lobbying for 3D and urging exhibitors to equip their theatres. While he had initially counted on an installed base of 3,000 to 5,000 3D theatres, he soon realised that the chances of reaching this goal were dim. The film was released in March 2009 in 4,104 locations, 1,550 of which were 3D sites. The lack of sites led to a cannibalisation effect – that is, the availability of screens did not allow simultaneous 3D releases. Though the film was a turning point for 3D releases, both in terms of total 3D digital theatre count and box-office take,[9] it became clear that the scarcity of 3D screens was not only disturbing the distribution strategy and release plan, it was also thwarting 3D-only releases. DreamWorks Animation, for instance, was forced to move the digital 3D release of *Monsters vs Aliens* from May to March 2009 and delay that of *Dragons* from November 2009 to March 2010 in order to avoid competing with *Avatar* (whose release was also pushed from May to December 2009).[10] One month before *Avatar*'s release, Disney was forced to release *A Christmas Carol* on barely 1,800 equipped screens in the USA.

For animation studios, the first to have invested in 3D in the USA, the market of 3D exhibition represents a considerable stake. With the DVD sales shrinking, the overall domestic consumer spending on pre-recorded home-entertainment content – the area from which the studios have been drawing their biggest revenues since 1986 – declining and exhibition windows reducing, animation studios saw in the 3D exhibition market a chance to invert the trend and create new revenue streams by charging higher ticket prices.[11] As *Variety* noted in April 2009, 'The biz has shifted back to the traditional box-office-based model, now enhanced by the rise of 3D.'[12] In May 2010, Katzenberg recognised that, as far as his studio was concerned, the income generated by 3D screenings, where prices were much higher than those applied in standard exhibition,[13] was sufficient enough to compensate for the drop of the home video market in 2009.[14]

By late 2009, 3D still lacked legitimacy. In December, Cameron explained:

> I'm waiting to see if 'Avatar' will legitimize 3D for other filmmakers who otherwise might have said, 'I don't want to make a 3D movie because it's for kids, or animation, or horror. I'm a serious filmmaker who makes serious films with big actors and I don't want my cred to be eroded by a 3D gimmick movie that is not a legitimate part of the cinematic art.'[15]

For *Avatar*'s launch, Cameron and Fox decided to go a different way to Katzenberg's approach. In the months prior to the release of *Monsters vs Aliens*, Katzenberg became the highest-profile 3D ambassador adopting a hard-selling approach towards exhibitors. 3D, he claimed, was the greatest opportunity for growth and expansion of the entertainment business he had seen in years, as well as the answer to the critical issue about piracy and video windows, but, for this to happen, exhibitors needed to be innovative and entrepreneurial,[16] meaning switching to digital and charging premium for the format. *Monsters vs Aliens*' aggressive marketing campaign put most of the emphasis on promoting 3D as part of the moviegoing experience, with Katzenberg comparing the 2D experience to 'the equivalent of vinyl records'.[17] James Cameron, producer Jon Landau (*Titanic*, *Avatar*) and Fox chose instead to let the film's prototypical status in terms of subject, visual universe and large-scale technological innovation speak for itself.[18] The basic message here would be 'Go digital, *Avatar* is coming!' Cameron insisted:

> The film should not be marketed first and foremost as a 3-D experience. The film should be sold on its merits, and the consumer should be informed that they can purchase the experience in 2-D or, for a couple extra bucks, in 3-D. It should be like ordering at Starbucks. Lots of choices. If the new media of the last decade has taught us anything, it is that people like choices, and they like control.[19]

20th Century-Fox and Cameron decided not to overplay the 3D element in *Avatar*'s communication strategy. Rather than using the hyperbolic language reminiscent of Cinerama's claims of envelopment and the active audience,[20] they chose to sell the 3D experience by repositioning it in relation with the digital technology and the new immersive media in order to attract a new generation of audiences more engaged with video games than films. The method was to invest in early audience engagement and create an *Avatar* fan community, notably through a viral campaign, long before the release, thus putting further pressure on exhibitors all around the world to invest in 3D digital equipment before *Avatar* opened in theatres. This resulted in a form of conversion marketing, targeting the professional group of cinema exhibitors and mixing public relations and event marketing focusing on the movie theatre experience.[21] As Tomas Jegeus, co-president of 20th Century-Fox International, said: 'We have to convert their minds so they can then start converting their theatres.'[22]

Building Up the '*Avatar* Day'

We may argue that conversion marketing really began when, in the years following *Titanic*'s release, Cameron became increasingly involved in deep ocean exploration and underwater documentary 3D film-making. He notably directed two IMAX 3D documentaries: *Ghost of the Abyss* (2003)[23] and *Aliens of the Deep* (2005). After having first developed *Project 880 – Avatar*'s working title – in 1994–5, Cameron took it up again in June 2005. At around the same time the first third-party non-exclusive virtual print fees (VPF) deals with studios and exhibitors in the USA were being announced (in November 2005); 3D projection was also making a comeback at commercial theatres with Real D launching its 3D business early in 2005 and Disney partnering with Lucas's Industrial Light and Magic and Dolby Laboratories in June to convert *Chicken Little* into 3D.[24] Indeed, shooting in 3D from inception entails increased production costs. The added cost above a film's core budget has been estimated somewhere between 10 per cent and 30 per cent, depending on the film.[25] For live action/CGI hybrid productions such as Tim Burton's *Alice in Wonderland* (2010) and James Cameron's *Avatar*, the cost of 3D represented an estimated one third of the film's budget.

The majority of films originally shot in 3D was animation – for which the extra cost was less important[26] – and franchises, or both. The eight highest-grossing 3D films released in 2009 and 2010 were the animated features *Despicable Me*, *How to Train Your Dragon*, *Monsters vs Aliens*, *Up!* and the animated franchises *Toy Story 3*, *Shrek Forever After* and *Ice Age: Dawn of the Dinosaurs*.

In February 2006, Cameron revealed *Project 880*'s true identity and in July he announced the film's release for 2008.[27] Fox greenlighted the project in October 2006.[28] From 2007 on, the buzz around *Avatar*'s production began to spread over internet and the press. The film entered production phase in April 2007. Cameron, counting on *Titanic*'s hyper-hyped performances in 1997, continuously promoted 3D to American and European exhibitors, still very reluctant regarding digital's added value for their theatres. He met with the American exhibitors during NATO/Showest in 2005, promising them a 'new age of cinema' and 'a stunning visual experience which "turbocharges" the viewing of the biggest, must-see movies',[29] and again in April 2006 during the National Association of Broadcasters' (NAB) Digital Cinema Summit. At Cinema Expo in 2006, Cameron cut together a reel showing what eleven films (including footage and clips from *Star Wars* [1977], *King Kong* [2005], *Chicken Little* and *Robots* [2005]) would look like 'dimensionalised' in 3D. It was a strong argument coming from one of the world's most bankable directors. Even though Cameron spoke very little of *Avatar* at that stage, he successfully built anticipation for his upcoming feature which would represent 3D's 'moment of truth for live action 3-D'.[30] A few months before the release, *Avatar*'s advertising campaign got a strategic boost when Katzenberg, speaking at the 3D Entertainment Summit in September 2009, said *Avatar* 'will be the "dam-buster" that does for live action S3D film-making what "The Wizard of Oz" did for colour, showing the artistic, creative and commercial potential of the format'.[31]

Anticipation for the film's release was further building up as *Avatar*'s communication revealed very little of the film's visual universe. At the end of 2008, no official trailer, photograph or official poster – except for a teaser poster, which revealed nothing but the film's title – had been publicised. However, the closely guarded project was feeding the buzz on the internet as reports of film-makers and industry insiders having seen footage of the film and calling it a revolution reached the press. In May 2009, a first trailer accompanying the release of *Transformers 2* was revealed to the American public. But it did not unveil any 3D element, which further fed speculation. *Avatar*'s first photograph was released mid-August 2009, first in *Entertainment Weekly*, then online,[32] five months before the film's release. But it was not until October, that the first exclusive images reached the press, in *Empire*. The exhibitors had had their first glance only in June. Fox's marketing strategy was motivated by a decision to hold back, but also by the lack of material, as production experienced delays.

In the most important trade shows, Cameron, Landau and Fox's marketing team showed previews with a clear message: 'Hurry! *Avatar* is coming.' In June, at Cinema Expo 2009 in Amsterdam, Cameron 'teased' *Avatar*, screening a twenty-four-minute promo assemblage to an estimated 1,250 total attendees from the European movie industry. Arguing that the 3D renaissance he had announced three years before had arrived, he urged exhibitors to upgrade to digital 3D before the film's release.[33]

Although, officially, Fox had urged the media not to report details of the film or interview audience members for reactions, comments on the footage were spread instantly and anonymously to many websites and blogs, building further excitement among fans and intensifying audience anticipation.

One month later, Cameron and Fox 'teased' *Avatar* to American exhibitors. The twenty-four-minute promo clip was screened before an audience of 6,000 hardcore fans at the San Diego Comic-Con annual convention, where the director and the studio announced an unusual and most innovating marketing event they called '*Avatar* Day', planned for 21 August. The operation was designed to build a global fan base for the film while pushing exhibitors to install more digital equipment and 3D screens in time for the opening. From 17 August, American hardcore fans were able to book seats on the film's official site to attend one of *Avatar*'s fifteen-minute free screenings. The *Avatar* Day operation took place in 101 IMAX theatres domestically and 238 abroad (including thirty IMAX venues),[34] gathering thousands of fans worldwide around what became the largest preview screening ever. To help boost the pre-event buzz, Fox financed the production of nearly 2,000 Ultra-3D movie posters, which were located in theatres and high-traffic venues throughout the USA and internationally.[35] *Avatar*'s 129-second teaser trailer – as well as the official game trailer – was released online to create additional word of mouth for the event and instantly became the most downloaded trailer on apple.com, registering over 4 million streams in its first day.[36] For the release of the three and a half minute trailer early in November 2009, Fox adopted a 'red-carpet approach', literally promoting the trailer that would promote the film. It premiered on the Diamond Vision screen[37] during a Dallas Cowboys football game at Cowboys Stadium in Arlington, Texas, and was simultaneously seen by millions of viewers tuning into Fox NFL to watch the match.[38]

Assessing the *Avatar* Strategy

This strategy calls for several remarks. Traditionally, audiences' first contact with a film in its launching phase takes place via printed media (teaser poster, official photos) and its teaser trailer, both in theatres and online. For *Avatar*, Fox made limited use of outdoor communication,[39] favouring the internet, mobile, theatre and television advertising. The actual education of audiences and exhibitors to the 3D experience took place within the movie theatres. While advance screenings of a film's footage for the press or at events such as Comic-Con are common practice for big-budget Hollywood fare, for the first time on a worldwide scale, audiences were given the opportunity to test the film on a big screen several months before its actual premiere. The *Avatar* Day thus provided Fox and the exhibitors with immediate and large-scale feedback of audience reaction to *Avatar*'s 3D well ahead of the film's December release. It also motivated fans to engage in online word of mouth anticipation, social coverage and deliver recommendations while at the same time creating media buzz – massively relayed on the internet – which added to pressure on exhibitors to install more 3D screens.

Second, *Avatar*'s trailers did not highlight one of the film's main characteristics: 3D. Only the trailers projected in IMAX 3D theatres clearly made reference to it. With a few exceptions, such as Italy and Greece, the film's poster, besides the special 3D poster for

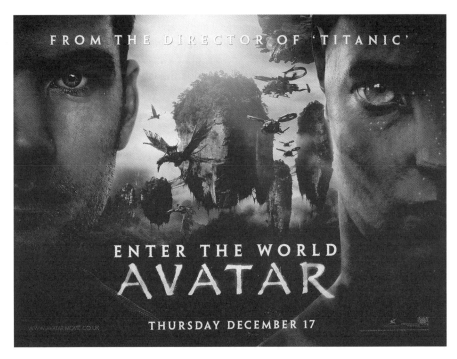

The 'world' of *Avatar* (2009)

Avatar Day, did not even mention the 3D element. Only the US televised trailers alluded to it. The emphasis was clearly put on the film's visual universe and the story told, and on the director. Attention was drawn specifically to his box-office power with the enumeration of his notable hits. The construction of the television trailer as described above provides further evidence of Cameron's 'high concept' auteurism.[40] The absence of any reference to 3D clearly aimed at differentiating the *Avatar* campaign from the 1950s 3D cinema campaign and its overused pop-up effects. It seemed to be telling audiences and exhibitors that *Avatar* was, above all, 'James Cameron's latest technological breakthrough reinventing the movies' and not just a '3D spectacle directed by James Cameron'. This was a radical departure from the marketing strategies of Cinerama and 3D movies in the 1950s whose purpose was to build a 'technological star'.[41]

Finally, *Avatar* Day proved to be a key component to conversion marketing, fulfilling Fox's predictions. Not only did it act as a catalyst of social conversation, virally increasing movie attendance, but, by reducing some of the uncertainty regarding the movie's capacity to spark the interest of a much wider audience, it also contributed to the impressive spread of 3D digital systems through mimetic adoption. The movie's upcoming release became the ultimate trigger for the pragmatic 'early majority'[42] of exhibitors all over the world to upgrade to digital, precipitating a cycle of adoption even during economic hardship. All over the world, exhibitors rushed to order digital equipment and 3D screens to be ready in time for the most awaited and talked-about film. In Europe, between December 2008 and November 2009, there was a sudden surge in the demand for digital equipment[43] as the number of major cinema chains announcing digital 3D installations increased significantly. In the USA, *Avatar* was released on 2,032 3D screens, including 191 IMAX 3D venues, out of the 3,124 3D total screens available. It was, at the time, the biggest 3D release. In the rest of the world, the film was released on 3,935 3D screens (eighty-one IMAX 3D).[44] The 'Avatar effect' was particularly perceptible in the French market, which emerged as the leading 3D digital market in Europe.[45] In 2009, there was an estimated 277 per cent increase in digital screens in France, 400 per cent in Spain and 86.4 per cent internationally, due to Avatar.[46] In the USA, the number of digital screens almost doubled between November 2009 and November 2010, from 6,336 to 12,802, or 33 per cent of the total screen count. Exhibitors rushing to get installations done in time for Avatar's release led to reaching a critical mass of 3D digital screens, and the number of 3D releases rose from eight in 2008 to thirty-eight in 2012 in the USA. In 2010, as the number of 3D screens had dramatically spread and Avatar was on the verge of a record-breaking performance, Cameron confirmed his motivations to make Avatar: 'Films can change people's minds, and the aim with "Avatar" was to introduce the industry to the possibilities of 3-D … I decided, let's go make a movie that they can't ignore.'[47]

When the September 2009 Panasonic–Avatar sponsorship deal to promote both 3D television technology and awareness for the film was announced, Panasonic's Masayuki Kozuka told Associated Press: 'We want to get global interest rolling. For people to want to watch 3D at home, the movie has to be a blockbuster.'[48] Kozuka's statement illustrates the constructed nature of Avatar as a game-changing event, while it draws attention on the fact that selling the 'Avatar revolution' was no longer about the movie itself and its director but about driving and legitimising more forcefully and convincingly 3D technology's penetration in the home, as well as in the movie theatre. Just like Avatar Day invited fans to test the movie along with the experience of 3D technology in the theatre, Panasonic organised the '3D Full HD Home Theater Tour' in Europe and the USA to allow consumers to experience clips from the movie before its release through the Panasonic 3D TV technology.[49] The Japanese firm also ensured exclusive distribution rights to the Avatar 3D Blu-ray edition until 2012, which was bundled with Panasonic 3D Blu-ray player hardware and 3D television sets.[50]

Such deals between Hollywood studios and electronics firms are not unusual and, in Avatar's case, they represent one of the components of a larger overall marketing approach, turning Avatar into a vehicle for selling new hardware. Furthermore, the construction of the movie as a game-changing event is also another way of promoting the game-changing character of new digital, multimedia and interactive communication technologies and implementing the latest media and high-tech corporations' business strategies. As Charles Acland suggests, Avatar 'effectively continues a primary mode of investment in changing media materials and processes'.[51]

While 3D movies continue to be very popular internationally, especially in China where 80 per cent of tickets sold are for 3D screenings,[52] accounting for a significant percentage of foreign box office for the studios, 3D earning as part of the total box-office gross has been declining since 2010.[53] The box office in the USA and Canada hit a record $10.8 billion in 2012, but 3D box-office takings have remained steady for the past two years at around $1.8 billion, as the novelty has been wearing off and audiences seem to have got tired of increased pricing for 3D screening,[54] a phenomenon also visible in Europe. 3D still appears as a viable format for event movies in theatres, whereas the 3D live broadcasting business model remains in its infancy. At the April 2013 NAB Show, CPG, Dolby Laboratories and Royal Philips Electronics announced a partnership to support 3D content and glasses-free 3D television and encourage consumer interest. Whether Cameron's business plans regarding 3D television will disrupt[55] the home entertainment market, the way Avatar's release proved a remarkably effective conversion accelerator for digital cinema worldwide, remains to be seen.

Notes

1. Daniel Biltereyst and Philippe Meers, 'Blockbuster and/as Events: Distributing and Launching *The Lord of the Rings*', in Ernest Mathijs (ed.), *The Lord of the Rings: Popular Culture in Global Context* (London and New York: Wallflower Press, 2006), pp. 71–87.
2. The author would like to express her sincere thanks to Nolwenn Mingant, Cecilia Tirtaine and Joël Augros for their advice and assistance in reviewing this contribution.
3. 'Avatar Soars on Fat Ad Spending, Mass Marketing', *Advertising Age*, 4 January 2010, http://adage.com/article/madisonvine-news/fox-movie-avatar-soars-fat-ad-spending-mass-marketing/141262/
4. Thomas Elsaesser, 'The Dimension of Depth and Objects Rushing Towards Us', *eDIT Filmmaker's Magazine*, 2010, www.filmmakersfestival.com/en/magazine/ausgabe-12010/the-dimension-of-depth/the-dimesion-of-depth-and-objects-rushing-towards-us.html
5. Charles Acland, 'The Impact of Technological Innovations on the Historiography and Theory of Cinema', international conference organised by GRAFICS (Université de Montréal) and ARTHEMIS (Concordia University), *Cinémathèque Québécoise*, 1–6 November 2011; 'Avatar as Technological Tentpole', *FlowTV* vol. 11, 22 January 2010, http://flowtv.org/2010/01/avatar-as-technological-tentpole-charles-r-acland-concordia-university/
6. 'James Cameron, Vince Pace Announce New 3D Venture', *Hollywood Reporter*, 4 November 2011, www.hollywoodreporter.com/news/james-cameron-vince-pace-announce-176951
7. In internet marketing, the concept describes a technique or process that aims to transform a website visitor to an actual paying customer.
8. 'Paramount Ponies Up 3D Deal', *Variety.com*, 22 January 2009, http://variety.com/2009/digital/news/paramount-ponies-up-3-d-deal-1117998968/
9. Only 44 per cent of the theatres in the first week were 3D, but they made up 74 per cent of the film's gross. In week six, 3D houses made up 80 per cent of the gross.
10. 'DreamWorks Pushes Back "Dragon"', *Variety.com*, 26 February 2008, http://variety.com/2008/digital/news/dreamworks-pushes-back-dragon-1117981491/; '"Monsters" Makes Room for "Avatar"', *Variety.com*, 19 September 2007, http://variety.com/2007/digital/news/monsters-makes-room-for-avatar-2-1117972295/
11. In 2008, 3D movies grossed $307 million at the domestic box office. 'Decade Changed Film Biz', 18 December 2009, http://variety.com/2009/film/news/decade-changed-film-biz-1118012975/
12. 'Lagging Libraries Shift Hollywood Mindset', *Variety.com*, 9 April 2010, http://variety.com/2010/film/news/lagging-libraries-shift-hollywood-mindset-1118017514/. In the late 2000s and early 2010s, the share of the domestic theatrical market in terms of the studios' total domestic revenues was estimated at around 20 to 25 per cent. 'Studios Hit with Homevideo Slump', *Variety.com*, 1 May 2010, http://variety.com/2010/digital/news/studios-hit-with-homevideo-slump-1118018573/
13. An extra charge of $3–4 for 3D digital theatres that belong to the big circuits and an additional $5 for IMAX 3D theatres.
14. 'Studios Hit with Homevideo Slump'.
15. 'Adding Depth to 3D: Cameron Talks About 3D's Industry Implications', *Variety.com*, 20 December 2009, http://variety.com/2009/film/news/adding-depth-to-3d-1118013000/
16. 'Heavy Hitters Bet Big on 3-D: Plexes to Upgrade with Top Directors', *Variety.com*, 15 June 2007, http://variety.com/2007/digital/news/heavy-hitters-bet-big-on-3-d-1117967068/;

'Katzenberg Offers Hollywood a Challenge: Dreamworks Animation Guru Delivers Keynote', *Variety.com*, 17 September 2009, http://variety.com/2009/digital/news/katzenberg-offers-hollywood-a-challenge-1118008778/

17. '3-D Transforming Tentpoles: Studios Prepare Future Franchise Instalments', *Variety.com*, 26 November 2008, http://variety.com/2008/digital/news/3-d-transforming-tentpoles-1117996536/

18. *Les Echos*, 16 December 2009, pp. 9, 13, 23.

19. 'James Cameron Supercharges 3D', *Variety.com*, 10 April 2008, http://variety.com/2008/digital/news/james-cameron-supercharges-3-d-1117983864/

20. For an analysis of both flat and 3D trailers of 3D productions of the 1950s and their emphasis on 3D technology, see Keith M. Johnston, *Coming Soon: Film Trailers and the Selling of Hollywood Technology* (Jefferson: McFarland, 2009).

21. In order to create a fan base long before the film was actually released, 20th Century-Fox opted for value-based marketing, adopting an experiential community (male technophile audience, hardcore players, Facebook, Twitter, Myspace etc.) and interactive approach (interactive trailers, webcasts, Tweeter contests, etc.).

22. Quoted in 'Stars Shine for Fox at Cinema Expo', *Daily Variety*, 24 June 2008, http://variety.com/2008/film/news/stars-shine-for-fox-at-cinema-expo-1117988001/

23. This short documentary was made for IMAX 3D theatres and specially outfitted for 35mm 3D theatres. It is the first of three documentaries to further explore the wreckage of the *Titanic*.

24. The plan was announced in June 2005 (for a release in November 2005). REAL D equipped eighty-eight theatres in the USA and supplied the glasses. The film launched 3D presentation in commercial cinemas.

25. Mainly because of the 3D camera system rental cost and the addition of two or more crew members such as the stereographer and the 3D rig technician.

26. '3D Fuels French Animation Boom', *Variety.com*, 11 December 2010, http://variety.com/2010/digital/news/3d-fuels-french-animation-boom-1118028543/

27. 'Cameron Comes Back with CG Extravaganza', *Hollywood Reporter.com*, 7 July 2006, retrieved from http://www.today.com/id/13759145/ns/today-today_entertainment/t/james-cameron-return-cg-extravaganza/#.VWH1i2bXfsF

28. 'King of the World (Again)', *BusinessWeek.com*, 21 January 2010, www.businessweek.com/magazine/content/10_05/b4165048396178.htm

29. 'Lucas and Cameron to Showcase Digital 3D at ShoWest', *Animation Magazine*, 15 March 2005, www.animationmagazine.net/events/lucas-cameron-in-3d-at-showest/

30. '3-D Transforming Tentpoles'.

31. 'Katzenberg Offers Hollywood a Challenge'.

32. 'First Official Photo for James Cameron's "Avatar"', *Thefilmstage.com*, 14 August 2009, http://thefilmstage.com/news/first-official-photo-for-james-camerons-avatar/

33. Cameron, however, precautiously underlining that '"Avatar" is going to play great in 3-D, 2-D, any "D."' 'Avatar Footage in Action at Cinema Expo', *HollywoodReporter.com*, 23 June 2009, www.hollywoodreporter.com/news/avatar-footage-action-at-cinema-85739

34. Tickets for the *Avatar* Day were free and given out during an online lottery. 'Big Splash for "Avatar" Clip', *Variety.com*, 23 August 2009, http://variety.com/2009/film/news/big-splash-for-avatar-clip-1118007626/

35. Source: Virtual Images, Inc.

36. 'How Digital Marketing Helped "Avatar" Break the Box-Office', *PBS*, www.pbs.org/mediashift/2010/02/how-digital-marketing-helped-avatar-break-the-box-office039.html

37. It is considered to be the world's largest high-definition video display because of the 11,393 square foot screen area.

38. 'Cowboy Crowd Gets "Avatar" Eyeful', *Variety.com*, 29 October 2009, http://variety.com/2009/film/news/cowboy-crowd-gets-avatar-eyeful-1118010556/

39. 'Executives Mull Art of Sell at Summit', *Variety.com*, 6 October 2010, http://variety.com/2010/film/news/executives-mull-art-of-sell-at-summit-1118025232/. Cameron has claimed that Fox's decision not to do any outdoor advertising stemmed from some negative comments on the blogosphere about the look of the characters.

40. Bruce Isaaks, 'Art, Image and Spectacle in High Concept Cinema', in Matthew W. Kapell and McVeigh Stephen (eds), *The Films of James Cameron: Critical Essays* (Jefferson: McFarland, 2011), pp. 90–108.

41. Keith, *Coming Soon*, pp. 32, 40.

42. Everett M. Rogers, in his 1962 seminal book *The Diffusion of Innovations* (New York: Free Press, 1995, 4th edn), distinguishes between five adopter categories on the basis of their innovativeness ('the degree to which an individual or other unit of adoption is relatively earlier in adopting new ideas than other members of the system'): innovators, early adopters, early majority (these first three categories adopting innovations prior to the average time of adoption), late majority and laggards.

43. Which continued beyond the film's release. The Xpand group, for instance, reported a 60 per cent increase in the demand for 3D screens in the USA between December 2009 and June 2010. 'Cinema Expo Eyes Alternative Content', *Variety.com*, 21 June 2010, http://variety.com/2010/biz/news/cinema-expo-eyes-alternative-content-1118020867/

44. 'Avatar Nabs $73 Million at Box Office', *Variety*.com, 20 December 2009, http://variety.com/2009/film/news/avatar-nabs-73-million-at-box-office-1118012991/. In the end, the film was distributed worldwide to a total of 17,163 screens, of which 5,354 were 3D screens.

45. In France, *Avatar* was released on 400 digital screens (which captured a 70 per cent market share), making more money than in any other country besides the USA. 'France Looks Towards Digital Future',*Variety.com*, 7 May 2010, https://variety.com/2010/digital/news/france-looks-towards-digital-future-1118018776/

46. At the end of 2009, 14.8 per cent of worldwide cinema screens had been converted to digital (of which 55 per cent had been also equipped for 3D). As *Screen Digest* observes, international exhibitors installed an additional 4,412 3D screens in 2009, representing more than four times the installed base of international 3D locations at the end of 2008 (1,022). North American 3D screens more than doubled at year end 2009, while in Western Europe the 3D-installed base marked an impressive growth of 614 per cent. 'Avatar and Alice in 3D Power Box Office to New Highs', Insight Report, *Screen Digest*, 24 March 2010.

47. 'Cameron's $1.7 Billion Aliens Have Studios Renting his Cameras', *Bloomberg*, 22 January 2010, www.bloomberg.com/apps/news?pid=newsarchive&sid=atMQxdF2u6WM

48. 'Panasonic takes James Cameron's Avatar on 3D Roadshow', *AVinteractive.com*, 24 August 2009, www.avinteractive.com/news/19719/panasonic-takes-james-camerons-avatar-on-3d-roadshow

49. In the USA, the company mounted three customised tractor trailers housing a theatre powered by Panasonic's 103-inch plasma technology and custom-built Blue-ray players, while in Europe the company erected mobile full HD 3D theatres within shopping malls and other locations.

50. Other big-brand consumer electronics companies, such as Samsung or Sony, have been also building their 3D technologies with Hollywood fare: the 3D Blu-ray version of

Monsters vs Aliens was bundled with Samsung Electronics' 46-inch set, while Sony got exclusive rights to Disney's *Alice in Wonderland* to sell its own television sets.

51. 'Avatar as Technological Tentpole'.
52. Press Release, International 3D Society, 14 May 2013.
53. '3 Signs that 3D Movies are the Way of the Future', *businessinsider.com*, 15 January 2013, www.businessinsider.com/3d-movies-have-a-future-in-hollywood-2013-1
54. Fitch ratings even projects a decline in 3D attendance in 2013. '3D Films Set for Popularity Slide in 2013', *Guardian*, 12 April 2013, www.theguardian.com/film/2013/apr/12/3d-films-slide-fitch-report
55. A disruptive innovation is an 'innovation that transforms an existing market or creates a new market, typically by trading off raw performance in the name of simplicity, convenience, accessibility, or affordability'. Clayton Christensen, 'Disruption Drives Growth: Ten Years After the "Innovators Dilemma"', *Strategy & Innovation* vol. 5 no. 3, 2007, p. 3.

'It's Africa. It's Arizona. It's Antarctica. It's Afghanistan. Actually, it's Alberta'

Marketing Locations to Film Producers

Ben GOLDSMITH

'Location production', meaning film production outside a film studio, has been common practice since the earliest days of cinema. Traditionally, film-makers have shot 'on location' – in real places rather than on a studio set or backlot – for reasons of aesthetics and authenticity, to secure arresting backdrops and novel or picturesque settings for their productions. In recent years, cost has become an increasingly important consideration. Techniques for transforming a place are well established, and it is no longer necessary – if indeed it ever was – for the production location to match the film's setting. Partly as a result of the malleability of locations, the competition to host film production has become fiercely contested. Hundreds of film commissions around the world, alongside other agents of the 'location interest' – those working to secure production in a particular place, as distinct from those acting in the 'design interest' of a particular production – pitch settings, infrastructure and incentives to film-makers. The competition is a consequence of and a catalyst for the enormous growth in itinerant film and television production in recent years, and is fuelled by the conviction that production confers a series of tangible and intangible benefits on a place. Locations are marketed via one of two strategies: low cost or product differentiation. The first involves tax incentives and other efforts to reduce film-makers' expenses, with some costs absorbed by locally domiciled taxpayers. This has produced a 'race to the bottom', as jurisdictions vie to outdo each other in the generosity of their offerings. The second strategy is more problematic. Unlike other forms of place marketing, a prospective film location is not typically promoted in terms of its distinctive qualities, but in terms of its malleability and similarity to other places. The most attractive locations for film-makers are often those that can be made over to substitute for somewhere else, or transformed into any place that the project requires. That is, a place's distinctiveness is not necessarily a primary selling point.

The recent boom in international production has encouraged more and more jurisdictions to establish new film commissions or modify the missions of existing agencies. Many are aligned with tourism or business development agencies. They have become more outward-looking (albeit in a limited way[1]), shifting focus from encouraging local film-makers to attracting incoming production. Their mission is built on creative industries and economic policy principles rather than cultural policy principles. The latter's emphasis on the relationship between film-making and local cultural identity has been replaced by a new discourse that prioritises the place's capacity to be transformed to fit incoming projects' needs. Film-making's economic and employment effects are now most highly valued. This is evident in the taglines and slogans adopted by commissions: 'It's Africa. It's Arizona. It's

DiscoverStillwater.com

Minnesota – Land of 10,000 Locations and 25% Cash Back

- Four distinct seasons
- Experienced crew
- Large and diverse talent pool
- Additional 20% regional incentive
- Equipment, Services and Support
- Lodging tax exemption

www.mnfilmtv.org      612.767.0095

Marketing Minnesota to film-makers (© Minnesota Film and Television)

Antarctica. It's Afghanistan. Actually, it's Alberta' (Alberta Film); 'Be wherever you want to be' (Panama Film Commission); 'Land of 10,000 locations and 25% cashback' (Minnesota Film and TV).

This chapter begins by outlining the dynamics of contemporary international film production and the inherent tension between 'design interest' and 'location interest'. A history of the promotion of particular places as film-making locations (including Hollywood) is presented, prior to the establishment of the first film commissions. The creation of international associations and their role in professionalisation, norm setting and the standardisation of offerings and activities is then described. The chapter concludes with a discussion of commissions' work, the emergent discourse of 'film friendliness' and the differences between location marketing and other kinds of destination marketing.

From 'Runaway Production' to 'Location and Design Interests'

North American critiques of the competition between locations have focused on the impact on Hollywood of 'runaway production', and on the precarious benefits such production offers to the locations to which it travels.[2] A 2001 US government report distinguished between 'creative' reasons for films to 'relocate' from Hollywood – to use particular locations, facilities, people or properties – and 'economic' reasons – principally access to non-unionised labour and tax incentives.[3] The powerful and emotive discourse of 'runaway production' has spawned protests and lobbying in Hollywood by representatives of those most at risk from declining production – those with limited capacity to relocate themselves, typically below-the-line workers, and most recently visual effects companies.[4]

It is clear from data produced by groups such as Film LA – a private company that is the closest thing in Hollywood to a film commission – that the volume of film-making there has declined in recent years, as production in newer locations – such as Louisiana – and more established places – such as Vancouver or London – has increased.[5] And yet, while persuasive, this is very much a 'view from the centre', built on the assumption that Hollywood is the 'natural home' of film production. Activity elsewhere is considered to have 'run away' and been 'lost' to Los Angeles. This does not completely account for what is happening within North America or beyond, nor does it enable us to fully understand the dynamics of contemporary global film production. It is historically inaccurate to claim that all production involving Hollywood studios is made in Los Angeles. 'Split location' production – in which a film is produced or post-produced in more than one place – is an industry norm. Furthermore, a vast amount of film production that places are competing to host is entirely independent of Hollywood. The 'runaway production' argument neither acknowledges the benefits that dispersed production brings to Hollywood and American cinema, nor accounts for the variety of reasons that may lie behind decisions about where films are made.[6] In casting the work of those who seek to bring production to particular places as mercenary and opportunistic, the discourse of runaway production is unable to objectively explain the work of location marketing.

As an alternative to the 'runaway production' paradigm, Goldsmith and O'Regan proposed the concepts of the 'design interest' and the 'location interest' to distinguish between those involved in creative decision-making who act in the interests of the project, and those who act in the interests of particular places to facilitate production there:[7]

> [T]he design interest is represented by the core creative and financial decision-making team whose objective is to create convincing 'story worlds' and who view the film or program as a project that could, in whole or in part, be made in a range of places … The location interest is the view of production from a particular place … A variety of agents or actors share an interest in facilitating – but not necessarily supervising or conceptualizing – production in a particular place; their role is to convince producers, whose principal interest is in the design of a project, to make some or all of that project in their location.[8]

To a great extent, location decisions are influenced by financial considerations including labour costs and the generosity of tax incentives and other subsidies. The role of financial incentives in attracting production to other places has been the principal focus of those lobbying for production in Hollywood for the last two decades, while promoting and managing these incentives has become a core component of the work of agents of the location interest, such as film commissions. But it is important to remember that location production has always been integral to film-making, and marketing locations for film production has a long history, particularly in the USA.

The History of Location Marketing
From the 1890s, the Lumière company dispatched Cinématographe operators to the far corners of the globe not only to screen films, but also to produce films in the locations they visited.[9] Pathé-Frères similarly encouraged its agents and affiliates to make films for local audiences that could also be distributed through the company's international network.[10] In the USA, while still very much driven by film-makers keen to distance themselves from New York and the hold that the Motion Picture Patents Company (the 'Trust') maintained over the industry, the establishment of Hollywood also owes much to the kind of supportive business environment that would soon become essential for other places to compete for the prize of hosting film production. Los Angeles in the early 1900s, Peter Hall argues, 'offered an ideal combination of cheap land and property, a cooperative Chamber of

Commerce, sun, diverse landscape, and remoteness from New York, plus nearness to the Mexican border' in case the Trust sought to pursue those film-makers working outside its control.[11]

Hollywood deal-makers' ambitions and expectations fuelled and directed the spread of production across the USA and around the world. The advantages of location shooting – from tax benefits for above-the-line workers, to the impression of authenticity and realism created by production beyond the studio and, after World War II, the opportunity to access funds that had been frozen in many countries in Europe – had to be weighed against the risks. As late as the 1980s, these included higher and less manageable costs of location production, a reduced ability to manage the appetites and egos of stars or labour demands away from Hollywood and the absence, in most places, of the requisite level of production facilities and ancillary services.[12] But the spread of production also owes much to individual agents of particular location interests. In 1938, one of the first non-Native American settlers in Monument Valley, Arizona, travelled to Hollywood in the hope of convincing someone to make a film there in order to help the Valley's desperately impoverished Navajo inhabitants. Harry Goulding struck lucky, meeting director John Ford and producer Walter Wanger almost immediately. Within days, Ford set off to scout locations, and within weeks was shooting *Stagecoach* (1939) in this remote landscape. As a backdrop for eight Ford films, Monument Valley would become *the* iconic Western setting.[13]

Ford and the Western genre played major roles in the establishment of the first American film commissions. In 1949, another enterprising rancher, George E. White, convinced Ford to locate production for his film *Wagon Master* (1950) in Moab, Utah. This coup was the catalyst for the establishment of the Moab Movie Committee – now the Moab and Monument Valley Film Commission – which is generally acknowledged to be the first modern film commission. White was a pioneer in this field; he travelled regularly to Los Angeles to attract film-makers to Moab, scouted locations and provided a range of services including offering his ranch as a set.[14]

A similar story provides the backdrop to the establishment of the first state film commission in 1969. Karol Smith, director and founder of the Colorado Motion Picture and Television Advisory Commission, was a location scout – that is someone, often a local of the area, who seeks out locations for specific scenes to recommend to film-makers – in Colorado in the 1950s and 60s. In 1958, Smith reconstructed the town of Buckskin Joe, which had thrived in the frontier period but had since been deserted. The town was recreated initially as a set for Westerns including *Cat Ballou* (1965), *The Cowboys* (1972), *True Grit* (1969) and *Comes a Horseman* (1978). It was later turned into a theme park, before falling again in to disrepair.[15] In 2010, the town was bought by billionaire energy magnate Bill Koch, and moved 200 miles west to his ranch to host his private collection of Wild West memorabilia.

Among the individuals who have played important roles in facilitating incoming production, few have been as influential as Dino De Laurentiis. In the 1950s and 60s he acted as a troubleshooter and intermediary for Hollywood productions in Italy while maintaining a prolific producing career and building his own studio complex, Dinocitta, outside Rome. In the 80s he played a leading role in establishing two new production centres, Wilmington in North Carolina, and the Gold Coast, in Australia. While not involved with these locations for lengthy periods of time, and while their rise to become significant 'satellite' locations for Hollywood and other production depended on the work of other, less high-profile agents of the respective locations' interests, De Laurentiis's role in each was crucial.[16]

Film Commissions and Location Marketing

The behind-the-scenes work of ensuring the suitability of local facilities and regulations, pitching to film-makers and attracting production has typically fallen to a range of more anonymous agents. Often this is the work of a non-profit film commission funded by local or national governments. Such commissions can represent areas in more than one country – for example, Oresund Film Commission, which covers the region around Copenhagen in Denmark as well as part of southern Sweden. Some are national bodies – for example, Jamaica Film Commission, a sub-unit of the national investment and export body, the Jamaica Promotions Corporation. Many represent regions – for example, Screen Flanders – or provinces – for example, Ontario Media Development Corporation – or states – for example, Screen New South Wales. And some serve an individual town or city – for example, Film London – or particular suburban areas – for example, the Ile-de-France Film Commission. Many, but by no means all, are members of international organisations such as the Association of Film Commissioners International (AFCI), or the European Film Commission Network (EUCN). All compete vigorously in an international 'locational tournament'[17] that shows no sign of diminishing in intensity.

The standardisation of work, and the task of minimising the risks to film-makers of working in several different places, was boosted by the establishment of the AFCI, the first professional organisation of film commissioners, in 1975. From an original base of seven, the AFCI, which describes itself as a 'non-profit educational association',[18] now boasts global membership of over 300 commissions. The AFCI has worked in succeeding years to promote the interoperability (if not the interchangeability) of locations, to encourage knowledge transfer and to institute norms and benchmarks for the services offered by commissions.

Under the banner of 'AFCI University', in 2007 the Association launched a series of courses and master classes culminating in the awarding of the designation 'Certified Film Commissioner'. AFCI membership currently costs $1,100 for the first year and $750 thereafter, with members required to complete the two 'basic courses' (Film Commission Fundamentals and Film Commission Professional) in order to gain full membership. To retain their accreditation, members must also gain a certain number of credits over a two-year period for achievements such as attending the annual conference, Cineposium and completing master classes.

The requirement to complete AFCI courses is one of the ways in which the Association seeks to set international norms. Another is through its annual trade show. Originally called 'Locations Expo', the convention, now known simply as 'Locations', was first held in California in 1986. Sixty-seven commissions attended to pitch their locations and services. The convention was held concurrently with the American Film Market until 1990, when the demand for exhibition space from over 160 commissions (including almost thirty from outside the USA) necessitated the creation of a separate event. In 1992, the issue that has since come to dominate professional discourse first became public when the Los Angeles County Film Office withdrew from the event held on its doorstep. Announcing that her office would not attend, the LACFO's deputy director explained: 'We feel that (AFCI's) goals and objectives are to take filming out of Los Angeles … We cannot support this.'[19] In 1993, 190 commissions attended, including forty-one commissions from nineteen countries. While the number of non-American commissions has grown steadily, particularly since 2000, almost half of current AFCI members are American, with twenty-three from California alone.

It is no coincidence that the period since 2000 has seen the global volume of peripatetic production rise dramatically as more and more places realise the perceived benefits of attracting and hosting large-scale film-making. Regional locations expos are now held in Busan, South Korea, as part of the BIFCOM Asian Film Market, and in Seville, Spain. In 2010, the Ile-de-France Location Expo was held for the first time, initially as a showcase for Parisian locations. In 2014 this was expanded to include locations throughout France with exhibitors including forty locations in the Ile-de-France, ten national organisations, twenty regional film commissions and seven professional associations.[20] In addition to these various locations expos, the major annual industry markets such as MIPCOM and MIPTV, held in Cannes, have also become venues for location marketing.

Hollywood studios and producers are still very much at the centre of the locational tournament, not least because of the enormous budgets that Hollywood blockbusters carry with them. But Hollywood is far from the only game in town; film-makers from India, France, South Korea, the UK – indeed from virtually all major producing countries – now routinely choose their locations on the basis of what particular places can offer. So what do film commissions and other agents of the location interest offer, and how do they distinguish themselves from their competitors?

Film Friendliness: Working in the Location Interest

Typical film commission offerings and activities include:

- Promoting locations at trade shows and markets;
- Providing general information on filming in the area, including assistance for film-makers in securing permits;
- Providing information on local and/or national incentives, and liaison with tax authorities;
- Lobbying local and national governments to 'improve' incentive programmes;
- Liaising with public services (police, fire, local government);
- Maintaining a portfolio of images of locations;
- Listing projects 'made' in area and testimonials from film-makers;
- Offering a 'News' feed on the commission's website, or via social media services such as Facebook, YouTube and Twitter;
- Providing a service for residents to list their homes/businesses as potential locations and informing such people about what to expect;
- Maintaining a listing of local crew and services.

'Film friendliness' has become the watchword for places seeking to attract film production. Film Friendly Michigan, a privately run agency established in 2008, offers 'training' to local communities, companies and service providers to smooth the path of incoming film-makers. In northern Europe, the Finnish Lapland Film Commission certifies local companies as 'Film Friendly' following training designed to 'give companies a boost on how to effectively deal with on-location filming and put their best foot forward in marketing their services and resources'.[21] Being film friendly 'is a state of mind, and more importantly, it is … a way of doing business'. Adherence to a Local Government Filming Protocol enables New Zealand local authorities to gain 'Film Friendly status'. By early 2014, thirty-one out of fifty local councils were recognised by the national film commission, Film NZ, as having 'the necessary processes and policies in place to meet screen production industry needs as they arise, without compromising the councils' statutory obligations'.[22] 'Film friendliness' is, then, a normative process; it is a deliberate strategy adopted by commissions and jurisdictions, rather than simply being a quality conferred by previous experience.[23]

Film friendliness is especially important for places with no history, or only a limited track record of hosting production. A place's reputation is a valuable commodity, and in its absence agents of new or aspiring locations must establish 'swift trust'.[24] They must be able to assure film-makers that the inevitable risks attending production in a place with limited infrastructures, crew base or talent pool can be offset by local advantages. These advantages can take several forms, and apply at different stages of the production cycle. In most cases, these advantages are not unique to a particular location, but rather are generic, equivalent to (or ideally better than) standard offerings or norms in more established locations. They are necessary to indicate that agents of the location interest are aware not only of the needs and expectations of film-makers, but also of international best practice.

Prior to pitching to prospective producers, agents of the location interest must prepare the location and the local community for the disruptions and demands of film-making. Stakeholders, locations and resources must be coordinated in pursuit of the location interest, and the film-makers' needs must be prioritised. Ancillary services such as hotels, catering, hardware supplies and equipment hire should be available and prepared to offer high-quality service to incoming productions. Poor-quality facilities and service can damage a location's reputation and make it more difficult to attract future production.

Some form of financial incentive programme is now virtually mandatory. Thirty-nine US states and Puerto Rico currently offer some kind of film incentive.[25] While some states and territories have wound back or abolished incentive programmes in recent years, others are expanding their offerings. The French government resisted pressure to institute financial incentives for incoming film-makers until 2009, partly on the grounds that such measures were costly and unnecessary given the French industry's size, the volume of French production and, perhaps, in part due to a view that international production was a secondary consideration behind domestic production. In 2009, a Tax Rebate for International Productions (TRIP) was established in France; in 2013, it was increased from €4 million to €10 million. In April 2014, New Zealand increased its baseline grant for international productions by 5 per cent from 15 to 20 per cent, and also introduced an uncapped Screen Production Grant.

In 2012, almost forty US states paid out roughly $1.5 billion in tax breaks, rebates and grants for film-related work. Ten years previously, the figure was just $2 million.[26] The sophistication of some tax regimes has even resulted in the creation of a secondary market for tax credits, whereby financial consultants broker the sale of film-makers' tax credits to other entities outside that are seeking to cut their tax liability. As the *Los Angeles Times* reported in 2013, 'The trade benefits both sides. The studios get their money more quickly than if they had to wait for a tax refund from the state, and the buyers get a certificate that enables them to cut their state tax bills as much as 15%.'[27] The size and make-up of tax credits, cash rebates that reimburse production companies for a percentage of qualifying local expenditures, exemptions from local sales or payroll taxes and other subsidies such as fee-free services provided by local and national authorities clearly affect production decisions. But these programmes need to be in place in advance of the pitch to producers. They require policy-makers to have been convinced of the benefits that will flow from incoming production and then legislation to be passed. These programmes are typically limited in value and timeframe, and commissions must be careful, particularly towards the end of a programme's life, not to over-commit to incoming projects. Although some jurisdictions like Michigan and Louisiana have made significant losses from their incentive programmes, not only do they appear to be essential mechanisms for any aspiring competitor, the massive growth in production in Louisiana in particular as a result of the introduction of a new incentives programme in 2001 is likely to convince many policy-makers to overlook the negative financial implications.[28]

Agents of location interest must be proactive in their relationships with film-makers. In addition to promoting their location at trade shows and markets, commissioners invest considerable time and effort in cultivating relationships with studio executives, producers and agents. Some – for example, the British Film Commission and the Ontario Film Commission – maintain offices in Los Angeles to facilitate close working relationships with key decision-makers who, as a result of the high executive turnover rate in Hollywood, may change at any time. In addition, some commissions will undertake extensive preparatory work prior to pitching to producers, including scouting locations for particular scenes or storylines, conducting some preliminary logistical planning and budgeting, and even engaging in some form of pre-visualisation work. Project representatives may be taken on an all-expenses paid 'familiarisation trip' to showcase local amenities and opportunities.[29]

We can think of location marketing and the competition for film production in terms of a combination of 'behind the camera' processes and activities (incentives, infrastructure, production services, crew depth) and 'in front of the camera' attributes – the profilmic or 'location space'. A place is valued as much for what it can stand in for, its fungibility or malleability, as it is for itself, as itself. One of the most valuable attributes of a place is a diversity of potential locations which can both 'play themselves' – that is, be represented on screen as wherever (or whatever) they are off-screen – but also play somewhere else. They must be able to 'stand in' for other, 'real' locations, or be capable of being made over or 'masked' to convincingly represent an imagined place. While some iconic locations can successfully trade on their 'real world' identity, for the most part success in the global competition to host footloose production – defined as the ability to attract and host production on a regular basis – will depend 'on the ability of places to successfully suppress their uniqueness and painlessly transform themselves into *whoever, whatever, whenever* sites' (emphasis original).[30]

It is commonplace for commissions to be subsidiaries of tourism bureaux, sometimes for financial reasons, but often as an indication of the priority given to the latter over the former. This can lead to misrecognition of the particularity of location marketing. 'Destination marketing' and 'experience marketing', or the promotion of a place for tourism or brand-building, typically emphasise a place's distinctiveness or uniqueness, and seek to generate an emotional connection between visitor and destination.[31] 'Place branding' aims 'to form a "unique selling proposition" that will secure visibility to the outside and reinforce "local identity" to the inside'.[32] Location marketing, by contrast, focuses on those aspects that render a place similar to or substitutable for somewhere else, and capable of being made over as required. Rather than 'reinforcing' local identity, identity is often suppressed in order for a location to become 'whoever, whatever, whenever'. Commissions must be committed to the prospect of masking or cloaking locations, and to highlighting their capacity to stand in for other places.

One of the essential elements of a commission's tool kit is a 'location gallery', a portfolio of images of a location that may be desirable to film-makers – from sandy beaches, to period buildings, to urban streets – and which are available and able to be transformed to suit a particular project's needs. Some agencies make the mistake of reproducing images used for tourism promotion, despite the fact that locations for film production are marketed to a very different target audience than place promotion for tourism. While agents of the location interest may aim to use films to attract future tourists, there is one fundamental difference between how prospective film-makers and prospective tourists will view images of a place. Tourists are presented with – and expect to find – a place as it really appears. A film-maker's focus is on how a place can be transformed to suit the specific needs of their project. Consequently, the kinds of images used and their aesthetics will differ. Film-makers are not looking for the perfect holiday destination; they are looking for a place in which they can work, and which can be put to work on film. If the film is an urban drama, for example, film-makers may need images of run-down inner-city areas, as well as generic settings – non-places[33] – such as motels, cafés, restaurants and police stations. While interior scenes may be built in a studio, exterior shots are almost always required, and are often easier to shoot on location. It is possible that after a film has been made these images may be used to promote film tourism, but while the association of a particular scene or image with a specific film may encourage future fan visitation, the very recognisability of a place may discourage other film-makers from shooting there.[34]

It is important, finally, to note that the institution of policies to attract film-makers represents a significant change in approach for many places and commissions. Traditionally, in countries like Australia, France and Canada, commissions were inward-looking, in that their mission was cultural: to nurture and promote local film-makers as part of the active construction of a national cinema. Incoming film-makers were not always welcomed:

> The 1975 Report of the Interim Board of the Australian Film Commission expressed an attitude to international production in Australia that bore the imprint of the cultural nationalism and anti-Hollywood views that had been voiced during the campaign to re-establish Australian film-making over the previous decade. 'Locations should not be given away to make decorations for overseas films, but kept as a vital part of those films to be made by Australians. … The Australian scene is as much a national resource as Australian minerals.' This idea, that Australian locations were a precious resource that might be exhausted, like minerals extracted from the ground if they were 'given away' to international producers, sits in stark contrast to the efforts of state and federal film agencies today to be 'film friendly'.[35]

The change in approach to embrace the locational tournament in part reflects the powerful policy influence of the creative economy discourse, with its emphasis on creative work as a driver of innovation and economic growth. This discourse has swamped protectionist and locally oriented film policies, in part because creative industries policy conceives film-making in terms of its revenue potential, while in more traditional film policy, subsidies and the virtual inevitability of financial loss are offset by the cultural value of local film-making.

The marketing of locations as sites for ongoing production requires a specific set of resources and expertise. Location marketing is not the same as tourism promotion, even though the goal of generating incoming visitation may appear to be the same, and even though the availability of tourism infrastructure like hotels and other ancillary services is essential for a place to become a regular production centre. A 'film friendly' policy climate and community is a prerequisite, despite the fact that production may not generate the promised long-term economic and employment benefits. For such benefits to be obtained, large investments are likely to be needed in permanent film-related infrastructure such as studio spaces and allied services.[36] The availability and depth of a local pool of below-the-line crew and service providers will also become important as places seek to take on more of the film-makers' costs in order to remain competitive. This, however, brings additional demands to attract or facilitate regular production work, by reducing labour costs and offering enhanced incentives. While new places are emerging as regular production locations, the dynamics of the global competition are likely to continue to favour large, established production centres including – despite the recent documented downturn in activity – Hollywood itself.

Notes

1. See Ben Goldsmith, 'Outwardlooking Australian Cinema', *Studies in Australasian Cinema* vol. 4 no. 3, 2010, pp. 199–214.
2. Toby Miller, Nitin Govil, John McMurria, Richard Maxwell and Ting Wang, *Global Hollywood 2* (London: BFI, 2005); Mike Gasher, *Hollywood North: The Feature Film Industry in British Columbia* (Vancouver: University of British Columbia Press, 2002); Aida Hozic, *Hollyworld: Space, Power and Fantasy in American Cinema* (Ithaca, NY: Cornell University Press, 2001).
3. United States International Trade Administration, *The Migration of US Film and Television Production: Impact of 'Runaways' on Workers and Small Business in the US Film Industry* (Washington, DC: US Department of Commerce, February 2001).
4. Michael Curtin and John Vanderhoef, 'A Vanishing Piece of the Pi: The Globalization of Visual Effects Labor', *Television and New Media*, published online before print, first published on 20 February 2014 as doi:10.1177/1527476414524285.
5. Film LA, *2013 Film Production Report*, www.filmla.com/uploads/2013%20Feature%20Production%20Report%20w%20Release%20030614_1394125127.pdf
6. Ben Goldsmith and Tom O'Regan, 'International Film Production: Interests and Motivations', in Janet Wasko and Mary Erickson (eds), *Cross-Border Cultural Production: Economic Runaway or Globalization?* (Amherst, NY: Cambria Press, 2008), pp. 13–44.
7. Ben Goldsmith and Tom O'Regan, *The Film Studio: Film Production in the Global Economy* (Lanham, MD: Rowman & Littlefield, 2005); Goldsmith and O'Regan, 'International Film Production: Interests and Motivations'.
8. Goldsmith and O'Regan, 'International Film Production', pp. 19–20.
9. Michael Chanan, 'Economic Conditions of Early Cinema', in Thomas Elsaesser (ed.), *Early Cinema: Space, Frame, Narrative* (London: BFI, 1990), pp. 174–88.
10. Marina Dahlquist, 'Global Versus Local: The Case of Pathé', *Film History* no. 17, 2005, pp. 29–38.
11. Peter Hall, *Cities in Civilization: Culture, Innovation and Urban Order* (London: Pheonix Giant, 1998), p. 534.
12. Hozic, *Hollyworld*, pp. 96–7.
13. Todd McCarthy, 'John Ford and Monument Valley', *American Film* vol. 3 no. 7, 1978, pp. 10–16; Nancy Lofholm, 'Moab's Scenery's Movie Magic Slips Out of Focus', *The Denver Post* no. 3, September 2000, n.p.
14. Ray Boren, 'Utah's Desert Hollywood', *Deseret News*, 6 November 1998, n.p.
15. Jane Harding, 'Celluloid Success', *Denver Business*, 1 May 1987, p. 12.
16. Ben Goldsmith, Susan Ward and Tom O'Regan, *Local Hollywood: Global Film Production and the Gold Coast* (St Lucia: University of Queensland Press, 2010).
17. Paul David, *High Technology Centers and the Economics of Locational Tournaments* (Stanford, CA: Stanford University, 1984).
18. Association of Film Commissioners International, 'History', www.afci.org/about-afci/history
19. Jeffrey Daniels, 'Jostling for Dollars at Expo 93', *Hollywood Reporter*, 26 February 1993, p. 4.
20. 'Ile-de-France Location Expo', *Daily Variety*, 12 February 2014.

21. Finnish Lapland Film Commission, 'Film Friendly Training', www.filmlapland.fi/home/film-commission/film-friendly/

22. Film NZ, 'Film Friendly New Zealand', www.filmnz.com/introducing-nz/film-friendly.html

23. Goldsmith, Ward and O'Regan, *Local Hollywood*, p. 154.

24. Debra Meyerson, Karl .E. Weick and Roderick M. Kramer, 'Swift Trust and Temporary Organizations', in Roderick M. Kramer and Tom R. Tyler (eds), *Trust in Organizations: Frontiers of Theory and Research* (Thousand Oaks, CA: Sage, 1996), pp. 166–95.

25. US National Conference of State Legislatures, 'State Film Production Incentives and Programs', www.ncsl.org/research/fiscal-policy/state-film-production-incentives-and-programs.aspx

26. Richard Verrier, 'Hollywood's New Financiers Make Deals with State Tax Credits', *Los Angeles Times*, 26 December 2013, www.latimes.com/entertainment/envelope/cotown/la-et-ct-hollywood-financiers-20131226-story.html

27. Ibid.

28. Vicki Mayer and Tanya Goldman, 'Hollywood Handouts: Tax Credits in the Age of Economic Crisis', *Jump Cut* no. 52 (2010), www.ejumpcut.org/archive/jc52.2010/mayerTax/index.html; Stephen R. Miller and Abdul Abdulkadri, *The Economic Impact of Michigan's Motion Picture Production Industry and the Michigan Motion Picture Production Credit* (Center for Economic Analysis, Michigan State University, February 2009).

29. Simon Hudson and Vincent Wing Sun Tung, '"Lights, Camera, Action …!" Marketing Film Locations to Hollywood', *Marketing Intelligence & Planning* vol. 28 no. 2, 2010, p. 199.

30. Hozic, *Hollyworld*, p. 89.

31. Hudson and Tung, '"Lights, Camera, Action …!"', p. 191.

32. Claire Colomb and Ares Kalandides, '"The *be* Berlin" Campaign: Old Wine in New Bottles or Innovative Form of Participatory Place Branding?', in Gregory Ashworth and Mihalis Kavaratzis (eds), *Towards Effective Place Brand Management: Branding European Cities and Regions* (Cheltenham: Edward Elgar, 2010), p. 175.

33. Marc Augé, *Non-Places: Introduction to an Anthropology of Supermodernity* (London and New York: Verso, 1995).

34. For example, the Wentworth Heritage Village in Rockton, Ontario, is so much associated with the four television mini-series made there that are based on Lucy Maud Montgomery's 1908 novel *Anne of Green Gables* that it would be difficult for other film-makers to shoot another project there. Even though the site is many hundreds of miles from the novel's and mini-series' settings on Prince Edward Island, the village still attracts tourists on the basis of its association with the television productions. See Shelagh J. Squire, 'Literary Tourism and Sustainable Tourism: Promoting *Anne of Green Gables* in Prince Edward Island', *Journal of Sustainable Tourism* vol. 4 no. 3, 1996, pp. 119–34.

35. Goldsmith, 'Outwardlooking Australian Cinema', pp. 209–10, citing Interim Board of the Australian Film Commission *Report of the Interim Board of the AFC*, Sydney, February 1975, p. 36.

36. Ben Goldsmith, '"If you build it …" Film Studios and the Transformative Effects of Migrating Media Production', in Greg Elmer, Charles H. Davis, Janine Marchessault and John McCullough (eds), *Locating Migrating Media*. (Lanham, MD: Lexington Books, 2010), pp. 103–30.

Select Bibliography

Acland, Charles, 'IMAX in Canadian Cinema: Geographic Transformation and Discourses of Nationhood', *Studies in Cultures, Organizations and Societies* vol. 3 no. 2 (1997), pp. 289–305.

Acland, Charles, 'Avatar as Technological Tentpole', *FlowTV* (http://flowtv.org) vol. 11, 22 January 2010.

Akrich, Madeline, Michel Callon and Bruno Latour, 'The Key to Success in Innovation: Part 1 The Art of Interessement', *International Journal of Innovation Management* vol. 6 no. 2 (2002), pp. 187–206.

Allison, Tanine, 'More than a Man in a Monkey Suit: Andy Serkis, Motion Capture, and Digital Realism', *Quarterly Review of Film and Video* vol. 28 no. 4 (2011), pp. 325–41.

Anderson, Benedict, *Imagined Communities* (New York: Verso, 1991 [1983]).

Araujo, Luis, 'Markets, Market-making and Marketing', *Marketing Theory* vol. 7 no. 3 (2007), pp. 211–26.

Athique, Adrian, 'The Global Dynamics of Indian Media Piracy: Export Markets, Playback Media and the Informal Economy', *Media, Culture and Society* vol. 30 no. 5 (2008), pp. 699–717.

Augé, Marc, *Non-Places: Introduction to an Anthropology of Supermodernity* (London and New York: Verso, 1995).

Augros, Joël, *L'Argent d'Hollywood* (Paris: L'Harmattan, 1996).

Augros, Joël and Kira Kitsopanidou, *L'Economie du cinéma américain: Histoire d'une industrie culturelle et de ses stratégies* (Paris: Armand Colin Cinéma, 2009).

Australia in the Asian Century Implementation Task Force, *Australia in the Asian Century: White Paper Canberra*, Commonwealth of Australia, 2012.

Basea, Erato, '*My Life in Ruins*: Hollywood and Holidays in Greece in Times of Crisis', *Interactions: Studies in Communication and Culture* vol. 3 no. 2, 2012, pp. 199–208.

Belleflamme, Paul and Martin Peitz, 'Digital Piracy: Theory', in *Oxford Handbook of the Digital Economy* (Oxford: Oxford University Press, 2012), pp. 489–530.

Belton, John, 'Digital Cinema: A False Revolution', *October* 100 (2002), pp. 99–114.

Biltereyst, Daniel and Philippe Meers, 'Blockbuster and/as Events: Distributing and Launching *The Lord of the Rings*', in Ernest Mathijs (ed.), *The Lord of the Rings: Popular Culture in Global Context* (London and New York: Wallflower Press, 2006), pp. 71–87.

Booth, Paul, 'Intermediality in Film and Internet: Donnie Darko and Issues of Narrative Substantiality', *Journal of Narrative Theory* vol. 38 no. 3 (2008), pp. 398–414.

Bordwell, David, *Planet Hong Kong 2.0* (Madison: Irvington Way Press, 2011).

Bordwell, David, Janet Staiger and Kristin Thompson, *The Classical Hollywood Cinema: Film Style & Mode of Production to 1960* (New York: Columbia University Press, 1985).

Bourdieu, Pierre, *The Field of Cultural Production* (New York: Columbia University Press, 1993).

British Film Institute, *BFI Statistical Yearbook 2012* (London: BFI, 2012).

British Film Institute, *BFI Statistical Yearbook 2013*, www.bfi.org.uk/sites/bfi.org.uk/files/downloads/bfi-statistical-yearbook-2013.pdf

Brown, Jo, Amanda J. Broderick and Nick Lee, 'Word of Mouth Communication with Communities: Conceptualising the Online Social Network', *Journal of Interactive Marketing* vol. 21 no. 3 (2007), pp. 2–20.

Bryman, Alan and Emma Bell, *Business Research Methods* (New York: Oxford University Press, 2007).

Bud, Alexander, 'The End of Nollywood's Guilded Age? Marketers, the State and the Struggle for Distribution', *Critical African Studies* vol. 6 no. 1 (2014), pp. 91–121.

Callon, Michel, 'Some Elements of a Sociology of Translation: Domestication of the Scallops and the Fishermen of Saint Brieuc Bay', in Mario Biagioli (ed.), *The Science Studies Reader* (London: Routledge, 1999), pp. 67–84.

Callon, Michel, 'What does it Mean to Say that Economics is Performative?', in Donald Mackenzie, Fabian Muniesa and Lucia Sui (eds), *Do Economists make Markets?* (Princeton, NJ: Princeton University Press, 2007), pp. 311–58.

Callon, Michel, Yuval Millo and Fabian Muniesa, 'An Introduction to Market Devices', in Michel Callon, Yuval Millo and Fabian Muniesa (eds), *Market Devices* (Oxford: Blackwell, 2007), pp. 1–12.

Camilleri, Carmel and Margalit Cohen-Emerique (eds), *Chocs de cultures: Concepts et enjeux pratiques de l'interculturel* (Paris: L'Harmattan, 1989).

Camilleri, Jean-François, *Le Marketing du cinéma* (Paris: Dixit, 2006).

CCNIC (China Internet Network Information Center), 'Statistic Report on Internet Development in China' (Beijing: CCNIC, 2014).

Chaffey, Dave, 'E-Marketing', in M. J. Baker and S. Hart (eds), *The Marketing Handbook* (Amsterdam: London: Elsevier/Butterworth-Heinemann, 2008, 6th edn), pp. 502–25.

Chanan, Michael, 'Economic Conditions of Early Cinema', in Thomas Elsaesser (ed.), *Early Cinema: Space, Frame, Narrative* (London: BFI, 1990), pp. 174–88.

Chu, S. C. and S. M. Choi, 'Electronic Word-of-mouth in Social Networking Sites: A Cross-cultural Study of United States and China', *Journal of Global Marketing* vol. 24 no. 3 (2011), pp. 263–81.

Clayton, Christensen, 'Disruption Drives Growth: Ten Years After the "Innovators Dilemma"', *Strategy & Innovation* vol. 5 no. 3 (2007), p. 3.

Colomb, Claire and Ares Kalandides, '"The be Berlin" Campaign: Old Wine in New Bottles or Innovative Form of Participatory Place Branding?', in Gregory Ashworth and Mihalis Kavaratzis (eds), *Towards Effective Place Brand Management: Branding European Cities and Regions* (Cheltenham: Edward Elgar, 2010), pp. 173–90.

Creton, Laurent, *Economie du cinéma: Perspectives stratégiques* (Paris: Armand Colin Cinéma, 2005 [1994]).

Croxson, Karen, 'Promotional Piracy', *Oxonomics* vol. 2 no. 1–2 (2007), pp. 13–15.

Curtin, Michael and John Vanderhoef, 'A Vanishing Piece of the Pi: The Globalization of Visual Effects Labor', *Television and New Media*, published online before print, first published on 20 February 2014 as doi:10.1177/1527476414524285.

Dahlquist, Marina, 'Global Versus Local: The Case of Pathé', *Film History* no. 17 (2005), pp. 29–38.

Dana, Martine, 'Marketing the Hollywood Blockbuster in France', *Journal of Popular Film and Television* vol. 23 (1995).

De Vany, Arthur, *Hollywood Economics: How Extreme Uncertainty Shaped the Film Industry* (New York: Routledge, 2004).

Delapierre, Michel and Christian Milelli, *Les Firmes multinationales* (Paris: Thémathèque, 1995).

Deprez, Camille, *Bollywood: Cinéma et mondialisation* (Villeneuve d'Ascq: Septentrion, 2010).

Desproges, Pierre, *Les Etrangers sont nuls* (Paris: Editions du Seuil, 1992).

Drake, Philip, 'Distribution and Marketing in Contemporary Hollywood', in Paul McDonald and Janet Wasko (eds), *The Contemporary Hollywood Industry* (Malden: Blackwell, 2008), pp. 63–82.

Duan, Wenjing, Gu Bin and Andrew Whinston, 'The Dynamics of Online Word-of-mouth and Product Sales – An Empirical Investigation of the Movie Industry', *Journal of Retailing* vol. 84 no. 2 (2008), pp. 233–42.

Durie, John, Annika Pham and Neil Watson, *The Film Marketing Handbook: A Practical Guide to Marketing Strategies for Independent Films* (Over Wallop: Media Business School, 1993).

Durie, John, Annika Pham and Neil Watson, *Marketing and Selling your Film around the World: A Guide for Independent Filmmakers* (Los Angeles: Silman-James Press, 2000).

Dwyer, Tim, *Media Convergence* (Maidenhead: McGraw-Hill and Open University Press, 2010).

Elberse, Anita and Jehoshua Eliashberg, 'Demand and Supply Dynamics for Sequentially Released Products in International Markets: The Case of Motion Pictures', *Marketing Science* vol. 22 no. 3 (2003), pp. 329–54.

Enticknap, Leo Douglas Graham, *Moving Image Technology: From Zoetrope to Digital* (London: Wallflower, 2005).

Entwistle, Joanne and Don Slater, 'Reassembling the Cultural: Fashion Models, Brands and the Meaning of "Culture" after ANT', *Journal of Cultural Economy* vol. 7 no. 2 (2013), pp. 161–77.

Epstein, Edward J., *The Big Picture, Money and Power in Hollywood* (London: Random House Trade, 2006, 2nd edn).

Epstein, Edward J., *The Hollywood Economist* (New York: Melville House, 2010).

Finney, Angus, *International Film Business: A Market Guide beyond Hollywood* (London: Routledge, 2010).

Flueckiger, Barbara, 'Aesthetics of Stereoscopic Cinema', *Projections* vol. 6 no. 1 (2012), pp. 101–22.

Fox, Kate, *Watching the English* (London: Hodder & Stoughton, 2004).

Friedman, Robert G., 'Motion Picture Marketing', in Jason E. Squire (ed.), *The Movie Business Book* (New York: Simon & Schuster, 1992 [1983]), pp. 291–305.

Ganti, Tejaswini, *Producing Bollywood: Inside the Contemporary Hindi Film Industry* (Durham, NC: Duke University Press, 2012).

Gasher, Mike, *Hollywood North: The Feature Film Industry in British Columbia* (Vancouver: University of British Columbia Press, 2002).

Gerlitz, Carolin and Anne Helmond, 'The Like Economy: Social Buttons and the Data-intensive Web', *New Media & Society* vol. 15 no. 8 (2013), pp. 1348–65.

Goldman, William, *Adventures in the Screen Trade: A Personal View of Hollywood and Screenwriting* (New York: Warner Books, 1983).

Goldsmith, Ben, '"If you build it …" Film Studios and the Transformative Effects of Migrating Media Production', in Greg Elmer, Charles H. Davis, Janine Marchessault and John McCullough (eds), *Locating Migrating Media* (Lanham, MD: Lexington Books, 2010), pp. 103–30.

Goldsmith, Ben, 'Outwardlooking Australian Cinema', *Studies in Australasian Cinema* vol. 4 no. 3 (2010), pp. 199–214.

Goldsmith, Ben and Tom O'Regan, *The Film Studio: Film Production in the Global Economy* (Lanham, MD: Rowman & Littlefield, 2005).

Goldsmith, Ben and Tom O'Regan 'International Film Production: Interests and Motivations', in Janet Wasko and Mary Erickson (eds), *Cross-Border Cultural Production: Economic Runaway or Globalization?* (Amherst, NY: Cambria Press, 2008), pp. 13–44.

Goldsmith, Ben, Susan Ward and Tom O'Regan, *Local Hollywood: Global Film Production and the Gold Coast* (St Lucia: University of Queensland Press, 2010).

Gray, Jonathan, *Show Sold Separately: Promos, Spoilers, and Other Media Paratexts* (New York: New York University Press, 2010).

Gray, Jonathan, 'Mobility Through Piracy, or How Steven Seagal Got to Malawi', *Popular Communication* vol. 9 no. 2 (2011), pp. 99–113.

Hagberg, Johan and Hans Kjellberg, 'Who Performs Marketing? Dimensions of Agential Variation in Market Practice', *Industrial Marketing Management* vol. 39 no. 6 (2010), pp. 1028–37.

Hall, Peter, *Cities in Civilization: Culture, Innovation and Urban Order* (London: Phoenix Giant, 1998).

Haynes, Jonathan (ed.), *Nigerian Video Films* (Athens: Ohio University Press, 2000).

Haynes, Jonathan, 'Nnebue: The Anatomy of Power', *Film International* vol. 5 no. 4 (2007), pp. 30–40.

Haynes, Jonathan, '*Close Up*: "New Nollywood": Kunle Afolayan', *Black Camera* vol. 5 no. 2 (2014), pp. 53–73.

Haynes, Jonathan and Onookome Okome, 'Evolving Popular Media: Nigerian Video Films', *Research in African Literatures* vol. 29 no. 3 (1998), pp. 106–28.

Hediger, Vinzenz and Patrick Vondereau (eds), *Demnächst in Ihrem kino. Grundlagen der Filmwerbung und Filmvermarktung* (Marburg: Schüren, 2005).

Hesmondhalgh, David, *The Cultural Industries* (New York: Sage, 2002).

Hesmondhalgh, David and Sarah Baker, *Creative Labour: Media Work in Three Cultural Industries* (Abingdon: Routledge, 2011).

Hills, Matt, 'Participatory Culture: Mobility, Interactivity and Identity', in Glen Creeber and Royston Martin (eds), *Digital Cultures: Understanding New Media* (Berkshire: Open University Press, 2009), pp. 107–21.

Hozic, Aida, *Hollyworld: Space, Power and Fantasy in American Cinema* (Ithaca, NY: Cornell University Press, 2001).

Hu, Kelly, 'Competition and Collaboration: Chinese Video Websites, Subtitle Groups, State Regulation and Market', *International Journal of Cultural Studies* vol. 17 no. 5 (2014), pp. 437–51.

Hudson, Simon, and Vincent Wing Sun Tung, '"Lights, Camera, Action …!" Marketing Film Locations to Hollywood', *Marketing Intelligence & Planning* vol. 28 no. 2 (2010), pp. 188–205.

Hunter, I. Q. and Laraine Porter (eds), *British Comedy Cinema* (London and New York: Routledge, 2012).

Hutchison, Tom, 'New Media Marketing', in Paul Allen, Tom Hutchison and Amy Macy (eds), *Record Label Marketing* (Burlington, MA: Focal Press, 2010), pp. 229–333.

Imanjaya, Ekky, 'The Other Side of Indonesia: New Order's Indonesian Exploitation Cinema as Cult Films', *Colloquy* vol. 18 (2009), pp. 143–59.

Iordanova, Dina, 'Digital Disruption: Technological Innovation and Global Film Circulation', in Dina Iordanova and Stuart Cunningham (eds), *Digital Disruption: Cinema Moves On-line* (St Andrews: St Andrews Film Studies, 2012), pp. 1–31.

Iordanova, Dina and Stuart Cunningham, *Digital Disruption: Cinema Moves On-line* (St Andrews: St Andrews Film Studies, 2012).

Isaaks, Bruce, 'Art, Image and Spectacle in High Concept Cinema', in Matthew W. Kapell and Stephen McVeigh (eds), *The Films of James Cameron: Critical Essays* (Jefferson: McFarland, 2011), pp. 90–108.

Jedlowski, Alessandro, 'When the Nigerian Video Film Industry Became "Nollywood": Naming, Branding and the Videos' Transnational Mobility', *Estudos Afro-Asiaticos* vol. 33 no. 1, 2, 3 (2011), pp. 225–51.

Jedlowski, Alessandro, 'Small Screen Cinema: Informality and Remediation in Nollywood', *Television and New Media* vol. 13 no. 5 (2012), pp. 431–6.

Jedlowski, Alessandro, 'From Nollywood to Nollyworld: Processes of Transnationalization in the Nigerian Video Film Industry', in Matthias Krings and Onokoome Okome (eds), *Global Nollywood: Transnational Dimensions of an African Video Film Industry* (Bloomington: Indiana University Press, 2013), pp. 25–45.

Jenkins, Henry, *Convergence Culture: When Old and New Media Collide* (New York: New York University Press, 2006).

Jenkins, Henry, Sam Ford and Joshua Green, *Spreadable Media: Creating Value and Meaning in a Networked Culture* (New York: New York University Press, 2013).

Johnston, Keith M., *Coming Soon: Film Trailers and the Selling of Hollywood Technology* (Jefferson: McFarland, 2009).

Jorgensen, Danny, 'Participant Observation: A Methodology for Human Studies', *Applied Social Research Methods Series* (London: Sage, 1989).

Kallinikos, Jannis, Paul Leonardi and Bonnie Nardi, 'The Challenge of Materiality: Origins, Scope, and Prospects', in Paul Leonardi, Bonnie Nardi and Jannis Kallinikos (eds), *Materiality and Organizing: Social Interaction in a Technological World* (Oxford: Oxford University Press, 2012).

Keegan, Warren J., *Global Marketing Management* (Upper Saddle River, NJ: Prentice Hall, 2002, 7th edn).

Keller, E., 'Unleashing the Power of Word of Mouth: Creating Brand Advocacy to Drive Growth', *Journal of Advertising* vol. 47 no. 4 (2007), pp. 448–52.

Kernan, Lisa, *Coming Attractions: Reading American Movie Trailers* (Austin: University of Texas Press, 2004).

Kerrigan, Finola, *Film Marketing* (Amsterdam: Elsevier, 2010).

Kimmeland, A. J. and P. J. Kitchen, 'Word of Mouth and Social Media', *Journal of Marketing Communications* vol. 20 no. 1–2 (2014), pp. 2–4.

King, Geoff, *American Independent Cinema* (New York: I.B.Tauris, 2005).

Kjellberg, Hans and Claes-Fredrik Helgesson, 'Multiple Versions of Markets: Multiplicity and Performativity in Market Practice', *Industrial Marketing Management* vol. 35 no.7 (2006), pp. 839–55.

Klaprat, Cathy, 'The Star as Market Strategy: Bette Davis in Another Light', in Tino Balio (ed.), *The American Film Industry* (Madison: University of Wisconsin Press, 1985), pp. 351–76.

Klinger, Barbara, 'Contraband Cinema: Piracy, Titanic, and Central Asia', *Cinema Journal* vol. 49 no. 2 (2010), pp. 106–24.

Koh, N. S., N. Hu and E. K. Clemons, 'Do Online Reviews Reflect a Product's True Perceived Quality? An Investigation of Online Movie Reviews Across Culture', *Electronic Commerce Research and Applications* vol. 9 no. 5 (2010), p. 374.

Kunz, William M., *Culture Conglomerates: Consolidation in the Motion Picture and Television Industries* (Washington, DC: Rowman & Littlefield, 2007).

Landy, Marcia, *British Genres: Cinema and Society, 1930–1960* (Princeton, NJ: Princeton University Press, 1991).

Larkin, Brian, 'Degraded Images, Distorted Sounds: Nigerian Video and the Infrastructure of Piracy', *Public Culture* vol. 16 no. 2 (2004), pp. 289–314.

Laroche, M., Z. Yang, G. H. G. McDougall and I. Bergon, 'Internet versus Bricks-and-mortar Retailers: An Investigation into Intangibility and its Consequences', *Journal of Retailing* vol. 81 no. 4 (2005), pp. 251–67.

Laurichesse, Hélène, *Quel marketing pour le cinéma?* (Paris: CNRS Editions, 2006).

Lefèvre, Raymond and Roland Lacourbe, *30 ans de cinéma britannique* (Paris: Editions cinéma 76, 1976).

Lehu, Jean-Marc, *Branded Entertainment: Product Placement & Brand Strategy in the Entertainment Business* (London: Kogan Page, 2007).

Lieberman, Al and Patricia Esgate, *The Entertainment Marketing Revolution: Bringing the Moguls, the Media and the Magic to the World* (New Jersey: Financial Times/Prentice Hall, 2002).

Litman, Barry and Hoekyun Ahn, 'Predicting Financial Success of Motion Pictures: The Early '90s Experience', in Barry Litman (ed.), *The Motion Picture Mega-Industry* (Boston: Allyn and Bacon, 1998), pp. 172–97.

Litwak, Mark, *Reel Power: The Struggle for Influence and Success in the New Hollywood* (New York: William Morrow, 1986).

Liu, Y., 'Word of Mouth for Movies: Its Dynamics and Impacts on Box Office Revenue', *Journal of Marketing* vol. 70 no. 3 (2006), pp. 74–89.

Lobato, Ramon, *Shadow Economies of Cinema: Mapping Informal Film Distribution* (London: BFI, 2012).

Lobato, Ramon and Julian Thomas, *The Informal Media Economy* (Cambridge: Polity, 2015).

Lukk, Tiiu, *Movie Marketing: Opening the Picture and Giving it Legs* (Los Angeles: Silman-James Press, 1997).

MacKenzie, Donald, 'Is Economics Performative? Option Theory and the Construction of Derivatives Market', *Journal of the History of Economic Thought* vol. 28 no. 1 (2006), pp. 29–55.

Marich, Robert, *Marketing to Moviegoers: A Handbook of Strategies and Tactics* (Carbondale, IL: Southern Illinois University Press, 2013, 3rd edn).

Mattelart, Armand, 'La nouvelle idéologie globalitaire', in Serge Cordellier (ed.), *La Mondialisation au-delà des mythes* (Paris: La Découverte/Poche, 2000), pp. 81–92.

Mayer, Vicki and Tanya Goldman, 'Hollywood Handouts: Tax Credits in the Age of Economic Crisis', *Jump Cut* no. 52 (2010), www.ejumpcut.org/archive/jc52.2010/mayerTax/index.html

McCall, John, 'The Capital Gap: Nollywood and the Limits of Informal Trade', *Journal of African Cinemas* vol. 4 no. 1 (2013), pp. 9–23.

McCarthy, Todd, 'John Ford and Monument Valley', *American Film* vol. 3 no. 7 (1978), pp. 10–16.

Medhurst, Andy, *A National Joke: Popular Comedy and English Cultural Identities* (London and New York: Routledge, 2007).

Meng, Bingchun, 'Piracy Cultures – Underdetermined Globalization: Media Consumption via P2P Networks', *International Journal of Communication* vol. 6, April 2012, p. 17.

Mestyán, Márton, Taha Yasseri and János Kertész, 'Early Prediction of Movie Box Office Success Based on Wikipedia Activity Big Data', *PLoS ONE* vol. 8 no. 8 (2012).

Meyerson, Debra, Karl E. Weick and Roderick M. Kramer, 'Swift Trust and Temporary Organizations', in Roderick M. Kramer and Tom R. Tyler (eds), *Trust in Organizations: Frontiers of Theory and Research* (Thousand Oaks, CA: Sage, 1996), pp. 166–95.

Miller, Steven R. and Abdul Abdulkadri, *The Economic Impact of Michigan's Motion Picture Production Industry and the Michigan Motion Picture Production Credit* (Center for Economic Analysis, Michigan State University, February 2009).

Miller, Toby, Nitin Govil, John McMurria and Richard Maxwell, *Global Hollywood* (London: BFI, 2001).

Miller, Toby, Nitin Govil, John McMurria, Richard Maxwell and Ting Wang, *Global Hollywood 2* (London: BFI, 2005).

Mingant, Nolwenn, *Hollywood à la conquête du monde: Marchés, stratégies, influences* (Paris: CNRS Editions, 2010).

Mingant, Nolwenn, 'A New Hollywood Genre: The Global-Local Film', in Rohit Chopar and Radhika Gajjala, *Global Media, Culture and Identity: Theory, Cases and Approaches* (New York and London: Routledge, 2011).

Mingant, Nolwenn, 'A Peripheral Market? Hollywood Majors and the Middle East/North Africa Theatrical Market', *Velvet Light Trap* vol. 75 (2015).

Molloy, Claire, *Memento* (Edinburgh: Edinburgh University Press, 2010).

Moretti, Enrico, 'Social Learning and Peer Effects in Consumption: Evidence from Movie Sales', *The Review of Economic Studies* vol. 78 no. 1 (2011), pp. 356–93.

Moretti, Franco, 'Planet Hollywood', *New Left Review* vol. 9, May–June 2001, pp. 90–101.

Naficy, Hamid, 'Self-Othering: A Postcolonial Discourse on Cinematic First Contacts', in Fawzia Afzal-Khan and Kalpana Seshadri-Crooks (eds), *The Pre-Occupation of Postcolonial Studies* (Durham, NC: Duke University Press, 2000), pp. 292–310.

Nightingale, Virginia, 'New Media Worlds? Challenges for Convergence', in Virginia Nightingale and Tim Dwyer (eds), *New Media Worlds: Challenges for Convergence* (Melbourne: Oxford University Press, 2007), pp. 19–36.

Ohmer, Susan, *George Gallup in Hollywood* (New York: Columbia University Press, 2006).

Okome, Onookome, 'Nollywood: Spectatorship, Audience and the Sites of Consumption', *Postcolonial Text* vol. 3 no. 2 (2007), pp. 1–21.

Okome, Onookome, '"The Message is Reaching a Lot of People": Proselytizing and Video Films of Helen Ukpabio', *Postcolonial Text* vol. 3 no. 2 (2007), pp. 1–20.

Olukoshi, Adebayo O. (ed.), *The Politics of Structural Adjustment in Nigeria* (Oxford: James Currey, 1993).

Pang, Laikwan, *Creativity and Its Discontents* (Durham, NC: Duke University Press, 2012).

Papadimitriou, Lydia, 'Travelling on Screen: Tourism and the Greek Film Musical', *Journal of Modern Greek Studies* vol. 18 no. 1 (2000), pp. 95–104.

Pardo, Alejandro, *The Europe–Hollywood Coopetition: Cooperation and Competition in the Global Film Industry* (Pamplona: Ediciones Universidad de Navarra, 2007).

Perren, Alisa, '"A Big Fat Indie Success Story?" Press Discourses Surrounding the Making and Marketing of a "Hollywood" Movie', *Journal of Film and Video* vol. 56 no. 2 (2004), pp. 18–31.

Perren, Alisa, 'Last Indie Standing: The Special Case of Lions Gate in the New Millennium', in Geoff King, Claire Molloy and Yannis Tzioumakis (eds), *American Independent Cinema: Indie, Indiewood and Beyond* (London: Routledge, 2012), pp. 108–20.

Purse, Lisa, *Digital Imaging in Popular Cinema* (Edinburgh: Edinburgh University Press, 2013).

Pype, Katrien, 'Religion, Migration and Media Aesthetics: Notes on the Circulation and Reception of Nigerian Films in Kinshasa', in Matthias Krings and Onookome Okome (eds), *Global Nollywood: Transnational Dimensions of an African Video Film Industry* (Bloomington: Indiana University Press, 2013), pp. 199–222.

Ray, Manas, 'Bollywood Down Under: Fiji–Indian Cultural History and Popular Assertion', in Stuart Cunningham and J. Sinclair (eds), *Floating Lives: The Media and Asian Diasporas* (St Lucia: University of Queensland Press, 2000), pp. 136–79.

Real, Brian, 'From Colorization to Orphans: The Evolution of American Public Policy on Film Preservation', *The Moving Image: The Journal of the Association of Moving Image Archivists* vol. 13 no. 1 (2013), pp. 129–50.

Reiss, Jon, 'A New Path to Engage Film Audiences and Create Careers: An Introduction', in Jon Reiss and Sherri Chandler (eds), *Selling Your Film Without Selling Your Soul: Case Studies in Hybrid, DIY and P2P Independent Distribution* (Los Angeles: The Film Collaborative, 2011).

Reiss, Jon, *Think Outside the Box Office: The Ultimate Guide to Film Distribution and Marketing for the Digital Era* (Los Angeles: Hybrid Cinema, 2011).

Roschk, H. and S. Große, 'Talk About Films: Word-of-mouth Behaviour and the Network of Success Determinants of Motion Pictures', *Journal of Promotion Management* vol. 19 no. 3 (2013), pp. 229–16.

Sadikov, Eldar, Aditya Parameswaran and Petros Venetis, 'Blogs as Predictors of Movie Success', Proceedings of the Third International ICWSM Conference, March 2009.

Screen Australia, *Common Ground: Opportunities for Australian Screen Partnership in Asia* (Canberra: Screen Australia, 2013).

Segrave, Kerry, *Product Placement in Hollywood Films: A History* (Jefferson: McFarland, 2004).

Sibley, Brian, *Peter Jackson: A Film-Maker's Journey* (London: HarperCollins Entertainment, 2006).

Smith, Michael D. and Rahul Telang, 'Piracy or Promotion? The Impact of Broadband Internet Penetration on DVD Sales', *Information Economics and Policy* vol. 22 no. 4 (2010), pp. 289–98.

Smith, Michael D. and Rahul Telang, 'Assessing the Academic Literature Regarding the Impact of Media Piracy on Sales', *Social Science Research Network*, 19 August 2012, http://ssrn.com/abstract=2132153

Stark, David and Verena Paravel, 'PowerPoint in Public Digital Technologies and the New Morphology of Demonstration', *Theory, Culture & Society* vol. 25 no.5 (2008), pp. 30–55.

Street, Sarah, *British National Cinema* (London: Routledge, 2009 [1997]).

Thompson, Kristin, *Exporting Entertainment: America in the World Film Market, 1907–1934* (London: BFI, 1985).

Thompson, Kristin, *The Frodo Franchise: How The Lord of the Rings Became a Hollywood Blockbuster and Put New Zealand on the Map* (London: Penguin, 2007).

Tirtaine, Cecilia, 'Le Nouvel essor du cinéma britannique (1994–2004): Facteurs conjoncturels et structurels', PhD Dissertation, Université Paris Ouest Nanterre, 2008.

Toder-Alon, A., F. F. Brunel and S. Fournier, 'Word-of-mouth Rhetorics in Social Media Talk', *Journal of Marketing Communications* vol. 20 no. 1–2 (2014), pp. 42–64.

Tomlinson, John, *Cultural Imperialism: A Critical Introduction* (Baltimore: Johns Hopkins University Press, 1991).

Trice, Jasmine Nadua, 'The Quiapo Cinémathèque: Transnational DVDs and Alternative Modernities in the Heart of Manila', *International Journal of Cultural Studies* vol. 13 no. 5 (2010), pp. 531–50.

Trumpbour, John, 'Hollywood and the World: Export or Die', in Paul McDonald and Janet Wasko (eds), *The Contemporary Hollywood Film Industry* (Malden, MA: Blackwell, 2008).

Tryon, Chuck, *Reinventing Cinema: Movies in the Age of Media Convergence* (New Brunswick, NJ: Rutgers University Press, 2009).

Tryon, Chuck, 'Video from the Void: Video Spectatorship, Domestic Film Cultures, and Contemporary Horror Film', *Journal of Film and Video* vol. 61 no. 3, 2009, pp. 40–51.

Tryon, Chuck, 'Digital Distribution, Participatory Culture, and the Transmedia Documentary', *Jump Cut: A Review of Contemporary Media* vol. 53, 2011, http://www.ejumpcut.org/archive/jc53.2011/TryonWebDoc/

Tsika, Noah, 'From Yorùbá to YouTube: Studying Nollywood's Star System', *Black Camera* vol. 5 no. 2 (2014), pp. 95–115.

Turnock, Julie, 'Removing the Pane of Glass: *The Hobbit*, 3D High Frame Rate Film-making, and the Rhetoric of Digital Convergence', *Film Criticism* vol. 37/38 no. 1 (2013), pp. 30–59.

Tzioumakis, Yannis, *Hollywood's Indies: Classics Divisions, Specialty Labels and the American Film Market* (Edinburgh: Edinburgh University Press, 2012).

Tzioumakis, Yannis, '"Independent", "Indie" and "Indiewood": Towards a Periodisation of Contemporary (post-1980) American Independent Cinema', in Geoff King, Claire Molloy and Yannis Tzioumakis (eds), *American Independent Cinema: Indie, Indiewood and Beyond* (London: Routledge, 2012), pp. 28–40.

Tzioumakis, Yannis, 'Reclaiming Independence: American Independent Cinema Distribution and Exhibition Practices beyond Indiewood', *Mise au point* (online), published 26 June 2012, www.map.revues.org/585, paragraph 7, accessed 11 October 2012.

Ulin, Jeff, *The Business of Media Distribution: Monetizing Film, TV, and Video Content* (Burlington: Focal Press, 2010).

United States International Trade Administration, *The Migration of US Film and Television Production: Impact of 'Runaways' on Workers and Small Business in the US Film Industry* (Washington, DC: US Department of Commerce, February 2001).

Vasey, Ruth, 'Foreign Parts: Hollywood's Global Distribution and the Representation of Ethnicity', *American Quarterly* vol. 44 (1992), pp. 617–42.

Vasey, Ruth, *The World According to Hollywood (1918–1939)* (Madison: University of Wisconsin, 1997).

Vonderau, Patrick, 'Beyond Piracy: Understanding Digital Markets', in Jennifer Holt and Kevin Sanson (eds), *Connected Viewing: Selling, Sharing, and Streaming Media in the Digital Era* (New York/London: Routledge, 2013).

Waldfogel, Joel, '*Lost* on the Web: Does Web Distribution Stimulate or Depress Television Viewing?', *Information Economics & Policy* vol. 21 no. 2 (2009), pp. 158–68.

Waldfogel, Joel, 'Copyright Research in the Digital Age: Moving from Piracy to the Supply of New Products', *American Economic Review* vol. 102 no. 3 (2012), pp. 337–42.

Wang, Shujen, *Framing Piracy: Globalization and Film Distribution in Greater China* (Lanham, MD: Roman & Littlefield Press, 2003).

Wasko, Janet, *How Hollywood Works* (London: Sage, 2005).

Wickham, Phil, *Producing the Goods? UK Film Production Since 1991, An Information Briefing* (London: BFI National Library, 2003).

Wickham, Phil, Erinna Mettler and Elena Marcarini, *Back to the Future: The Fall and Rise of the British Film Industry in the 1980s, An Information Briefing* (London: BFI National Library, 2005).

Wiese, Michael, *Film & Video Marketing* (Stoneham, MA: Focal Press, 1989).

Wyatt, Justin, *High Concept: Movies and Marketing in Hollywood* (Austin: University of Texas Press, 2003 [1994]).

Xiao Wu, Angela, 'Broadening the Scope of Cultural Preferences: Movie Talk and Chinese Pirate Film Consumption from the mid-1980s to 2005', *International Journal of Communication* vol. 6 (2012), pp. 501–29.

Yin, Robert, 'The Case Study Crisis: Some Answers', *Administrative Science Quarterly* vol. 26 no. 7 (1981), pp. 58–65.

Zhao, Elaine Jing and Michael Keane, 'Between Formal and Informal: The Shakeout in China's Online Video Industry', *Media, Culture & Society* vol. 35 no. 6 (2013), pp. 724–41.

Zhao, J., J. Lui, Don Towsley, X. Guan and Y. Zhou, 'Empirical Analysis of the Evolution of Follower Network: A Case Study on Douban', IEEE INFOCOM WKSHPS (2011), pp. 924–9.

Zhu, Ying, *Two Billion Eyes: The Story of China Central Television* (New York: New Press, 2012).

Zone, Ray, *3-D Film-makers: Conversations with Creators of Stereoscopic Motion Pictures* (Oxford: Scarecrow Press, 2005).

Websites

www.allocine.fr

www.bfi.org.uk

www.boxofficemojo.com

www.cbo-boxoffice.com/

www.chinesefilms.cn

www.filmla.com

www.filmlapland.fi/

www.filmmakersfestival.com/en/magazine/

www.imdb.com

http://inatheque.ina.fr/

www.indiewire.com/

www.screenaustralia.gov.au/

www.screendaily.com

http://variety.com

Index

Note: Page numbers in **bold** indicate detailed analysis. Those in *italic* refer to illustrations.
n = endnote. *t* = table/diagram.

List of Illustrations

While considerable effort has been made to correctly identify the copyright holders, this has not been possible in all cases. We apologise for any apparent negligence, and any omissions or corrections brought to our attention will be remedied in any future editions.

Four Weddings and a Funeral, © PolyGram Filmproduktion GmbH; Top Gun, © Paramount Pictures Corporation; Black Swan, © Twentieth Century-Fox Film Corporation/Dune Entertainment III LLC; Bhaji on the Beach, Channel Four Films/Umbi Films; Maybe Baby, © Carlton Jarvis/© Pandora Investment S.a.r.l.; Ice Age Live, © Radio Hamburg; Fatal Attraction, Paramount Pictures Corporation; The Hobbit: An Unexpected Journey, New Line Cinema/Metro-Goldwyn-Mayer/WingNut Films; The Blair Witch Project, © Haxan Films Inc.; Uncovered: The Whole Truth About the Iraq War, © Carolina Productions; Project X, Green Hat Films/Silver Pictures; Avatar, © Twentieth Century-Fox Film Corporation/Dune Entertainment III LLC.